D0492722

THE LAST ASSAULT

Also by Charles Whiting

Bloody Aachen
Massacre at Malmédy
Hitler's Werewolves
The End of the War
Hunters from the Sky
A Bridge at Arnhem
Decision at St Vith
The Battle for Twelveland
Operation Africa
The Three-Star Blitz
Forty-Eight Hours to Hammelburg

The Battle of the Ruhr Pocket
The Hunt for Martin Bormann
The War in the Shadows
Operation Stalag
The Battle of Hurtgen Forest
The March on London
Operation Northwind
Bounce the Rhine
Siegfried: The Nazi's Last Stand
Slaughter over Sicily

THE LAST ASSAULT

The Battle of the Bulge
Reassessed

by

Charles Whiting

BCA

LONDON   NEW YORK   SYDNEY   TORONTO

This edition published in 1994 by
BCA by arrangement with
LEO COOPER
an imprint of
Pen & Sword Books Limited

Copyright © Charles Whiting, 1994

CN 3888

Typset by CentraCet Limited, Cambridge

Printed by Redwood Books Limited
Trowbridge, Wiltshire

THIS BOOK IS DEDICATED TO TOM DICKINSON,
JIM THORPE (USA) AND MIKE TOLHURST (UK) –
MY STALWART RESEARCHERS.
WITHOUT YOU, I COULDN'T HAVE DONE IT.

CW.

Contents

'This is undoubtedly the greatest American battle of the war and will, I believe, be regarded as an ever-famous American victory.'

Winston Churchill, addressing the
House of Commons, January, 1945.

'I am unalterably opposed to making any effort to publicize at this time any story concerning the Ardennes Battle or even of allowing any written explanation to go outside the War Department.

General Dwight D. Eisenhower to
Robert Patterson, Secretary of War,
18 December, 1945.

'I believe the main feature of this operation (Ardennes Battle) – the events leading up to it, the incidents of the fighting and the outcome – should be made known to the American people. Otherwise they will hear nothing but fault-finding and many of them will think the Army is covering up.'

Patterson to Eisenhower, 19 December, 1945.

THANK YOU!

It is customary for the author to call his tribute to those who have helped him 'acknowledgements', but that is too weak a word. How can you 'acknowledge' the 80-year-old veteran of the 4th Infantry Division, who excused his poor handwriting 'on account of my hands being badly frostbitten in the Ardennes', still suffering half a century after the battle? Or that other 80-year-old of the 28th Division who would 'fly over and tell you everything I know, but I can't because I've got to look after my wife who has Alzheimer's. No, it has to be '*thank you*'.

In particular I would like to thank Messrs Marshall, Mattocks, Walsh, Rutledge, Pennino, Cornell, Howe, Hale, Malinowski, Martin, Dillard, Thomson, Russo, Klimick, Boykin, Dalyen, Beck, Bigger, Petersen, Cope, Kreisle, Ausland, Perry, Schorr, Barton, Arn, Hall, Ciccinelli, Calvert, Chance, and Mrs Milnarich – veterans all.

I'd also like to thank the editors of some thirty newspapers and journals from the *New York Times* to the *Jewish Veterans of WWII*. In particular, I'd like to extend my sincere thanks to the *Washington Post*. Its publication of my appeal for information brought in many replies.

My thanks are also due to the staff of the following institutions for their unfailing help and courtesy: U.S. National Archives, Washington, D.C.; Suitland, Maryland Military Archives, Carlisle, Pennsylvania; Boeing Aircraft Corporation Archives, World War II Branch, Seattle, Washington; U.S. Air Force Historical Research Agency, Maxwell Air Force Base, Alabama; The Eisenhower Library, Abilene, Kansas; University of Maryland, McKeldin Library, College Park, Maryland.

C. Whiting
York, England
Bleialf, Germany
March, 1994

'Life to be sure is nothing much to lose.
But young men think it is and we were young.'

A. E. Housman.

Author's Note

Twenty-odd years ago now I set off on an overcast morning from that Devon coastal village to climb up the fields to the remote farm where he lived. The locals had told me that there was a track to it, but it was muddy and probably too narrow for my car. So I walked. I crossed a couple of stiles, scattered a flock of sheep and then the farmhouse came into view. It was built, probably in the 18th century, of that mellow, yellowish stone common to that part of Devon. But it was terribly rundown. The roof obviously needed repairing. I walked into the drive, lined with tumbledown wooden sheds and rusting farm implements, wondering how a man who had once dealt with a prime minister and a future president of the United States could have landed here.

Once he had been a ranking SIS agent. He had met Hitler, Hess, Goering and the like while spying in Germany. He it was who had pioneered the spy overflights which would lead to satellite surveillance and which would make his profession almost superfluous. A very important man.

I knocked. He opened the door himself. He was tall, a little bent and his face was still handsome. I guessed he was in his mid-seventies. In one of those English upper-class voices used to giving orders and having them obeyed he said, 'We'll feed you. There's plenty of meat. No wine afraid. Just home-made stuff. But it'll do, won't it?'

Thus, for the first time, I met Group-Captain (thought it was not a rank he was entitled to) Fred Winterbotham, one-time head of Air Intelligence in the Secret Intelligence Services – a man, who knew where the bodies were buried, a man who perhaps knew too much.

How much I didn't discover until the scotch which I had brought with me started to have its effect. He was bitter, of course. He had been released from the Service after the war 'without a penny piece'. He had not received a 'K', as some of the others had. The 'gong' he'd received was 'hardly worth bothering about'. But he had a manuscript he was working on.

'What kind of manuscript?' I asked. 'If it's interesting, you ought to send it to a publisher.'

Winterbotham frowned. 'The boys would send me to the Tower if I did,' he said very seriously.

'At your age?' I exclaimed, wondering if by 'the boys' he meant members of his old Service.

'It's all very hush-hush still, even after all these years,' he replied hesitantly. 'You see our people could read the German secret codes all throughout the war. We knew what Hitler wanted them to do just as soon as his own generals did.'

That afternoon I had stumbled, quite by chance, on one of the greatest secrets of the Second World War. What I was hearing in that remote Devon farmhouse would soon mean, when the secret was made public, that the history of the Second World War would have to be re-appraised, in parts completely re-written. For I was listening to the story of the Ultra Secret.*

At the time I thought that was the last great secret of the War which would ever be revealed. Here and there during the course of that long bitter conflict there were still minor mysteries, grey areas, nagging little questions still to be resolved, but there could be nothing of the same magnitude of the Ultra Secret. Those amazing decodes coming from Bletchley had influenced the course of great battles, even whole campaigns. Wasn't it said that Crete had been lost because General Freyberg, the Commander of the island, had not dared to reveal to the Germans that he already knew they were coming? If he'd altered the dispositions of the defenders the enemy would have been alerted that their codes were being read. Ultra was more important than Crete!

In 1992, when I started the research for this book, I began to be not quite so sure that Ultra was the last great secret. My original brief had been to refute the standard argument that the Battle of the Bulge had begun with an American defeat around St Vith, in which a whole US corps was shattered, and ended in a brilliant victory, kicked off by Patton's relief of the 'battered bastards of Bastogne.'

---

* When *Ultra Secret* became such a success in 1974, Fred Winterbotham wrote to me that he had been round the world twice, had his hips replaced and re-roofed the farmhouse.

My idea was that I would prove that General Bruce Clarke's stubborn defence of St Vith for seven long days gave the Allies time to set up a blocking position on the west bank of the Meuse and harden the 'shoulders' of the Bulge to north and south. By the time St Vith fell, the Germans had already lost the battle.

Naturally the survivors of the ill-fated 106th and 28th Infantry Divisions and the 14th Cavalry Group, who had borne the brunt of the German 'surprise' attack and who wrote in answer to my appeal, were bitter. Many of them seemed to regard themselves as 'fall guys' who, back in December, 1944, had been placed in untenable positions with no back-up and with no warning of what was going to strike them. Why had it happened? Why had the Top Brass never heeded their numerous reports that something strange was going on in the German positions opposite them in Eifel?

Conventional wisdom after 1974 was that the Top Brass had relied too much on the Ultra decodes. When they dried up prior to the German 'surprise' attack, the Top Brass was left in the dark. But there *were* Ultra signals still coming in, detailing the scores of *Luftwaffe* fighters being sent to the front when they were vitally needed to defend Germany's much bombed cities in the north. Ultra had also cracked the German *Reichsbahn* code, so the Bletchley boffins knew that the German State Railway was sending hundreds of troop trains to the front.

The Top Brass also received another vital source of signal intelligence: the 'Magic' decodes of Japanese messages from Berlin to Tokyo. As far back as September, 1944, Baron Oshima, the Japanese Ambassador in Berlin, was reporting to Japan that 'Herr Hitler' had told him he would counter-attack in the West soon.

What did the Top Brass make of the reports sent in by Air Vice Marshal E. B. Addison's 100 Group of the Royal Air force? With the most advanced technology in the world at that time, those early AWACs, with their air-to-ground radar, were constantly flying over the future battleground. What was made of their reports of troop and armour concentrations, poised right in front of what was supposed to be a recuperation and training area for US troops, eighty miles of front held by a mere four divisions?

Had the Top Brass been blind in the autumn of 1944? Or had it been a case of complacency – the Germans were finished? They would never attack again in the West. They were virtually beaten. The boys might well be coming home for Christmas! Or had it been gross negligence right at the top? All these reports, from whatever the source, had finally come to rest in Eisenhower's desk in Versailles. Why hadn't Ike acted? What had gone on in Versailles that autumn?

In 1966 a law was passed in the United States giving its citizens access to Federal files. The Freedom of Information Act seemed to offer a great opportunity for researchers to see how a democratic United States worked. America was to be shown as a free society, not like Great Britain with its Officials Secret Act and all the other restrictions which went with it. Of course, it didn't work like that. Most requests were marked by decade-long delays, which ended in denials on the grounds that disclosure would greatly damage 'national security'. Those countless cartons of documents stamped 'top secret' remained firmly behind double-locked steel doors with their classified combinations.

The author's attempts to tap these sources went, of course, much further back than the U-2 incident, the Cuban crisis or the start of the Cold War. I was trying to find out about events which took place half a century ago – the details of a battle of which the US Army could be proud. Why should there be any secrecy about that famous victory?

But in 1992 when I requested details of the US Army Inspector General's investigations into the actions of the first US units to be hit by the German 'surprise' attack, the Secretary of State for Defense's representative stated 'there are no records re your request'. Had the US Army lost valuable historical records dealing with the activities of some 20,000 American soldiers in December, 1944? They hadn't, of course. Those records were declassified, somewhat mysteriously, in February, 1993. Dating back to an inquiry held in January, 1945, they turned out to be perfectly harmless – no more than a whitewash job. But why the mystery?

It was the same with documents held by the National Security Agency. Dating back nearly half a century, they had been declassified for a decade, but parts were still censored in 1993. Why were files, such as the decodes of Japanese diplomatic traffic between their European embassies and Tokyo, and there were many thousands of them, so jumbled up and disorganized that only the most dogged and knowledgeable researcher could ever find his way through them? It was as if someone, at one time or other, had made it almost impossibly difficult for the researcher. Why? Could it be, half a century after the end of the Second World War, that there was one last secret that had to remain hidden? Who would have had the power back in 1945–46 to start the process which would ensure that key documents were missing, intelligence files doctored, papers remain classified or censored right up to the present, possibly for ever.

By September, 1944, after the Allies' sweep across France, Belgium and Luxembourg, the supposedly defeated German *Wehrmacht* had stopped them dead on the borders of the Reich. That September and October the Allies, and the Americans in particular, had tried time and again to bull their way through the fixed defences of the Siegfried Line on which the British had wanted to hang out their washing five years before. The reduction of the German defences around Aachen had taken seven weeks at a very high cost. In the Hurtgen Forest an American infantry division lasted, on average, two weeks before it was withdrawn, a third of its number killed, captured or wounded and another third succumbed to combat fatigue, trench foot or respiratory diseases.

The butcher's bill was tremendously high. As one weary GI said after reading a headline that the *Westwall* was manned by old men of the German Home Guard and boys, 'I don't care if the guy behind that gun is a syphilitic prick who's a hundred years old. He's still sitting behind eight feet of concrete and he's still got enough fingers to press triggers and shoot bullets!'

Now, as General Eisenhower personally took control of his land armies in the first week of November, his most urgent problem was to break through the Siegfried Line or to get the Germans to come out of their fixed defences and fight in the open where he could use his superior armour and aerial capacity. But how to do it?

In the second week of that month Eisenhower toured his frontline, showing himself to his hard-pressed soldiers and visiting divisional corps commanders. For three days during that period he was virtually incommunicado. The man who commanded armies numbering many millions sent out not one *single* message. What was going on at the front which was so important?

On 8 November, together with General Bradley, his army group commander, Eisenhower conferred with General Middleton, the VIII US Corps Commander. Under his control Middleton had three battle-experienced divisions, manning a frontline which stretched over eighty miles from Germany, through Belgium and into Luxembourg. Middleton's front was the most exposed of all the corps on the Western Front. And significantly Middleton had no reserves, save one green armoured division. Behind his thinly held frontline there was nothing but the natural water barrier of the River Meuse, which itself was unguarded.

In other words, Middleton's corps was wide open to attack. Asked at a meeting Middleton and Eisenhower held in the Luxembourg town of Wiltz what he would do if the Germans attacked his corps, Middleton boasted, 'It would be the best thing that could happen to us. I have nothing of value to lose between the front and the River Meuse. If they come through we can trap them and cut their head off, shortening the war by several months!'

It was a bold answer which must have pleased Eisenhower, but not for the reasons one would have expected. Here was a Supreme Commander who knew that three powerful German armies were being assembled to strike westwards – all his intelligence reports indicated that, probably through Middleton's Corps. Yet he did nothing to reinforce Middleton, ready for the blow to come. Indeed his Corps seemed to have been *purposefully* weakened in the weeks following Eisenhower's visit. By the time the Germans did strike, that long front was being held by two divisions which had been decimated in the Hurtgen Forest, each having suffered some 5,000 casualties, and the greenest infantry division in the whole of Europe, with only five days' experience in the line.

Why had Eisenhower done nothing? The answer is quite simple. He *wanted* the Germans out in the open. He had to force them out of their Siegfried Line defences into an area of his own choice – the Ardennes. Later, as part of the cover-up, much was made of the sluggishness of Eisenhower's response to the 'surprise' attack. On the first day of the German assault Eisenhower had two armoured divisions, one in the north, one in the south, moving to the attack. On the second day he had his two airborne divisions moving. On the third a whole British corps, four divisions strong, was on its way to the battlefront and three US divisions still in Britain were alerted for Europe. On the fourth, Patton's Third Army, which that flamboyant general had alerted to move north into the Ardennes *four days* before the 'surprise' attack had begun, was on its way too. Eisenhower's response was decidedly sharp and quick.

By the end of the first week of the Battle of the Bulge, as Churchill would soon call it, the Germans were beginning to admit defeat. Their losses were too high. Their fuel was beginning to run out, as Eisenhower had known from his intelligence before the battle that it would, and the weather was turning in the Allies' favour. Eisenhower had lured the Germans out of their fortifications and had inflicted upon them a great defeat, from which the *Wehrmacht* would never really recover.

But what of the bait? What of the young soldiers of Middleton's Corps – 60,000 of them, one third of whom were killed, wounded or captured in the first week of the Bulge – what of them? How could Eisenhower explain away their sacrifice? What would the Great American Public say if it ever found out that the Supreme Commander and future President of the United States had known the Germans were coming, but had done nothing *because he wanted them to come*?

In 1972 President Richard Nixon welcomed the Freedom of Information Act with a proclamation stating: 'The many abuses of the security system can no longer be tolerated. Fundamental to our way of life is the belief that when information which properly belongs to the people is systematically withheld by those in power, the people soon become ignorant of their own affairs, distrustful of those who manage them, and – eventually – incapable of determining their own destinities.'

Two years after making that promise, Nixon lost the presidency because he, too, had used the sword and shield of secrecy for his own protection. Eisenhower, on the other hand, has been more fortunate. He has managed to hide his secret for nearly half a century. Now I think the time has come to reveal how thousands of young American lives were sacrificed for a strategy. That is what this book is about – deceit in high places, sacrifice in lower ones. It is not a pretty tale. But in that dark December fifty years ago there were no pretty tales.

PROLOGUE

'If the other fellow would only hit us now! I'd welcome a counter-attack. We could kill many more Germans with a good deal less effort if they would only climb out of their holes and come after us for a change.'

General Bradley to General Smith,
8 October, 1944.

Before the Storm

All that November it had rained – a thin, bitter drizzle which turned the fields where the Blacks buried the dead into a quagmire. When the 'meat wagons' brought in their daily loads of dead from the 1st Army front, Captain Shomon's men worked up to their ankles in the thick, grey mud. There they stood sorting out the hundreds of dead Americans sprawled in great piles, their blood-stained, torn uniforms soaked black with the rain so that they looked like heaps of abandoned rags.

Shomon's Blacks, or as he called them 'my colored boys', had arrived for duty in the first week of that month. Shomon, all ruddy cheeks and glistening white teeth, had ordered his mess sergeant, Sergeant Brennan, to give the new arrivals a hearty meal before they were paraded in the burial fields just outside the tiny Dutch village. The white Captain thought it was better they had some hot food in their stomachs before they were confronted with the dead.

Then the white medical sergeants paraded the black workers in the mud and the rain. Before them on mattress covers lay the dead. There were hundreds of them, sprawled out grotesquely in the cold drizzle. Joe Shomon welcomed them to his 611th Quartermaster Graves Registration Company and told them that this was going to be 'their' cemetery. They would see it grow. The work was unpleasant, he knew, but all the same they were fortunate. They were not the victims. They were alive and well. Now and then they'd be given leave to go away and enjoy themselves.

Captain Shomon could see that the new arrivals were 'likeable chaps', but he could see, too, that they were mesmerized, perhaps horrified, by the piles of dead bodies lying before them. Indeed some of them couldn't take this first sight of the bodies of men killed in battle (by the time they were finished they would have buried 21,000). They broke ranks without orders and rushed to the latrines.

One of the remaining Blacks broke the ice, however. He looked at one of the white medical sergeants who had been doing this job since Normandy and said, 'Gruesome, aint it? Sho' is gruesome. Ah cant stand workin' hyar. Ah's gonna dig graves. Yassuh, give me a shovel. Ah's gonna dig graves.' Thereupon he grabbed a spade, stepped over the nearest body and started to trudge through the mud, shaking his head all the while. One by one they followed him to the open fields. They were in business.

Shomon's 'colored boys' began work outside the little Dutch village of Margraten, not far from the German frontier city of Aachen, where the line was. Now each day the US First Army's 'meat wagons' brought back the dead, splattering mud everywhere as the vehicles skidded and bounced their way to where the medical sergeants and the Blacks, shovels in hand, waited for them.

Swiftly the medical noncoms went to work on the corpses. For no one, especially the Blacks, wanted to leave the dead unburied overnight. Shomon knew his Blacks wouldn't have stood for that. Expertly the white sergeants slit the two sides of the dead man's uniform with their scalpels. All personal possessions were taken from the corpse and placed in a little canvas bag to be sent back home to the dead man's kin. Dirty pictures, condoms, things which might offend the sorrowing relatives, were tossed to one side. The dogtags came next. One was cut off for dispatch to the rear. The other was placed in the dead man's mouth which was firmly closed. This would help in any later identification.

That done, the bodies were handed over to the Black burial details. The corpses were loaded into mattress covers and taken to where the graves were being dug. Shomon's boys worked long and hard, but they had one strange failing. They seemed to eat all the time. It wasn't just the regular three hot meals a day served by Sgt Brennan. It was the turnips in the fields, even raw cabbages and raw potatoes. They appeared to be stuffing their mouths with food of some sort all the time. In the end Shomon concluded vaguely that it had something to do with their macabre job.

The mixed team of Whites and Blacks worked well together. In an army which was totally segregated, this was unusual. There was absolutely no racial prejudice. Black and White, the men often prepared the same body together. Complications arose only when they had to deal with 'X' bodies. These were corpses which had not yet been identified. Blacks hated working on them. Fluid had to be injected into the tips of the dead fingers so that a set of prints could be taken. Rigid jaws had to be forced open in order to make a dental chart for identification purposes. Now and again these 'X' corpses lacked both hands and heads.

There was one of Shomon's boys whose morale never wavered. He was a 'short, silent, bowlegged character' called Henry. No one ever seemed to know his surname. Henry had the most dangerous job of all. It was his task to carry away any ammunition found on the dead. Whenever one of the sergeants on 'the stripping line' called, 'Henry – *Hen-ree*, take this ammo down to the pit and watch them grenades,' he would come ambling up carrying his basket and tape. He'd stick down the grenades' levers with his tape, put them in the basket and trot off to the pit, muttering to himself, 'Lawdy, lawdy. If these aint dangerous taties, plumb dangerous. Yassuh.' As Joe Shomon recalled after the war, 'None of us envied Henry, but we all liked him.'

But now, as November gave way to December, the rains gave way to icy winds, blowing in straight from the east where the front was. They brought with them the ominous boom of the permanent barrage. Now the ground was iron-hard. Sometimes it took the sweating Blacks four hours to dig a single hole. The work was so hard that the officers often gave a hand and wielded a pick. It was one way to keep warm in those freezing fields of death.

Despite the cold the medical sergeants on the 'stripping line' continued to work without surgical gloves. They were too cumbersome. But working without gloves on putrid bodies which might have lain on the ground for days brought danger with it. The prescribed sterile techniques were almost impossible to maintain among so much putrification. Frequently the medical sergeants were rushed to the nearest field hospital. Blue streaks were spreading up their forearms and there'd be the telltale hard knots under their armpits: both sure signs of blood poisoning.

But with December and the arctic cold, the number of casualties from the front started to drop rapidly. In November the meat wagons had brought them back in their hundreds. Now they came in trickles, perhaps only a couple of dozen a day. The men had more time to spend in the warmth of their quarters in the village. Passes were issued to Paris and Liège. Happy young men, showered and shaved, the stink of death eradicated from their bodies and uniforms, boarded the 'deuces-and-half' which would take them to those cities for a 'seventy-two hours'. There they'd enjoy their brief spell of freedom with 'boocou' beer and the women who worked the red light district behind Liège's main station or in Paris' 'Pig Alley' (*Place Pigalle*). But in the end they had to return to face the meat wagons and the stripping line once again.

Of an evening now, with the pressure off, Joe Shomon and Lt Donovan, his second-in-command, played bridge with his host, Burgomaster Bouckers, and the local priest, Father Heynen. The latter always said the last rites over the daily delivery from the front, whatever the weather. They played in the warmth of the Burgomaster's living room, conversing in an awkward mix of French, English and German (all the villagers spoke a German dialect).

Now the front had stabilized. The US 1st Army had finally admitted, after horrendous casualties, that it was stalled on the Siegfried Line. From Aachen right down to Trier, with the exception of the bitter fighting in the Hurtgen Forest, hardly a shot was being fired. It was no different further south. There, Patton's Third Army's attack on the same fortifications in the Saar had come to a halt. After two months he was still trying to take the French fortress city of Metz. The front, in general, seemed to have gone to sleep.

The only activity seemed to be the overflight of the German buzz bombs which were being launched at Liège, Antwerp and London from just over the German frontier. During the evening card sessions they came over at regular intervals. At first they had taken to rushing outside when they heard the ominous put-put of the flying bombs. But after a couple had exploded prematurely nearby they had taken to the safety of the Burgomaster's cellar. There they would sit until the danger had passed.

But as the last Christmas of the war approached, even the buzz bombs seemed to have ended their nightly flights. At the front the heavy guns had ceased firing, too. Now the dead came in in mere trickles. The only activity was *behind* the front. On both sides of Highway One, which ran from Maastricht to Aachen, where the front was, the great dumps of shells intended for the next 1st Army offensive mounted daily. Mountains of full jerricans were everywhere. In the village itself thousands of tons of high explosive were stacked. They came 'right up to our front yard,' as Shomon remembered. Whole batteries of guns – 105mm, 155s and 140s – were sited under their camouflage nets on either side of the key highway to the front.

*

A hundred miles further south, at the end of the 1st Army's long front, it seemed no different. There in Luxembourg where the Rivers Our and Sauer – shallow enough to be waded in summer – formed the front line, with the Germans hidden in their bunkers on the hills only 150 yards away, nothing stirred, at least during daylight hours. The GIs of the 28th and 4th Infantry Divisions moved about freely. Occasionally a solitary shell or burst of machine-gun fire reminded them that a war was still going on, but that was about it.

It was something for which the 'Misfits', as they called themselves, were grateful. The 'Misfits' were the oddballs of the 28th's 707th Tank Battalion's Company B. On 21 November, 1944, the 28th Division had followed its neighbour, the 4th, out of the 'green hell' of the Hurtgen Forest. Both divisions had lost well over 5,000 men, nearly one third of their strengths. Now as they rested in peaceful Luxembourg, they were sorely in need of new weapons and replacements.

The 'Misfits' felt they needed more rest than their comrades, for they had seen some terrible things in those woods. They had seen their C.O., Colonel Ripple, abandon his tanks. They had watched as one of their officers had directed fire on his own attacking infantry. They had heard how battalion commanders had broken down with 'combat fatigue' and had refused to fight any longer. They had seen a fellow crew member killed in action in a 'particularly horrific manner'. The Misfits needed the rest all right. They had survived the 'death factory', with its conveyor belt slaughter of American divisions, one every two weeks. Now they could try to forget the war for a while.*

There were four Misfits. There was Pfc John Marshall, who hated all authority, especially when wielded by officers he thought cowards. To Marshall his C.O. was 'a bullshitter' and his platoon leader, Lt Carl Anderson, 'skinny, about 110 pounds, soaking wet,' always intent on reminding the men that he was 'an officer and superior to the enlisted men'.

Their driver was Corporal John Alyea from Indiana. He was likeable and very strong, 'with the endurance of an ox'. The loader for the Sherman's 75mm cannon was Pfc Jim Spencer. He was short and sturdy and hailed from a 100-soul hamlet somewhere in

---

* See C. Whiting, *The Battle of the Hurtgen Forest*, Leo Cooper Ltd, for further details.

remotest Kansas. He was always ready to do anyone a favour, even if it meant risking his own life to do so.

The gunner was Cpl Lennard McKnight from Arkansas. He talked very slowly and seemed, on the surface, somewhat dim-witted. He wasn't at all. He has a mind 'like a calculating machine'. At one time or another every man in the Misfits' B Company owed him money which he had won by his astute manner of playing poker. Even the mess sergeants were in his debt. This meant that *Bea Wain II*, as they called their Sherman tank, was always well supplied with 'goodies' intended for the company's officers. At all times Marshall kept the cavities intended for the tank's 75mm shells stocked with hams, canned goods, even, at one time, with canned oysters, taken from behind the officers' backs by the indebted cooks. That was something that gave Marshall particular pleasure.

Bea Wain II's commander was Sergeant Mike Kasovits from Chicago. He was 'strictly G.I.', unlike the other Misfits. But they admired him for his daring. Once in the Hurtgen, while they were under shell fire, the Sergeant had got tired of relieving himself in the empty ammunition box they kept for that purpose inside the tank. Although shells were bursting everywhere, he had clambered out of the turret and completed his business. Returning, he was hit by a burst of shrapnel. Hurriedly the crew had dragged him inside and stripped him. They discovered that bits of red hot shrapnel had penetrated right to his underwear, raising half a dozen ugly welts on his body. Otherwise he was completely unhurt. That had seemed to the Misfits like a miracle. Thereafter they always thought of him as 'Mac, the Invisible Shield'. Mac could be as 'G.I.' as he liked, but as long as they had him aboard the *Bea Wain II* they knew they never would be hit.

Now, with the enemy just on the other bank of the River Our, the Misfits relaxed. They were still wearing the same dirty uniforms they had worn in the Hurtgen Forest. What little ammunition they had left dated from that battle too. Nor had the fifth member of the crew who had been killed there been replaced.

Such matters didnt not seem to worry their C.O., Colonel Ripple. He sent so many officers and enlisted men on leave that there were always tanks without crews. Nor did he order any maintenance to be carried out on the battle-battered Shermans, though now, in this freezing December, maintenance was highly necessary. Indeed the Misfits had begun to light fires under the *Bea Wain II* to get it started in the morning. As John Marshall reported long afterwards: 'The tanks stayed idle although we could see the Germans across the river. I never had such a workfree time in camp. It was like a holiday, as though we'd never fight again.'

Only once were the Misfits ordered out on patrol. As they suspected, they had much difficulty in starting their Sherman. Only after lighting fires under her did they manage to get her rolling. So they ran along the River Our which was less than thirty yards wide at that spot.

Suddenly they spotted a German patrol. The thought flashed through Marshall's mind that their little idyll was going to come to an abrupt end. But the Germans didn't fire and their platoon leader *daren't* fire. Instead he gave that classic order that the Misfits had heard often enough in the Hurtgen, when it looked as if trouble was coming their way: 'Let's get the hell outa here.' They did.

Now, as Christmas approached, the first presents from the States began to arrive at Company B. Some of the men started buying up the local Diekirch beer and schnapps, which had a kick like a mule. They were planning to have a company smoker on Christmas Day. They thought they deserved it, for most of them had not spent a Christmas at home since 1942. As Marshall recorded many years afterwards, 'It was a fun time, *while it lasted*!'

Even the new boys of the 106th US Infantry Division, moving for the first time into the centre of the long American line in the second week of December, found it totally different from what they had expected. The 'Golden Lions', as they called themselves after their divisional patch, were taking over positions from the veteran 2nd Division in the captured Siegfried Line bunkers in front of the key Belgian road and rail centre of St Vith.

The 2nd had spent two months here, where the Allied forces had penetrated deepest into Germany. They had made the most of their time in this quiet sector, where there had been no fighting since the previous September. Now the Golden Lions found that they were not going to live in damp foxholes as they had expected. Instead they were housed in Siegfried Line bunkers of massive concrete and steel, or in wooden huts which the 2nd had built from the plentiful timber of the forests which surrounded their positions.

20-year-old Staff Sergeant Petersen of the 422nd Regiment's mortar team arrived in the line to be told by the 2nd Division sergeant from whom he was taking over, 'There's the stakes [for aiming the mortars] and there's the latrine. Bye.' That was the extent of Petersen's briefing. Minutes later a bemused Petersen entered his new home, a Siegfried Line bunker, and found it 'almost homey'. 'There were tables on which to write and eat. Steel bunks [were] hanging from the walls and there was a wood-burning stove in the corner.' To Petersen it looked 'almost like a boy scout camp back home.' He was soon to be disillusioned.

Pfc Harry Martin also arrived at the front with the 106th's 423rd Regiment that cold Monday afternoon, 11 December, 1944. He was a tall, skinny boy of 18 who was blind in one eye. For years as a child Harry been the butt of his father's scorn and temper. Old Mr Martin had gone overseas in the First World War. When angry he would rage, 'You bigfooted, skinny, four-eyed bastard. I wish I had been killed in the war in 1918 and then none of this would have happened!'

Drafted for 'limited service only', young Harry Martin had volunteered for the infantry because he knew that would annoy his father, who so far had kept bombarding him with letters urging him to keep to that 'Good Old Narrow Path'. It did. In August, 1944, he had received a letter stating, 'If you haven't already taken the last letter I wrote to you to your company commander, DO SO AT ONCE! You do not belong in the infantry and I DO NOT WANT YOU IN THE INFANTRY! Do not volunteer to stop in the infantry as your chances with the enemy are all in his favor, especially in HAND TO HAND COMBAT!'

Martin had ignored his Father's advice. He loved the camaraderie of the infantry, their macho toughness, their ribald jokes and dirty marching songs. One in particular always gave him a charge as he sang it lustily on route marches. Always he imagined what the 'Old Man' would say if he heard him bawling out:

> Momma's on the bottom,
> Poppa's on the top,
> Baby's in the crib shouting,
> 'Give it to her, Pop!'

He liked the last verse best of all and he sang it with particular gusto:

Goddam Christ Almighty,
Who the fuck are we?
We're the raiders of the night.
WE'D RATHER FUCK THAN FIGHT!

Now as the teenage, one-eyed machine gunner surveyed his new positions, he thought the last line was particularly apt. On this 'ghost front' there'd be no fighting, he had been assured. Soon they'd be on leave somewhere to the rear, where there were women, and everyone knew that foreign women were easy lays.

Again like the 422nd, the 423rd didn't have to go into foxholes. Instead they were housed in log huts and in Martin's there were 'bunks, blankets and a wood-burning stove'. Like Petersen, Martin thought, 'It was like being in boy scout camp, not the frontline. We had three good meals a day, served by the company cooks, "Marmalade" Martin and "Peanut Butter" Rosen, and a comfortable place to sleep.'

But at night things changed dramatically. The Second had strung empty cans filled with pebbles along the barbed wire to their front. This was to warn them if any German attempted to sneak up on their positions during the hours of darkness. In the night wind these cans rattled constantly. That started the nervous new boys on sentry duty shouting to each other for reassurance. The Germans would respond by firing parachute flares over the line or with long bursts of tracer. Usually the Americans returned the fire and, in the darkness beyond, the German observers would mark down another '*Ami*' position on their charts.

Even when off duty at night, Pfc Martin was often scared. He had a horror of being run through by a German bayonet. 'The thought of that long steel blade going through my body was bad enough, but the worst part would be when he violently withdrew the bayonet, taking my guts with it.' One night in his snug wooden hut he dreamed that a German fighter was coming zooming in, machine guns chattering. He could actually see two 50 calibre bullets heading right for his forehead, shattering his brain. A comrade shook him awake, telling him he had been shouting out in his sleep. He had a headache for two days after that, 'and carried that vision with me for a long time. I kept hoping it was not a premonition of my death'.

But in the morning the Germans, real or imaginary, had vanished. The front would be quiet again and 'Marmalade' Martin and 'Peanut

Butter' Rosen would be serving scalding hot java and buckwheat flapjacks with plenty of syrup. Once more the front just seemed like a large boy scout camp, where there was absolutely no danger. Wasn't this the ghost front? Here divisions came to train for combat or rest after it.

Not all the Golden Lions were so sanguine. General James, the 51-year-old commander of the 106th, was one such. He was a somewhat overweight officer with that Don Ameche type of moustache popular with Regular Army officers of the time. Now he had set up his HQ in the *Sankt Josef's Kloster* school in St Vith itself. There he had mentioned his doubts to General Robertson of the Second.

The latter knew that, although Jones had been in the army for nearly 30 years, he had never heard a shot fired in anger. He sought to calm Jones, saying, 'Take it easy. Those Krauts won't attack even if ordered to.' What Robertson didn't tell Jones at the time was that he, too, had been unhappy with his divisional position in the Eifel for the two months they had been there. He had appealed to General Middleton, commander of the VIII Corps to which they both belonged, for permission to change his position. Troy Middleton had turned him down flat. He wasn't to yield an inch of territory, however dangerous or exposed it seemed to him.

One of Robertson's subordinates, Colonel Boos, did, however, reveal to his opposite number, Colonel Cavender of the 106th's 423rd Regiment, that the 2nd had not been happy with their dispositions. He told Cavender, one of the handful of Golden Lions who had actually seen action, albeit as a GI in the First World War, 'Come on, I have something to show you.' Together the two colonels went up into the line and from a height overlooking the foremost village held by the Americans – beyond on the ridge line were the Germans – Boos had pointed in the direction of Prum, the largest town in the area beyond the horizon and had said, 'That's the way the Krauts will come. Through that corridor. In the direction of Bleialf.' Colonel Boos was to be proved right.

Next morning Cavender had set out with his executive officer, Lt-Colonel Nagle, to inspect his positions which covered seven of the total twenty-seven miles held by the new 106th Division. That was about five times the length of front which should have been held by troops facing first class soldiers like the Germans. What he saw didn't please Cavender. After his release from a German POW camp, he would write: 'I realized that we were up against a problem with some seven miles of frontage. By necessity, it was thinly held with no depth and without a mobile reserve.'

Cavender took the matter up with General Jones. He asked for the return of his 2nd Battalion which was in the divisional reserve. Jones refused. Then Cavender asked what armour he could call upon in case of trouble. Jones answered that he had posed the same question to the Corps Commander, General Middleton. His answer had been, 'There is no armour. There is no help in case of an attack in force up there. You are to stay in place and slug it out with them.' With that General Jones departed, saying cheerfully over his shoulder, 'Good luck. I'll be seeing you.'

When the two men did meet again the war was over and their world had fallen apart. In the eyes of the US Army they had disgraced themselves; there was no future in that Army for them. Jones would never get another division. Cavender would never receive that first general's star for which he had worked so hard ever since General Pershing had picked him out of the trenches in the Argonne in 1918 and sent him back to West Point to become an officer. In the winter of 1944 the US Army, rightly or wrongly, would have no time for losers.

In April, 1918, when Cavender was still a private in France, 26-year-old Captain Troy Middleton was desperately trying to get out of his job of training recruits in the States. He wanted to rejoin his old outfit, the 4th Infantry Division, so that he could go with it to France. Already he was wise enough in the ways of the Army to know that rapid promotion came on the battlefield and not in a base camp.

In due course he managed to convince his C.O. to relieve him. He hastened to the 4th (the 'Ivy League Division' as it was called from its divisional patch) where he took over his old company from a certain Captain Hurley Fuller, 'a cantankerous fellow, but a good fighter' in Middleton's words, of whom we shall hear more. Thus, at the head of his old company Middleton sailed for France. Six months later he was a regimental commander and the youngest colonel in the US Army.

Thereafter the years of peace passed slowly with the Army being progressively run down, while promotion came tardily. In the end Middleton took retirement in the same rank that he had obtained twenty years before. But in 1941, immediately after Pearl Harbor, he rallied to the flag. He gave up his job as an administrator at the University of Southern Louisiana in Baton Rouge and rejoined the army. He asked for a fighting command, but again he was given the task of training troops.

Not for long. Soon he was given command of the green 45th Infantry Division, a National Guard outfit. With it he took part in the invasion of Sicily, its first battle. Thereafter he led the Division in Italy, where it was to become one of the US Army's most experienced outfits.

Middleton, however, didn't stay with the Forty-Fifth during its long, hard slog up what Churchill called 'the soft underbelly of Europe' (the hard-pressed troops had another name for it). Instead he was sent to England, where he took over command of the US VIII Corps. The VIII Corps, as part of Patton's Third Army, played a large part in the conquest of Brittany and, in particular, in the protracted siege of Brest. After the French seaport finally fell in September, 1944, Middleton's VIII Corps was sent to take over the Eifel-Ardennes sector of the US 1st Army's front.

Here the big, burly, bespectacled General, now in his mid-fifties, was responsible for the front stretching from Losheim in the north on the German-Belgian border to Echternach in the south on the German-Luxembourg frontier. In December, 1944, Middleton had under command four divisions to cover this very long front. In the south there was his old 4th Infantry. Next to it came the 28th Division. Both had just returned from the 'Green Hell of the Hurtgen', where they had suffered grievous casualties. In the centre lay his green 106th Division, which was linked to its neighbour in General Gerow's V Corps, the equally inexperienced 99th Infantry Division, by the 14th Cavalry Group. The 14th, which had fought one small action in France, were, in essence, cavalrymen acting as infantry.

As his reserve Middleton had the bulk of the 9th Armored Division, which was also green and which he was keeping behind the front near his headquarters at the Belgian town of Bastogne. In essence, therefore, Middleton had some 60,000 men in the line, of which some thirty per cent had combat experience. They were commanded by officers, right down to the company commander level, who had little or no battle experience.

The thinness of his troops on the ground and their lack of combat experience didn't seem to worry Middleton greatly. The terrain was, in his opinion, and apparently that of the High Command, unsuitable for the kind of mobile warfare which the Germans favoured with their 'blitzkrieg' techniques. (All of them had apparently forgotten that German armour had swept through the Eifel-Ardennes back in 1940 to strike a death blow at the French Army, dug in in the Maginot Line.)

To attack Middleton's key positions, the Germans would have to breach a front line formed by the Rivers Our and Sauer. Thereafter, apart from the five-mile-broad 'Losheim Gap' guarded by the 14th Cavalry, the attackers would have to scale wooded heights everywhere to reach the main road connecting St Vith and Luxembourg, known to the troops as 'Skyline Drive'. If the attackers succeeded in this, then they could advance along the few roads leading westwards to the River Meuse at the back of VIII Corps and all these roads were channelled through either St Vith or Bastogne. In Middleton's considered opinion, an attack on his VIII Corps would be a very tough proposition for the Germans. Besides, this was the 'Ghost Front' where there had been no German activity, save patrolling, for over three months. Nothing could happen to his VIII Corps.

There is a US Signal Corps photograph extant which shows Middleton in a small office near the Luxembourg town of Wiltz on the late afternoon of Wednesday, 8 November, 1944. Next to him on his right is General Leonard of the 9th Armored Division. On his left is General Bradley, Commander of the US 12th Army Group, complete with combat jacket and a revolver slung under his left armpit. Sitting on the desk in the corner, sipping coffee out of a chipped cup, is the Supreme Commander, General Eisenhower himself. As usual he had one of the sixty cigarettes he smoked every day clenched in his right hand.

Middleton has his head bent slightly to one side and his hand raised as if he is making a point, while Eisenhower and Bradley seem to be listening attentively. But what is that point? Neither of the two most senior officers there that late winter afternoon ever mentioned what it was. For some strange reason the Supreme Commander filed no messages during his tour of the front between 8 and 10 November. Volume Five of his Despatches is completely blank for this period. Nor did General Bradley, in two volumes of biography, ever mention it!

But we *do* know what Bradley told General Bedell Smith, Eisenhower's Chief-of-Staff, that month. For three months now Bradley's armies had been battering their heads against the German defences in the Siegfried Line. Casualties had been high, with very little success. The Germans were still in place and Allied advances were measured not in miles, but in metres. Understandably Bradley could explode to Bedell Smith, 'If the other fellow would only hit us now! I'd welcome a counter-attack. We could kill many more Germans, with a good deal less effort, if they would only climb out of their holes and come after us for a change!'

We know, too, that at that Wednesday meeting in Wiltz there was some discussion of the vulnerability of Middleton's front. Eisenhower, it has been suggested, asked Middleton, 'How serious a problem would we have if Hitler were to attack through the Ardennes?'

Was this the point Middleton was making with his raised hand at that moment when he replied fervently, 'It would be the best thing that could happen to us. I have nothing of value that I can't afford to lose between the front and the Meuse River. If they come through we can trap them and cut their head off, shortening the war by several months.'

With what he already knew of German intentions, was this just a rhetorical question on Eisenhower's part? Was General Middleton's bold answer the one he was expecting? If Eisenhower's question was not rhetorical and Middleton's answer is to be taken at face value, what provision would be made for those divisions at the front through which the Germans would strike? As of that Wednesday there seemed to be none. A lot of questions, but few answers.*

Thereafter, one by one Middleton's veteran divisions departed for other fronts to be replaced by green or very tired soldiers. It seemed as if Middleton's already extended front in the Ardennes was being deliberately weakened. He had little to do. In early December he was asked by 1st Army to use 23rd Special Troops to attempt to fool the Germans into believing that a new division, the 75th Infantry, was moving into VIII Corps area. The Special Troops did their usual stunts with sound trucks, extra radio traffic, etc, but the Germans

---

* It seems strange, even suspect, that Eisenhower, commanding the destinies of some four million men, should remain incommunicado for seventy-two hours while visiting his frontline commanders. Was there not *one* single message which needed to be sent his 5,000-strong HQ in Versailles?

opposite weren't fooled. They had enough agents in Middleton's area, where everybody spoke German, to know exactly what was going on there.

Christmas approached. At Middleton's HQ in Bastogne, a remote provincial town where, in peacetime, the only excitement had been the annual nuts festival, Middleton's staff officers prepared a slap-up party for the local kids. General Middleton occupied himself with matters other than military. Indeed he seemed so unconcerned about the situation that one of the last letters he sent out from APO 208 before the storm broke reads:

'Colonel E. Monnot Lanier came by my headquarters today and left me a file of correspondence and his reply regarding the Louisiana State University William Helis oil lease. Colonel Lanier has requested me to express my views.

'Not having the lease before me I cannot recall the exact provisions. I can state, however, that at no time did the Finance Committee of the Board of Supervisors signify a willingness to alter the terms of the lease. The committee took the stand that, without further ado, the contracting parties abide by the terms of the lease.'

So the Corps Commander dealt with the business of his old university, apparently confident that his front was secure. Soon he would have other more pressing problems on his mind.

In the second week of December, 1944, the little German officer who was soon to cause General Middleton so much trouble moved his headquarters to the little Eifel hamlet of Dachscheid, some ten miles behind the German frontline. The hamlet was located in what the military called the '*Grünzone*' (green zone), from where the locals had not been evacuated. So, in order not to attract attention, the little officer did not wear the uniform and badges of rank to which he was entitled. Instead he wore that of a lowly colonel of infantry. Most of the locals had friends or relatives on the other side of the border in Belgium and he wanted no loose tongues wagging.

Although he stood five foot two, the little officer had a determined walk. His face was hard and energetic, with powerful eyes. All in all, he looked like a man who was used to giving orders – and having them obeyed – *immediately*. Even the villagers, who over the last few months had seen a lot of colonels of infantry come and go, were impressed by him.

Not that they saw much of him. For the little officer spent only nights at his farmhouse HQ, where the animals lived under the same roof as the staff officers. Early each morning, accompanied by an aide and a driver, armed with a machine pistol, the little officer was off to visit yet another frontline outfit. Here in the *Rotzone* (red zone) there were few civilians. Most of them had been evacuated back in September when the *Amis* had first made their appearance on the frontier of the Reich. Still the little officer stuck to his disguise.

Once he spent a night in a freezing bunker opposite the positions of the 28th Division's 110th Regiment, to which the Misfits belonged. He noted that as soon as dusk fell the *Amis* fell back to the shelter of their villages on the heights along 'Skyline Drive'. It was a particularly useful piece of information. He made a note of it; he would use it in due course.

On another occasion he slipped into the Eifel village of Weinsheim, which housed the HQ of the *18th Volksgrenadierdivision*, facing the newly arrived Golden Lions. Not that the little officer was particularly interested in the 106th. He knew as much about them and their dispositions as he needed. The Division's path across France and into Belgium had been covered by 'sleepers', paid agents left behind by *Obersturmbannfuhrer* Skorzeny, head of the *SS Jagdkommando** during the German retreat of the previous September.

What did interest the little officer was the road network in and around the 106th's positions. With the commander of the 18th, he studied the positions of the *Grünschnabel*, or 'greenbeaks', as the latter called the 106th contemptuously. For the most part the 106th seemed to have grouped themselves to the north-east of the road that led from the American-held village of Bleialf, which ran in two directions – one to Auw and over the frontier to the Belgian village of Schönberg, the other directly to Schönberg. From here it went on to St Vith, which he vitally needed to capture on the first day of the great surprise attack.

Again his study of the 106th that winter's day provided him with a piece of information of great importance. Colonel Hoffmann-Schonborn, the commander of the 18th *Volksgrenadier*, told him that day that his patrols had discovered a two-mile gap in the area defended by the 14th Cavalry group between the 99th and 106th Divisions. It was exactly at the spot where the *Ami* V and VIII Corps

---

* Literally 'hunting commando'. Best equivalent would be the British S.A.S.

joined – an ideal place for an attack. The little man made a quick note of the information.

That late December afternoon with the light already beginning to fade as he motored back to his HQ, the little man found himself travelling through a desolate landscape abandoned by man. There was hardly any sign of human activity, military or otherwise. That pleased him. His plan of concealment was working splendidly, it appeared. For he knew better than most that the dense fir woods on both sides of the winding road to Prüm and then on to Dachscheid concealed a whole army, *his*.

Under camouflage nets on both sides of the road lay huge piles of ammunition, petrol, shells, etc, etc. Deeper in the forests there were whole regiments of tanks, huge lumbering Tigers, the quicker Panthers and the old reliable Mark IVs. Battery after battery of artillery was hidden there too. And everywhere there were soldiers camping out in the woods, some 200,000 of them, all under the strictest orders not to reveal themselves to the *Ami* artillery spotter planes.

They were not allowed to light fires unless they had smokeless fuel. If they didn't, they had to wait till after darkness when the cooks brought up the great hayboxes filled with the German *Landser*'s favourite 'fart soup', peasoup made from great green bricks of dehydrated peas, accompanied, if they were lucky, by slabs of sausage.

Despite the growing darkness, with a hint of snow in the air, the little *Ami* spotter planes, out looking for targets for their artillery, were hopping in and about the green hills. But, as the little German officer noted with satisfaction, they found none. The men were obeying his orders to the letter.

Of course discipline was draconian. Only the previous week, Hoffmann-Schonborn had had a message read to each battalion of his 18th *Volksgrenadierdivision*. It named six of his grenadiers who had deserted to the *Amis* and stated: 'Those bastards have given away important military secrets. The result is that the Americans have been laying accurate artillery fire on your positions, your platoon and company headquarters, your field kitchens and your message routes. Deceitful Jewish mud-slingers taunt you with their pamphlets and try and entice you into becoming bastards who let them spew their poison. As for the contemptible traitors who have forgotten their honour, rest assured the Division will see that they never see their loved ones any more. Their families will have to atone for their treason. The destiny of a people has never depended upon traitors and bastards. The true German soldier was and is the best in the world. Unwavering behind him is the Fatherland. 'Long live Germany! Heil the Führer!'

It was strong stuff. The concept of *Sippenhaft* (arrest of the kin of the accused) was totally unfair. But desperate times needed desperate measures. If men could be stopped from deserting to the enemy, especially at this juncture, by the threat to their families, well and good. For the utmost secrecy was necessary for the success of what was to come.

Tired but satisfied, the little man returned to his smelly farmhouse HQ, with the usual steaming manure pile under the kitchen window. It was the way the local farmers showed how prosperous they were; the bigger the heap, the richer he was. Here, as usual, he would change into a cleaner uniform and become for the evening Colonel-General Hasso von Manteuffel, veteran of battles on all Germany's fronts over the last five years, and now commander of the Fifth Panzer Army.

Now there would be a few schnapps, perhaps a couple of bottles of Moselle to go with the same fare that his soldiers ate. Thereafter the bemedalled tunics would come off and they would resume working over their maps until the small hours when their eyes would blur and their heads would be ringing with fuel tonnages, supply routes, march columns and all the other complicated logistics of an army preparing for a big attack. Still it had to be done. Time was running out.

Artilleryman Klaus Ritter was one of the many thousands of men of the Fifth Panzer Army under the command of von Manteuffel, though the young soldier in his twenties had heard of neither. He had come on emergency leave to the Eifel from Russia to help clear up the wreckage of the family home at Weinsheim after the little farm had been hit by an *Ami* bomb. That job completed, it had seemed wiser to him to stay in this quiet front rather than go back to the shooting war in Russia. He had asked to join the *18th Volksgrenadierdivision* and had been accepted.

Now he and the other crew members of their 105mm cannon team, towed by a captured Russian tractor, lived deep in the forest. Their billet was a deep hole they had dug and covered with logs.

They called it their *Gartenlaube* (the bower), beloved by German weekend gardeners in peacetime. The place was plagued by rats, but it was warm and comfortable and lined with carpets looted from bombed and abandoned houses.

They didn't go short of food either. At first there were ample supplies of abandoned cattle, pigs and chickens. These they looted and brought back to their elderly sergeant. He belonged to '*Volksliste III*', a designation given by authorities to ethnic Germans who were not regarded as absolutely trustworthy. The sergeant, who had been a butcher in civvie street in his native Alsace, had become a German in 1940 when Hitler had annexed that province from France. The NCO soon carved up their booty and the cannon crew held regular feasts in their 'bower'.

It was a rough-and-ready sort of existence, but young Klaus Ritter wasn't complaining. He had escaped Russia with a whole skin, had been posted to a quiet front where nothing ever happened and twice a week he could go to the next village and luxuriate in a hot bath. What more could a *Landser* want in this year of 1944?

But by the beginning of December Ritter began to notice changes in the Eifel. On 1 December all ethnic Germans were removed from the 18th *Volksgrenadier*. That day their Alsatian sergeant was replaced by a much younger and more energetic NCO. More and more troops started to pour into the Eifel. These days when he went for his fifteen minute bath, he'd encounter some of them and they would tell him how they had been called into the infantry the previous September from the Navy, Air Force, flying schools, universities, factories and the like. It had been a *levée en masse*, ordered by Hitler personally. Why, the new arrivals didn't know.

But they did tell him that their journey to the front had been carried out with the utmost secrecy. Always they had arrived at night. In Kyllburg, Wittlich and Bitburg, the main railheads behind the Fifth Army front, they had been picked up by truck or in some cases by local farmers driving their oxen-towed carts and wagons. This transport would take them from the 'Green Zone' to the 'Red Zone'. Here they would dismount and carry out the last leg of their journey to the front on foot.

They marched, they related, down a specifically designated road, the stamp of their marching feet deadened by the straw covering the road's surface and the roar of low-flying fighter planes zooming down at regular intervals. Each road was 'commanded' by a 'road officer', who was answerable to a court martial if anyone breached the security of 'his' road by lighting a fire or flashing a torch.

Now Klaus Ritter, one of the 'old hares', as the veterans of the *Wehrmacht* called themselves, who had thought the war was lost, sensed new hope. The new boys were very green and not well trained, but they were well armed with the latest machine pistols and assault rifles. Their uniforms were clean and brand new, not like his ragged tunic and down-at-heel boots. They were young and fit. They impressed him because 'they projected optimism and confidence. Perhaps there was hope for Germany after all?' He could not fail to notice the rising tension and undercurrent of suppressed excitement as more and more troops flooded into his native Eifel. Something was going to happen.

Perhaps the only man in the whole of the Eifel who could have answered that question in full was Colonel General Hasso von Manteuffel. For even the latter's staff did not know the full extent of the plan. Each officer knew only as much as von Manteuffel was prepared to tell him. For the Führer had insisted on the strictest security. Everything was based on a 'need-to-know' policy, one with which von Manteuffel agreed. After all, even the Army Commander himself was ruled by the threat of *Sippenhaft* if he did anything wrong.

On Tuesday, 12 December, von Manteuffel, with all the other senior German commanders involved, had been subjected to a long lecture by Hitler on the objectives of the great attack. Stooped, pale and puffy-faced, with shaking hands that might indicate he was suffering from Parkinson's Disease, Hitler had given them the rationale behind his decision to launch one final great attack on the Western Allies. He said, 'In the whole of world history, there has never been such a coalition which has consisted of such heterogeneous elements with such diametrically opposed objectives as the present hostile coalition against us. On the one hand, ultra-capitalistic states; ultra-Marxist states on the other. On one side, a dying empire, that of Great Britain; on the other a 'colony', the United States, anxious to take over the inheritance. The United States is determined to take Britain's place in the world. The Soviet Union is anxious to lay hands on the Balkans, the Dardanelles, Persia and the Persian Gulf. Britain is anxious to keep her ill-gotten gains and make herself strong in the Mediterranean. These states are already at loggerheads and their antagonisms are growing visibily from hour to hour. If Germany can now deal a few heavy blows, the artificially united front will collapse at any moment with a tremendous thunderclap.'

Von Manteuffel was not particularly interested in Hitler's political reasoning. To him it sounded a bit like wishful thinking, based on the break-up at the very last moment of the military coalition against the Prussian King, Frederick the Great, in the 18th century. What interested him was *his* part in dealing out those 'heavy blows'.

In the end, after hours of talk, Hitler enlightened him. Three armies, which would finally amount to 600,000 men, would attack the American positions between Monschau in the north and Echternach in the south. This great force was to steamroller its way through the American VIII Corps and drive for the River Meuse to the rear of that corps. Once they had crossed the river, they would head for the capital, Brussels, and the huge Allied supply base at Antwerp.

If successful, this drive would split the Anglo-American forces. Britain, Hitler reasoned, would not have the resources – it was already scraping the manpower barrel – to make good its losses in men. The French coalition under General de Gaulle would probably fall and America would be left isolated on the Continent with its armies shattered and its rear areas in total disarray. The result, Hitler hoped, would be a better peace offer from the Western Allies than the present one of 'unconditional surrender'. Then he would be free to deal with Russia.

Most of the senior commanders listening to the Führer expounding his plans in his Ziegenhain HQ in the Hessian hills, close to where a certain Eisenhaur had emigrated from his poverty-stricken village to America in the 18th century, were far from convinced of the successful outcome of his plans. But if the *Wehrmacht* did manage to reach the Meuse, it would be a splendid victory and perhaps delay the inevitable defeat until Hitler introduced his much vaunted, war-winning 'wonder weapons'.

Colonel-General Jodl, Hitler's pasty-faced chief-of staff, now took over. He explained that Dietrich's Sixth SS Panzer Army to the north of Manteuffel's Fifth would take the lead and be given the most important objectives. The Führer owed it to his loyal SS. They should achieve the greatest laurels. But von Manteuffel's Fifth would also play a great role.

Four divisions of General Brandenburger's Seventh Army would protect von Manteuffel's flank in the south. They would move across the Sauer River into Luxembourg and form a blocking position there, in case – as was expected – the *Amis* attacked with Patton's Third Army from the Saar. Protected thus, the Fifth Panzer Army would drive forward and capture the two major rail-and-road centres in the US VIII Corps area, St Vith and then Bastogne, before driving on to the Meuse where they would cross at Namur.

A thoughtful von Manteuffel nodded his agreement. In the wintry conditions soon to be expected, the road network which radiated out from St Vith would be vital to the success of his operation. He would need to capture St Vith on the first day of the attack. His armour would be stalled if the infantry did not succeed in driving the *Amis* out of the place. Besides, the longer it took to clear St Vith, the sooner the *Amis* would recover from their surprise. They would use that same road network to bring up their own troops. St Vith had to be his number one priority.

As von Manteuffel listened to Jodl's exposé, he realized that Hitler and his staff had planned the operation in unusual detail. Normally such planning was left to subordinate staffs. Not now. Hitler had concerned himself with units down to the level of a brigade and, in one case, down to one single heavy tank company. Now von Manteuffel was told he could have a whole panzer corps to attack the 28th Infantry Division's 110th Regiment. This attack would be proceeded by a heavy artillery bombardment. The Army Commander objected. He told Hitler and Jodl he had personally observed the 110th's positions. They were empty at night. Instead of alerting the *Amis* by artillery fire, he preferred to cross the River Our in silence and reach the 'Skyline Drive' without the *Amis* being aware that they were being attacked.

Surprisingly Hitler agreed. In the 106th area, he agreed to an artillery bombardment, but before it came he wanted to infiltrate his units into the 'Golden Lions' positions using artificial moonlight. This was a device first used by Montgomery. Searchlight beams were bounced off low cloud to illuminate the ground below.

Hitler gave the General a wintry smile. 'How do you know there *will* be clouds, *Herr Generaloberst*?' he asked.

Cockily von Manteuffel replied 'Because, *mein Führer, you* have decided there will be bad weather that morning.'

On that note, with Hitler wagging his finger at von Manteuffel, the latter's part in the conference had ended. He set off on the long journey back to his remote Eifel HQ, his shaven head buzzing with new information. One thing was crystal clear to him, however. He must maintain absolute secrecy to the very end. That was vital if he were to achieve his first-day objectives. The *Amis* must know nothing until it was too late.

Three weeks before, on the night of 28/29 November, a young Luxembourg housewife, Madame Linden-Meier, her brother and two other Luxembourg civilians were surprised by a German border patrol at the little hamlet of Bivels. They were driven into Germany where they were taken to the village of Geichlingen. Here they noted many German soldiers and lots of vehicles. An hour later they were questioned by their German captors on the habits of the *Amis* in the border villages before being sent to the nearest town, Bitburg.

Here in the ruined Eifel town, still smoking from the last Allied air raid, they received an unpleasant surprise. They were confronted by the notorious Gestapo Official, Kloecher, who, up to the previous September, had ruled the nearby Luxembourg city of Diekirch with a rod of iron.

Kloecher didn't waste time. He knew his Luxembourgers. Peasants that they were, they were slow and stubborn, but gifted with what the Germans called *Bauernschläue* (peasant cunning). They needed to be treated firmly right from the start. A hail of questions descended upon the frightened housewife and her companions. *How many troops did the Amis have in Vianden? Where were their positions? What was their relationship with the locals?* There seemed no end to questions.

Finally he let them go and they were sent to Bernkastel, famous for its wines, where Madame Linden-Meier and three other Luxembourg women who had also been kidnapped by German patrols were put in the charge of Luxembourg collaborators who had fled with the retreating Germans the previous September. Their renegade fellow countrymen called them 'Ami Huren' (American whores) and said that the days of their type were numbered. Soon the Germans would be returning and Luxembourg would be part of the Reich once more. Not only that, the Germans would be back in Paris by Christmas!

Terrified as she was, the slim dark-haired housewife noted all she had seen and heard and when, on 9 December, she managed to escape, she reported everything to the first officer she met. But in Diekirch the Americans did not seem particularly interested in the number of German troops she had seen on the other side and they laughed outright when she reported that the renegades had told her the Germans would be back in Paris for Christmas. She went away, wondering if she had imagined it all or whether the Americans were complete fools.

But her report was forwarded to General Middleton in Bastogne, as was that of another Luxembourg woman who was captured by a German patrol but managed to escape. The report on the latter, a Madame Dele, read: 'Report received at 18.00. Information received from a woman who crossed into Germany . . . and was arrested . . . She is vouched for by the Luxembourg police as thoroughly reliable. She saw many horse-drawn vehicles, pontoons and boats and other river-crossing equipment coming from the direction of Bitburg. In Bitburg she heard some military personnel say they had taken three weeks to get there from Italy. There were also troops in the town with gray uniforms with black collar patches, the uniform of the SS troops. She also stated she had seen many artillery pieces, both horse-drawn and carried on trucks.'

These *appeared* to be the first indications that something was stirring on the Eifel-Ardennes sector. But there were many others prior to that period coming in from aerial reconnaissance, the US radio detection units and US patrols, as well as from deserters and civilians.

As far back as 18 September, 1944, an order from the German High Command was picked up, stating that a new Sixth SS Panzer Army was to be set up. Shortly thereafter the four key SS panzer divisions, the 1st, 2nd, 3rd and 12th, disappeared from German Order-of-Battle kept by Allied Intelligence. Three weeks after that von Manteuffel's Fifth Army was similarly 'lost'. On 20 November Captain Liddell Hart, the British strategist who thought of himself as the 'father of the Blitzkrieg', gave a vague hint in the *Daily Mail* that the Germans had managed 'to pull out their panzer divisions for refitting', implying that any future counter-offensive would, therefore, have a greater punch. Later, when the new 6th SS Panzer Army was 'found' moving over the Rhine to the general area south of Aachen, deep into the Eifel, no one at the top in the Allied camp seemed to be alarmed by the information.

In 1973, when the Ultra secret was finally revealed, writers on the Battle of the Bulge were now able to explain the supposed Intelligence failure to detect the coming German attack by the fact that virtually no Ultra intelligence was coming through in November and December. Right from the start, Hitler had ordered that landlines would be used for transmitting commands instead of the Enigma coding machine used up to that time. That excuse simply doesn't hold water. Indications of what was to come were flooding in to Supreme HQ until the very last hours before the great assault.

On 4 December, for example, a German soldier captured by a patrol of the 28th Division reported that the Germans were preparing to assault Siegfried Line positions currently in US hands. He meant those occupied by one of the 28th's regiments and the others soon to be taken over by the 106th Division.

On 10 December a prisoner classified by 1st Army Intelligence as 'an extremely intelligent PW whose other observations check with established facts' reported that all possible means were being used to collect forces for a coming all-out attack. Two days later 1st Army's Intelligence Bulletin recorded: 'Train movements indicate that the build-up of enemy forces on the western slope of the Moselle valley continues. *Grossdeutschland* Division,* a crack infantry division of the Germany Army, has again been reported in the area by PWs. A conservative estimate would place at least two *Volksgrenadier* and one *Panzergrenadier* division in the enemy's rear area opposite VIII US Corps.'

The following day a POW captured by the 14th Cavalry patrolling the gap between the 99th and 106th Divisions reported that a parachute division in the area was soon to be relieved by the elite 12th SS 'Hitler Youth' Division, part of the 'refound' 6th SS Panzer Army.

In the same week as Colonel Reeves, Middleton's Chief-of-Intelligence, wrote in his report that 'the enemy can continue his active defense of his present positions . . . until the VIII Corps goes on the offensive,' he was warned by a leading citizen of Bastogne that the Germans would attack. Everyone in the city knew it. His fellow citizens had observed light signals at night. Germans in civilian clothes had been observed placing panels in the fields to mark dropping zones. (There were plenty of German civilians in that

---

* This was in fact the Führer Escort Brigade, intended for the attack on St Vith.

area of the Ardennes who had been evacuated from the front in Germany the previous September.) Colonel Reeves laughed at the information. As the Belgian civilian commented long afterwards, 'American casualness prior to the offensive was only equalled by their roughness once it had been launched.'

Although Allied Intelligence officers, much senior to him, including Colonel Dickson, 1st Army's Intelligence Chief, and Brigadier Strong, Eisenhower's own Chief-of-Intelligence, now suspected something was afoot in the Eifel-Ardennes, Reeves stuck to his belief, with almost perverse stubbornness, that all was well on the VIII Corps front. Even when Lt-Colonel Stout, the senior Divisional Intelligence Officer of the 106th Division, reported that at night there was 'the sound of vehicles all along the front, barking dogs, motors, etc,' Reeves took no notice. His sole comment was a cynical 'the Krauts are playing phonograph records [of troop movements] to frighten your new boys'. That was all.

On the late afternoon of Friday, 15 December, a badly wounded SS man was brought into a 106th Division's field hospital. Up to now the green medics had only treated trench foot – there had already been forty cases within the Division – and traffic accidents: young men, so the medics thought, always seemed to drive their jeeps recklessly. Now they were seeing their first wounded man, a German SS man.

In the event he turned out to be a Pole who had stepped on a mine while trying to desert from the 12th SS up in the 14th Cavalry area. An American soldier was found who could speak to the Pole in his native language. The man was in shock – part of his right foot had been blown off by the mine – but he was coherent and ready to talk. What he had to say frightened, and at the same time excited, the young medics.

The man said he had been pressed into the SS and had been recently transferred to this front from the East. He didn't want to fight the Americans, so he had deserted. Now he wanted to tell them all he knew.

Hanging on to the interpreter's words, 20-year-old Sergeant Thorpe thought that, although the man might be attempting to curry favour with his captors, he was genuine enough. He was too shocked by his wound to be in a position to lie easily. He was speaking the truth all right.

He told how his unit and others had been quietly moved into the

Eifel at night from the railheads at Wittlich and Bitburg. Now these units, fully equipped and up to strength, were hidden in the forests just east of the frontier village of Losheim. He didn't know when the attack would take place exactly, but he knew it would occur at night. The Germans would use searchlights to bounce their beams off the clouds and illuminate the ground over which they would attack.

His long and somewhat rambling statement was greeted with gasps of amazement by the medics attending him, but Sergeant Thorpe could see that the young Intelligence officer who had been hastily summoned to take down his statement took it seriously enough. For as soon as the Pole was finished he belted for his jeep and sped away up the hill in the direction of St Vith and the headquarters of the Divisional Commander, General Jones.

Then the doctors gave the Pole a sedative and the medics drifted away to other duties. Their excitement had given way to a sudden sombre mood, each man wrapped in a cocoon of his own thoughts. Abruptly they realized they were vulnerable. They had thought they had come to a quiet front to be prepared for combat. Suddenly combat was imminent – unless Division pulled something out of the hat.

Until the day he died in 1983 and was buried in the uniform he had worn as a young soldier in the 106th, Sergeant Thorpe, who would go through Korea and Vietnam, could never understand why nothing was done about the information given to them by the Pole. Why hadn't it been forwarded to General Middleton's HQ? Why had Colonel Stout, the 106th's Chief-of-Intelligence, sat on this vital news?

Already those civilians who had reason to fear the return of Germans were leaving St Vith. Those who favoured the German cause were now openly contemptuous of the *Amis*. On the day that General Jones had set up the 106th's HQ in the town, every window had borne patriotic pictures of Roosevelt and Churchill. American, British and Belgian flags had been everywhere. Suddenly overnight the pictures and flags had disappeared. Why?

Colonels Stout and Reeves, trained Intelligence men with large staffs at their command, did not seem to know what the simple Belgian civilians all around obviously did – the Germans were coming back! Nor apparently did the Supreme Commander, with his even greater intelligence resources, which stretched from the front line to Paris and then on to London and Washington, even as far as Australia.

Or did he?

About midnight on 15/16 December, 1944, Klaus Ritter and his eight comrades started up their captured Russian tracked vehicle which towed the cannon and set off for the hamlet of Brandscheid. It was set right in the midle of the *Westwall*, opposite the positions of the 106th. Everywhere, as they moved up the winding road to the hamlet set on top of a hill, Ritter caught glimpses of infantry advancing, all heading westwards.

Once on their way they were stopped by a traffic jam. A young officer spoke to the men in the stalled column. He offered them words of encouragement. He said proudly, 'In four weeks we'll be in Paris. Nothing can stop us. Hundreds of aircraft will support our attack!'

Rations were handed out and, to Ritter's astonishment, the young officer gave each man a pack of 20 cigarettes. There was also a bottle of Moselle wine for every two men.

Brandscheid was reached. In the previous September it had been taken and lost eight times. The Germans had called it the 'little Verdun of the Eifel'. Now it was in total ruin, the houses shattered and empty as the first flakes of snow started to drift down. They clattered over the potholes in the village road. Beyond on the height two kilometres away lay Bleialf. There, Ritter told himself, were the *Amis* asleep in their warm bunks, totally unaware of what was soon going to happen to them.

They were ordered to stop at a bunker to the right of the road and were told they could rest inside for a couple of hours. The crew pushed inside, lay down on the concrete floor and fell asleep straightaway. It had been a long day.

At about four thirty they were ordered back to their vehicle. They were conscious in the cold wind of dark figures moving down the long slope into Bleialf, bent as if they were moving against a storm, weapons held at the high port. No orders were given. No one spoke. The only sound was that of their boots on the frozen ground and their heavy breathing.

Time passed leadenly. Then it was five o'clock. Half an hour to go still. The driver started up and they clambered aboard. The driver let out the clutch.

They were moving. The artillery was moving. It was half past five. Suddenly the whole horizon was lit up as if someone had thrown a gigantic switch. Men were running through the fields on all sides. They were on their way into battle.

The stage was set. The actors were in place. The drama of the last assault had begun.

DAY ONE:

Saturday, 16 December, 1944.

Weather: Generally foggy to misty in the morning. Visibility too poor for air activity over the Ardennes. Sunrise 0829. Sunset 1645.

'On the day of battle Truth stalks naked. Thereafter they put on their little dress uniforms.'

General Sir Ian Hamilton.

The dawn sky to the east erupted into flame. Virtually everywhere on VIII Corps' eighty-mile front the scarlet flashes of gunfire merged into sheets of fire. The whole horizon was ablaze as some 2000 guns, ranging from 81mm mortars to giant 240mm railway cannon, smashed into ear-splitting life. In the 99th's lines to the north, a cook mixing batter in a tent leaped in the air with surprise as great holes were suddenly ripped in the fabric. He recovered himself, tugged his foot out of the can of batter into which he had plunged it and continued beating the mix for the breakfast pancakes.

Further back, at divisional HQ, Master Sergeant Beck of Intelligence knew exactly what to do when the first shells began falling. Hurriedly he began to burn top secret documents; he knew the Krauts were coming. As he did so, he was astonished to see movie star Marlene Dietrich, minus all make-up, clattering down the stairs. She knew what would happen to her if Hitler's soldiers captured her.

In the lines of the 14th Cavalry, linking the 99th with the 106th, Sergeant McIntyre from Oregon, who was used to forest fires, thought at first that the forests all around had caught fire.

Further south the 28th Division's Misfits were just lining up for breakfast, wondering what all the shooting was about when Lt Sarn rushed in. Knocking the canteens out of the hands of the startled Misfits, he yelled, 'Get to your tanks! Get to your tanks! The Krauts are coming!'

It was a little different in the positions of Middleton's most southerly division, the 4th Infantry. There the bombardment was not so heavy because the German Seventh Army who were doing the attacking possessed little artillery. By the time the men of the 4th's 12th Infantry Regiment were aware of what was going on, the Germans were already across the River Sauer. Standing at his post in the village of Dickweiler, young Marc Dillard, a survivor of the Hurtgen, could see 'them already moving through the fields and woods to our front'.

Minutes earlier they had crossed on either side of the little stone bridge, now wrecked, which had once linked Luxembourg with Germany. Soon they were advancing into Echternach. They stole by the great basilica from which in the Dark Ages St Willibrord had left to convert the heathen Germans across the river. Now they were coming back, the heathen Germans, with a vengeance.*

General Jones awoke with a start in his HQ on the hill overlooking the positions of his 424th Regiment. Already the shells from the 240mm railway gun in the sidings at Niederprüm, some 15 kilometres away, were smashing into St Vith. This was clearly no small-scale attack. As he clattered down the stone stairs to the command room, telephones were beginning to ring. Outside in the freezing cold, frantic drivers tried to start reluctant motors. Trucks, jeeps, armoured cars wheezed and coughed into life. A courier jeep, splattered with mud from the front, bounced up the cobbled *Hauptstrasse* towards the HQ.

Already the half-dressed staff officers were being flooded by grim tidings. '*0550-from 423d Infantry. Anti-tank Co shelled by artillery since 0530.*' . . . *2nd Battalion 423d Inf. alerted . . . lines out to anti-tank Co . . . From 28th Div-receiving heavy shelling by artillery . . . 0623-from 99th Inf. Div. Taking heavy shellings all along sector.*' It was one message of gloom after another.

Then, as abruptly as it had started, the shelling stopped. In the echoing silence which followed, white-faced, half-dressed staff officers stared at each other in bewilderment. Behind them telephone operators frowned at their instruments. Suddenly, for some reason, they had gone dead. 'What the hell is going on at the front?' was the unspoken question in everyone's eyes.

Normally Corps Commander Troy Middleton was a poor sleeper. He suffered from bursitis, which kept jolting him awake. But, the night before, his HQ had celebrated the first anniversary of VIII Corps' arrival in England on 15 December, 1943. There had been *beaucoup de champagne*, not to mention stronger waters. As a result the Commanding General had slept unusually well. It had taken the sentry's heaving pounding on the door of his caravan to waken him.

* St Willibrord was, incidentally, an Englishman.

Now he hurried outside, reaching for his teeth and glasses as he did so.

The horizon to the east glowed a faint pink, broken by sudden electric flashes. There was also the rumble of heavy artillery which he knew wasn't American. The Germans were attacking in force; of that he was sure.

At about this time, Jones's Intelligence Officer, Colonel Stout, came on the line to Middleton's HQ. He reported that the Germans were attacking everywhere. St Vith was also monitoring reports from both its neighbours that they were being attacked as well. Stout was told to be calm. A little later he called again to tell Reeves that he was forwarding a plan just captured by the 424th Regiment. It was a detailed account of the enemy's intentions. Again no real reaction from Middleton's HQ. *Why?*

The Germans attacked the 14th Cavalry's foremost outpost at Krewinkel without covering fire. The dismounted cavalrymen were nervous, but they held their fire. The Americans let them come to within twenty yards of the perimeter. Then they opened up with everything they had. It was as if the attackers had run into an invisible wall. They went down on all sides,. In an instant the field was littered with dead and dying as the survivors broke and ran.

Soon they rallied and came in again, urged on by young officers carrying machine pistols. The defenders wondered at their fanatical courage. Were they drunk or drugged? All that morning they attacked time and again, leaving the wintry fields around the tiny border village littered with their dead. In the end there were 375 of them.

For a while there was a break in the close-combat fighting. Then the Germans began to soften up the garrison with their fearsome multiple rocket mortars. With a frightening wail they surged into the grey sky, trailing black smoke behind them. Then with a tremendous crash six heavy rockets descended upon the US positions at one time, making the very earth tremble.

By mid-morning they had forced the defenders back and had captured half the village, almost up to the battered church. But a determined counter-attack by the cavalrymen threw them out once more.

Now all the 'hedgehogs' (fortified villages) held by the 14th Cavalry group were under attack. No 3 platoon at Roth reported by radio – all land lines were out – that the Krauts were in the village and a tank seventy-five yards away from the platoon command post was 'belting us with direct fire'. Colonel Mark Devine at the 14th Cavalry's command post at Manderfeld in Belgium sent light Honey tanks to help out. They didn't get far. An 88mm cannon tore the air apart like the noise of a giant piece of canvas being ripped. The Germans had spotted them coming from their positions in Auw. Mushrooms of earth spouted up on both sides of the road. The Honey tanks thought it would be wiser to go no further.

At 1100 hours Captain Stanley Porché, in charge at Roth, signalled, 'We are moving back. Your friends to the south are moving back too'. He meant the 422nd Infantry, commanded by Colonel Deschenaux of the 106th Division. Porché never made it. He and 87 of his men surrendered to the Germans minutes later.

Colonel Mark Devine, who commanded the 14th Cavalry Group, which guarded the link between the 99th and 106th Divisions, was a strict, zealous man in late middle age with dark piercing eyes. His men were pretty scared of him, for he was a stickler for discipline and spit-and-polish. Back in the States he had ordered that the men's hair and the grass lawns around their quarters should not be longer than one and a quarter inches. Once when there had been an outbreak of coughs on the post, he had ordered that there would be no more coughing at his briefings from now on. Captain Kreisle, a 26-year old Harvard graduate and now one of the Group's surgeons, remembers, 'Thereafter we had a run on cough medicine at the dispensary. No one wanted to get into Colonel Devine's bad books.'

Now on this cold, dark morning in Manderfeld, with his outposts under attack everywhere, Colonel Devine seemed to be losing his grip. The village was under heavy artillery fire and, watching him shouting out excited, contradictory orders, Dr Kreisle thought he was doing more harm than good. There was no doubt that he was a brave man, but with his 'unstable temperament and severe frustration at a situation over which he had no control, he was getting the troops upset. They were in trouble enough as it was.'

They were. For now they were dealing not only with Hoffmann-Schonborn's triumphant grenadiers of the 18th Volksgrenadier Division, but also the advance guard of the elite of the elite *Kampfgruppe Peiper* of the 1st SS Panzer Division, 'the Adolf Hitler Bodyguard'.

*

At eleven o'clock, unaware of what was heading for Manderfeld, Colonel Devine made a quick tour of his command. Then he returned to his CP. He found it in a state of panic. His staff were tossing their gear into their vehicles. The nervous drivers were gunning their engines impatiently, as if they couldn't get away swiftly enough. Inside the CP clerks were burning secret papers and destroying files. Contact with the 99th Infantry Division to the north had been lost. The reserve squadron he had ordered up seemed to have disappeared.

Devine tried to restore some order. Dr Kreisle, with nothing to do as yet, could see he was failing. The men were too concerned about their own safety. Hurriedly Devine called Jones and asked for an infantry attack 'to save us'.

Jones, who was occupied entirely with the problems of his own command, replied that he could give no infantry support 'at this time'.

Devine then said that if he received no infantry support he would have to withdraw entirely to a new defence on the ridge behind Manderfeld.

The line went dead and Devine realized that it was up to him. For the first time in his long career in the US Army he must have known that he was finally in a decisive combat situation where the only one who could make the decision was he. There were no superiors to whom he could turn. It was up to him. In the event, he made the wrong one.

Things worsened rapidly. Men were struggling back from the fortified 'hedgehogs', obviously in panic. Behind them they could hear the rumble of heavy tanks. The defenders of Krewinkel pulled back at last. On the road to Manderfeld they were jeered by the reserve squadron making their way up to the front. It wouldn't be long before the reserve squadron was moving back too, though, then, there would be no jeering.

Now the Germans were trying to slip around the flanks of the 14th Cavalry in Manderfeld. They bumped into the reserve squadron. A fierce fire fight broke out. Scarlet flame stabbed the grey gloom. Tank guns thumped. Armour-piercing shot hurtled through the air. There was the clang of metal striking metal. The reserve squadron started to pull back.

Colonel Dugan, Devine's executive officer, called Jones. There was a note of despair in his voice. 'The Germans are passing south-west,' he reported. 'They're moving towards the Our.' Then he asked permission to withdraw the 14th Cavalry to a line of ridges between Manderfeld and Andler which was on the road to St Vith and protected somewhat by the line of the River Our. Reluctantly General Jones gave his permission, not realizing that he was hammering another nail in the coffin being prepared for his 106th Division.

It was not a moment too soon in the opinion of Dr Kreisle. Although so far he had not caught a single glimpse of a German soldier, shells and mortar bombs were hitting Manderfeld from all quarters. As he waited with his sergeant beside their Red Cross halftrack, a shell howled out of the sky. The two men flopped to the ground in the same instant that the shell exploded. Deafened and groggy, Kreisle rose to his feet to see, a few yards down the street, a young woman gasping with pain. Both her legs had been blown off and he could see the thigh bones gleaming brightly through the bloody gore. Beside her lay her three dead children.

Thereafter, as he noted at the time, 'Never in my life have I departed from any place more willingly.' Once on the road in his jeep, leading his own little column of medics, he remembered he still had his pipe in his teeth, a dangerous thing to do in an open jeep. Reaching up to remove it, he found to his astonishment that only a stub of the stem remained between his tightly clenched teeth. In the tension of the withdrawal from Manderfeld he had bitten clean through it!

Behind them there was a hasty scramble to escape. A sergeant at headquarters, pouring gas over papers and other items which had to be left behind, lit a match too soon. Not only he, but the whole of the bottom of the HQ went up flames. Soon the whole of Manderfeld would be ablaze.

Now it was a case of *sauve qui peut*. The roads were already clogged with vehicles, fighting their way through disheartened, frightened men on foot. Trucks skidded off the slippery roads into ditches. Vehicles which ran out of gas were simply abandoned. Platoon leaders told the men to get rid of heavy equipment so that they could move westwards faster. They needed no urging. They couldn't get out of the death trap fast enough and always in the distance they could hear that ominous clatter and squeak of tank tracks. The Krauts were coming and the gap between the 99th and 106th Divisions was wide open.

*

So far not a single shot had been fired as Klaus Ritter and the other vehicles of the 18th Volksgrenadier Division advanced slowly towards Bleialf, their way illuminated by the ghostly light of the searchlights on the clouds above. He asked himself if that tremendous barrage had wiped out the *Ami* defenders. Or perhaps they had fled.

They started to roll over the little bridge across the River Alf* which gave the village its name, when suddenly there was the whine of a mortar bomb. The column stalled. The men of Colonel Cavender's 423rd Infantry belonging to the 106th Division had not abandoned Bleialf after all. There was going to be a fight.

Mortar bombs started to fall on all sides. Ritter flung himself from the Russian tractor and scrambled underneath the wheels of the cannon they were towing. Higher up, a truck containing ammunition was hit. It exploded with a furious roar. Another vehicle caught fire – and another. The whole front end of the convoy was burning within minutes, while white tracer shells from the ammunition truck zig-zagged crazily into the sky. All was chaos, confusion and sudden death.

A mortar bomb exploded close by. The ground rose up and slapped him in the face. There was a terrible howl of agony. Forgetting his own fear, Ritter scrambled from beneath the gun. He was appalled by what he saw. One of his comrades had been hit in the face by some sort of explosive bullet. It had torn away all of his jaw.

The men found a stretcher and placed their comrade, now unconscious, on to it and, ignoring the battle going on all around them, doubled back with him up the hill to Brandscheid. By the time they reached the nearest dressing station, their comrade was dead and the battle for Bleialf had started in earnest.

On Cavender's right flank, Colonel Reid's 424th Regiment of the 106th was also heavily engaged fighting off another thrust of the 18th Volksgrenadier. Somehow Harry Martin had slept through the heavy bombardment. Now a squad leader ran into the log hut Harry shared with his buddies yelling, '*The Germans are coming!*'

---

* *Blei* is the German for 'lead'. Lead had been found in the area in the Middle Ages and was mined there right up to and after the war. Bleialf means 'lead on the Alf'.

Harry and his buddy Bill rushed outside, grabbing their rifles and helmets as they did so. They pelted to their foxhole on the extreme left flank. The rest of the squad headed for the bunkers.

Now the two soldiers could see hundreds of shadowy figures coming over the crest of the hill in front of them. To Harry Martin they seemed drunk or drugged. For they all were screaming and shrieking. In minutes they'd outflank their company and start to sweep up the line of foxholes and bunkers to finish off the survivors.

Hurriedly Bill fixed a grenade to the muzzle of his rifle. He had never fired one before. Now the Germans were streaming in their hundreds towards them. Harry Martin felt as if the very life force had been drained from his skinny body. Sheer panic set in. He started blasting away with his M-I without thinking or aiming.

Still the Germans kept on coming. Harry was not hitting a thing. His eyes simply wouldn't focus, carried away as he was by his overwhelming fear. Inside the foxhole, still struggling with the rifle grenade, Bill kept crying, 'Are they close enough?' Harry didn't answer. He couldn't. The only thing he seemed able to do was to keep firing his rifle – without aiming.

The Germans closed on the company CP. They flung open the door and tossed in stick grenades. There was a series of muffled explosions. The company commander was dead; Harry knew it, and it was his fault!

Suddenly in the middle of this mayhem, a confident, calm voice inside Harry Martin's head said, '*Squeeze the trigger, Don't pull it. Squeeze the trigger!*' It was the advice musketry sergeants had always given in basic training. It had been drummed into them day after day. Now Harry Martin acted upon that advice. He started to take aim and fire. Germans to his front started to go down and he told himself he was a real soldier now. His father would be proud of him at last.

Thirty minutes later it was all over. Exhausted, Harry and Bill, bodies lathered in sweat despite the freezing cold, slumped in their foxholes, as the rest of the Germans fled. Heads began to pop out of bunkers and foxholes. A few men got out and started to wander around, looking at the dead Germans. And there among them was Captain Barthel! He hadn't been in the CP at all. He'd been further up with the rest of the company. Harry Martin felt a tremendous sense of relief sweep through his skinny body. He hadn't failed the C.O. after all.

But at the same time he felt different. In that strange silence that always follows a battle he knew he had changed. 'At this moment, I was a veteran combat soldier.'

Colonel Descheneaux, at 32 one of the youngest full colonels in the US Army, felt he had the situation in his own 422nd Regiment area well in hand. To his south he could hear from the volume of small arms fire that his two sister regiments, the 423rd and 424th, were engaged in heavy action. But apart from the action at Auw, there had been little fighting in his own sector. Little did he know that on the ridge line facing him, which was the German front line, there were fewer than a hundred Germans. Hoffman-Schonborn had taken a calculated risk. He had reasoned the 'greenbeaks' wouldn't attack. Therefore he could use all of his manpower for the attack on the 14th Cavalry on the northern flank of the 106 Division and the 424th Regiment on its southern flank. He was trying to achieve the classic pincer movement, which all professional soldiers dreamed of.

Deschenaux felt, too, that he was fortunate in having just behind his command post in a *Gasthaus* in the village of Schlausenbach, the regimental direct support field artillery battalion, the 589th. Behind it, beyond the road that ran from Bleialf to Auw, there was the divisional support battalion with their great 155mm howitzers, the 592, located at the hamlet of Laudesfeld.

Now it seemed to him that all he could do was to hold in place and at the same time to clarify what was happening in the Auw area held by a company of Colonel Riggs' 81st Combat Engineer Battalion. He was also worried a little by the fact that he was no longer able to reach the 14th Cavalry Group. He assumed, however, that the tremendous bombardment that morning had knocked out the land lines. But it was strange that he couldn't reach Colonel Devine's CP at Manderfeld by radio.

He dismissed the problem of the 14th Cavalry Group for the moment and concentrated on re-establishing the situation at Auw, some two miles south-east of Schlausenbach. Swiftly a small task force of some three hundred men was formed from two companies of his infantry and set off to do battle.

At first everything went well. The men were in good heart. There was no sign of the Germans. In the distance they could hear firing, but it didn't seem to concern them. They didn't appear to have anything to worry about. Now they could just glimpse the pointed slate steeple of Auw's tiny church, for most of the village lay hidden in a valley.

Above the sky was darkening rapidly. As they emerged from the woods to the left of the road, ready for the attack, they were engulfed by a fierce blizzard which reduced visibility almost to nil. Still they pressed on, heads bent against the wind, rifles held at the port.

Suddenly there came the high-pitched burr of a German MG 42 machine gun which could fire at the rate of 1,000 rounds per minute. A few men stumbled and went down, their blood staining the snow. In an instant the angry snap-and-crack of a small arms battle could be heard on all sides. Auw was held in force by the Germans and they had stumbled right into them!

Their leader's radio crackled urgently. They would have to do an about-face. German industry had been spotted east of Descheneaux's CP at Schlausenbach. All the 422nd had left to defend the place were cooks and clerks and a handful of riflemen. Cursing and bitching, the riflemen swung round and prepared for another hard slog back to the CP.

Behind them the acting commander of the 589th Artillery, a Major Arthur Parker, had spotted the danger to his own force on the left side of the little winding ridge road that led to Auw. He ordered some of his gunners out as local protection. One group under a Lieutenant Leach, struggled through the blizzard to within 300 yards of Auw. The German defenders spotted them. Tracer bullets sped across the snowy field. Leach and his group dropped into a ditch where they were pinned down. Leach called down fire on the area of the ditch. As the first shells started to plummet down, he and his group rose to their feet and pelted to the rear.

Hoffmann-Schonborn, who was commanding the attack of the 18th Volksgrenadier from the front (he had been ordered to do so by von Manteuffel), commanded a number of assault guns to root the American artillery out.

Lieutenant Eric Wood, 25-year-old son of a general on Eisenhower's staff and a former Princeton fullback, executive officer of A Battery, doubled forward to a knoll on the left flank. Standing upright in full view of the advancing German assault guns, he coolly passed back orders to Number 4 piece. Number 4, the only gun which could reach the three German assault guns, belched smoke and flame. Two shots were enough. The assault gun burst into flame and came to an abrupt halt. A moment later the second was hit and it scuttled off, belching smoke, with the remaining one.

Now Wood tackled the follow-up infantry. He ordered the woods to his front to be swept by short-fuse shells. Trees snapped like matchwood. Great holes suddenly appeared in the snow. Men were flung to all sides and the German attack came to a sudden halt.

Not for long. Hoffmann-Schonborn was determined not to give up. The *Amis* had to be driven off the Auw-Bleialf road. Von Manteuffel was already breathing down his neck to capture the road network that led to St Vith. He ordered his multiple mortars, which were carried on the back of a truck and were fully mobile, to begin firing on the artillery positions.

Moments later there came that now familiar howl, followed by trails of black smoke etching their way across the grey sky.

'Hit the dirt!' Wood yelled and flung himself down.

The artillerymen of the 589th needed no urging. Next moment the murderous barrage swamped their positions, clearly defined on the top of the hill. Fist-sized shards of gleaming steel hissed through the howitzer pits. Men went down everywhere. Within the hour, thirty-six men of A Battery would be dead.

As the 'Misfits' had predicted, *Bea Wain II* would not start up in an emergency. Now they were proved right. As the rest of B Company started to rumble away, the Sherman simply would not start. Frantically Mac, John, and Jim worked on the tank, cursing all the while. One primed the motor while the other two placed all the burners they had in or near the motor to help warm it up.

While that was going on Pfc John Marshall, that hater of authority, who felt they were being abandoned by their officers yet once again, hurriedly loaded the 75mm cannon with an armour-piercing shell. That done, he ran a belt of 30 calibre ammunition into the machine gun and then placed himself on the back of the tank, watching for the first sight of the enemy with his binoculars.

One by one the other tanks started to file by them, their crews averting their eyes as they passed the Misfits' vehicle, with three other Shermans which had similar problems in starting up. Years later John Marshall learned from a newly declassified report that an officer had stated, 'All remaining tanks in Pintsche were lost'. Marshall stated in disgust, 'That should have said "left".' But at that highly tensed moment, with the Germans almost up to their positions, he consoled himself with the thought that they had 'Mac, the invisible shield', their tough tank commander. He hadn't let them down yet.

Suddenly he jumped. What he had taken to be haystacks in the meadows were beginning to move. *Haystacks in December?* In an instant he tumbled to it. The 'haystacks' were camouflaged German tanks and they were moving straight in their direction. He cupped his hands and shouted down to the other three, 'Kraut tanks! Let's grab a gun and head for the woods!'

Mac, his face dirty with engine grease, shook his head. 'No deal. The only way we're gonna get out of here alive is in this tank. You keep lookout. We'll start the tank.'

John Marshall didn't believe that they would get the tank started in time, but he said nothing and resumed his task as lookout. Now he could see that the slow-moving German tanks, their guns swinging from side to side, were crawling behind a hill and disappearing. But soon they would emerge at the other side and see the stationary tanks. God, let *Bea Wain II* start, he prayed to himself.

John clambered into the turret. To Marshall's relief the Sherman started up the very first time. 'What a beautiful sound,' he gasped.

But the battle to get *Bea Wain II* moving was not won yet. *The transmission was frozen solid!*

In later years John Marshall always thought the episode was 'a real cliffhanger. You solve one problem and another comes up and all the time the enemy's coming ever closer.' But although 'everything worked against us', none of the Misfits panicked.

Now the lookout could see the German infantry running in and out of the village houses, searching the sheds and setting up a strongpoint at the crossroads. It was obvious they knew there were still Americans in the area and they were looking for them. All the same *Bea Wain II* was in an excellent defensive position. It could hit any German tank entering Pinsche before it saw them. Mac the invisible shield must have sensed something like this might happen when he had positioned *Bea Wain II* here after that abortive patrol the week before.

Down below one of the Misfits used a shovel as an axe to cut the sledgehammer the tank carried very short. As John, the driver, depressed the clutch, Mac struck the gear shift hard with the abbreviated sledgehammer which he could now wield with all his strength and forced it into gear.

1. Two aspects of Belgium in 1944. *Above:* a parade at the border town of St Vith, complete with SA and Hitler Youth — all Belgians. *Below:* a Resistance fighter of the 'White Army', so called because of the white uniform supplied by the British, as also was the sten gun. The helmet is German.

2. John Marshall of the 'Misfits' beside his tank.

3. The way they lived then: engineers building log huts in the woods for front-line infantry.

4. The 'poor bloody infantry' led a short and brutal life.

5. The sharp end: US medics tend a wounded infantryman.

6. A Weasel tries to tow out a stranded Jeep in the awful terrain in which they fought.

7. An American Stuart light tank advances through a shattered village. A dead German soldier lies in the foreground.

Now they were moving. They headed for the village. They knew the houses were full of Germans, but they felt safe from small arms fire. However, if the Germans were armed with the feared *panzerfaust*, which could go through a Sherman's armour like a knife through butter, they'd be in serious trouble. The Misfits prayed that wasn't the case.

They swung down the little country road to where the other three Shermans, which had now been started, were waiting for them. Their crews were all enlisted men and they knew Mac's reputation for brave leadership. In the turret, Marshall left his machine gun and dropped over the side. As he ran forward to guide the four tanks over a narrow bridge, he could hear one of the company's sergeants shouting from an upstairs window to the Germans that he wanted to surrender.

John Marshall pulled a contemptuous face but continued running. Now he waited on the bridge with the Germans all around him, waving on *Bea Wain II*. The Sherman rattled across the little structure safely. Marshall guided the second tank across and then he was pelting to where his own task was waiting for him, the driver gunning his engine impatiently.

The third tank crossed. Suddenly there was the hollow boom of metal striking metal. Marshall turned. The fourth tank had been hit. Now it was turning awkwardly and heading back to the house. Another hollow bang. A sheet of flame and the fourth tank rumbled to a stop.

Later Marshall found out that there had been Germans hiding under the bridge all the time. They had waited till the last tank had begun to rumble across. Then they had sprung from their hiding place and let the Sherman have it with a rocket from their *panzerfaust*. Both the gunner and the tank commander had been killed and the driver had turned in order to look for medical assistance. The Germans had fired again and that was that.

But the Misfits had no time to ponder the fate of their unlucky buddies. *They* had just been lucky. They daren't tempt the fates by turning back. So they rolled on, slugs pattering off their armour like heavy rain on a tin roof. It was grey and overcast. The tanks' radios were not working correctly and gradually they lost the other two, so *Bea Wain II* rolled on down the narrow valley roads, the heights on either side sheer and holed with the caves of primitive man who had once lived in them.

Time and again they spotted German patrols, but never a sight of Americans. The whole 28th Division seemed to have disappeared, but they could hear the sound of fighting to their front and reasoned that the 110th Regiment, to which they had been attached, had pulled back to the 'Skyline Drive' on the heights above.

In the end they decided that they had risked their necks long enough. Sooner or later they'd bump head on into a German patrol and that would be that. So they pulled off the narrow road and drove into a field. They rolled to a stop and John Alyea, the driver, turned off the engine.

Now all was silent save for the noise of the battle to their front. They were all alone behind the German lines. But they were bold, resourceful men who did not dwell on their precarious situation. Marshall depressed the 75mm cannon as far as it would go in order to prevent anyone rolling a grenade down it. Periodically during the coming hours of tense waiting and dozing, they would furtively open the breach to check whether the barrel had been plugged by anything lethal. Meanwhile John Alyea slipped outside and draped the torn, dirty tarpaulin they used for working underneath the Sherman over the long gun. Now it looked, so they hoped, as if *Bea Wain II* had been knocked out.

Now, with Alyea safely back inside, they 'buttoned up' and stopped the engine. They closed the turret cover, reasoning that a sentry standing in the turret would soon be spotted by the infantry who were now beginning to pass. So they settled in for their long wait, listening to the German infantrymen talking among themselves, crying '*Panzer kaput*' or yelling '*Deckung!*' (take cover) whenever a shell exploded along the road.

This was going to be the longest night of the war for them, *if* they survived. They all knew that. What the morrow might bring, they didn't ever dare consider. Let God see them through this one first. So the Misfits waited, four lonely Americans, caught up in a tragic disaster of world-shaking importance.

The officer whom fate had selected to defend the most sensitive sector of the 28th Division's front was that same 'cantankerous fellow but a good fighter' who had helped Middleton to wangle his way to war back in 1918. Hurley Fuller had not gone far in the Army since that time. He had come overseas as a regimental commander with the rank of full colonel, but had lasted in combat only ten days before his divisional commander had relieved him. For nearly five months he had languished in Europe without a job until finally Middleton took pity on him and gave him the command of the 28th's 110th Infantry Regiment. From the Hotel Claravallis in the picturesque tourist town of Clervaux where he had set up his HQ, he had attempted to get the badly beaten up 110th back into shape after it had been pulled out of the Hurtgen Forest.

That had all ended this morning at dawn. As German signallers radioed back bearings and directions from a room in the *Pharmacie Molitor* in the cobbled square of the little Luxembourg town, shells came raining down, accurately pinpointing American installations. The 120th's executive officer, Lt-Colonel Daniel Strickler, one of the few to escape from the débâcle to come, had rushed to Fuller's bedroom on the second floor of the hotel and asked for the C.O.'s reaction.

Fuller, without his briar pipe for once, answered with a question of his own, 'What do *you* make of it?'

Strickler shrugged. 'All this big stuff? It's a sure sign we're in for a fight.'

Strickler had been right. They were. Soon the regiment of which they were both so proud would be virtually wiped out.

Von Manteuffel's plan was to attack the Skyline Drive between the villages of Hosingen and Marnach. The first village was of particular importance to him because it had a road leading westwards to Clervaux and from thence to Bastogne, the other key road-and-rail centre.

Now virtually a full corps, including a panzer division, was being flung at the Americans defending the Skyline Drive hamlets and villages, all dotted along that key road which led from St Vith to Luxembourg.

German pressure was intense. Von Manteuffel was breathing down his commanders' necks. He brooked no delay. If the Luxembourg villages defended by the *Amis* could be circumvented, well and good. If they couldn't, they had to be steam-rollered over.

At the village of Consthum, for instance, which housed the 110th's 3rd Battalion, Sergeant Cope of the HQ's mess centre had known for a long time that the Germans were preparing to attack. He had fought through the Hurtgen, winning two purple hearts. He knew when the Germans were about to attack. All the same when they came blundering in out of the mist, he was caught by surprise.

49

With hands that had been badly frostbitten in the Hurtgen, he set about helping his C.O. to phone out his instructions and try to keep the battalion organized under the German attack. Although the 3rd was fully up to strength, it had absorbed hundreds of reinforcements to make up its severe losses in the Hurtgen. Not surprisingly the young soldiers, straight in only a few days before from the reinforcement depots, were decidedly shaky.

A shell hurtled through the CP. Major Milton, the C.O., ignored it. He had other things on his mind. His own artillery was not firing any more. A few minutes later they found out why. A captain from the battery made his appearance. He said the guns were getting too hot. Milton snarled, 'Fire the goddam things till they melt!'

Now the 3rd Battalion's outposts in the villages along the ridge road were under fierce attack, as von Manteuffel urged his troops to do their utmost for 'Folk, Fatherland and Führer'. Stealing forward under the cover of the fog, the Germans tried to infiltrate the positions in the white-painted, slate-roofed houses of the area. Now and again it was the Germans who were caught by surprise. In one case just outside Consthum, a German company walked straight into a position occupied by a battery of anti-aircraft gunners. They let the Germans come within 100 yards and then they opened up with their quadruple 50 calibre machine guns. At that range they couldn't miss. Germans were mown down on all sides. Afterwards the triumphant gunners counted the German dead. There were over a hundred of them. No wonder the GIs called the mobile anti-tank guns the 'meatchoppers'.

Still the Germans persisted and a worried Major Milton feared his positions were going to be overrun altogether if he didn't get some help. He alerted everyone in battalion headquarters – cooks, clerks, jeep drivers, even poor Cope with his frost-bitten hands, indeed anyone who could carry a rifle – and formed provisional rifle squads with them. At the same time he signalled for armoured support; 'little friend', the infantry, needed 'big friend', the tank, as soon as possible!

By now the Germans had penetrated to the outskirts of Consthum itself. Alerted by the crackle of a small-arms firefight close by, Captain John Mitchell of the artillery stepped outside to see what was happening. To his horror he saw a German, in a long greatcoat which reached almost to his ankles, coming down the battle-littered village street, snapping off bursts from his Schmeisser at houses on both side.

Instinctively Mitchell raised his carbine and fired off a shot from the hip. It missed. The German swung round. He spotted Mitchell. He pressed his trigger. Slugs peppered the walls all around Mitchell. Mortar and wood splinters rained down on him. He dived through the open door. The civilians inside fled in terror. The German followed. Mitchell ran for the barn. He scurried into the dark corner to the rear and waited there, heart pounding, carbine raised, head cocked for the slightest sound.

There it was. The sound of hobnailed boots approaching his hiding place. The footsteps paused just outside the window of the barn. Mitchell hardly dared breathe for now he could hear a second man walking outside. And he was German too, for Mitchell could hear him whispering to the first soldier.

Mitchell steeled himself. He could just see out of the window and there he saw two German helmets, barely glimpsed, but definitely German. He controlled his breathing. Raising his carbine above his head and holding it out at arm's length, he fired several shots in double-quick time. There was a gasp, followed by the heavy thumps of bodies falling to the wet cobbles outside. But Mitchell had little time to savour his victory. He was too busy fighting off a cow which had panicked at the firing.

But there weren't too many humorous incidents that grim Saturday. It was clear by that afternoon that the three regiments that made up the 28th Division were being forced apart, with the 112th Regiment wheeling north-west in the direction of St Vith, while its sister regiment the 109th was pushed south-west into the positions held by the Fourth Infantry Division. In the middle, still fighting desperately, the 110th Regiment, commanded by Colonel Fuller, was being split into separate groups, with the enemy attempting to bull his way through to Clervaux and then on to the 28th Division's HQ at Wiltz. Later the Germans would claim that the 28th was 'shattered'. In the sense that its commander, General Cota, was losing direct control of his three regiments, it was. Yet it continued to fight as separate units, even down to the level of companies, many of which were virtually cut off by now.

Here and there the men of the 'Bloody Bucket' division, given its name from the divisional insignia, which did look like a bloody bucket, actually counter-attacked. Despite the overwhelming strength of the enemy, lost strongpoints were retaken and Germans forced out of villages and hamlets they had just taken. But the cost was high and in most cases the 28th's infantry casualties were replacements, not too skilled in the difficult business of house-to-house fighting.

Colonel Rudder, the commander of the 109th, had been a Ranger. He had fought on D-Day and in the Hurtgen. He was particularly aggressive and didn't give up ground easily. In one case he ordered his infantry to counter-attack and drive off some Germans who were threatening his artillery positions. To help the infantry in their assault, he gave them two tanks from the 707th Battalion.

But the infantry, all reinforcements save their commander, a Lieutenant James Christy, were not too happy with the assignment. Still they moved forward, upset by the losses they had already suffered that day, and hungry. Even as he led them towards the enemy the young officer 'could sense the uneasiness of the soldiers'.

They had almost reached their objective when the lead Sherman stopped abruptly. Christy went forward to see what was the cause.

The tank commander told him plainly that he was not going to risk being shot up by 'some Kraut kid' armed with a *panzerfaust*. He wanted riflemen up front to protect the vehicle.

Christy went back to where his senior NCO, Sergeant Wieszcyk, was slumped waiting. The NCO was also a replacement: a mess sergeant ('Listen Lieutenant, I got these stripes for running a combined mess hall at Camp Fannin, Texas.') who had been hurriedly retrained in a few days and sent to the infantry. Now Christy told him to get a rifle squad up in front of the tank.

Sergeant Wieszcyk protested, 'The guys have had more than enough today. They won't go.'

Christy gulped. He didn't want to have to shoot the NCO. What was he to do? Suddenly he had it. He turned to the tank commander and yelled, 'How many men do you want in front of the tank to move it?'

The tanker replied that *one* good soldier would do.

Christy nodded grimly. 'You've got him,' he snapped, 'Follow me.' He set off alone.

He had gone only a short way and the tank had only just begun to move when Sergeant Wieszcyk shouted, 'Okay, Lieutenant, you've made your point.'

Christy turned and grinned with relief. The big NCO was following him. Behind him came the entire 1st Squad.

*

52

Rudder's neighbour, the most southern of Middleton's units, the Fourth Division's 12th Regiment, was not as heavily shelled as the men of the other two divisions. All the same, the Germans had the advantage of surprise and long before the offensive they had plotted all the main US positions, in particular their headquarters.

The 12th Infantry, however, veterans of the Normandy landings (though again made up to strength with hundreds of reinforcements) dug in everywhere as the Germans surged through their positions. In particular, they knew it was important to hold the road from Echternach to Luxembourg. For there was the headquarters of the Army Group Commander, General Bradley, and at first it was thought this was the German intention: to rush the city and capture him at his HQ in the Hotel Alpha, just opposite the railway station.

So the 'Ivy League' men, as they were called after their divisional patch, dug their heels in. By mid-morning all of the 12th's forward companies had been surrounded. There they were ordered by the Divisional Commander, General 'Tubby' Barton to stand fast. There would be 'no retrograde movement' in the 12th Infantry Sector.

In the event the hard-pressed infantrymen didn't have a chance to do that, even if they had wished. They were surrounded everywhere. The only alternative was to fight or to surrender. But in most cases they were holding off the Germans and giving as good as they took. They held out in hat factories, a ruined castle, a luxury hotel and, in the case of the men of the 12th's 3rd Battalion defending the village of Dickweiler, a collection of farm outhouses and cottages, including what the locals called the 'plumpsko' in dialect an earth closet.

19-year-old Pfc Marc Dillard, who had fought with the Fourth since Normandy, was one of the few veterans among the defenders. He and his crew set up their 81mm mortar in the yard of one of the little cottages when a German shell cleared the house and dropped right in front of the mortar. Somehow they escaped and then the Germans were upon them.

Now all of them functioned as riflemen. But there were so many targets and so much firing to be done that one man loaded the M-I while the other fired. As Dillard recalled afterwards, 'It was like in the old cowboy movies when the wagon train was attacked by the Injuns. There were so many targets and we daren't let up our fire for one minute.'

In that first assault the Germans lost fifty men. For a while an uneasy silence reigned, broken only by an odd shot or a burst of angry machine-gun fire. Three Shermans with fifteen riflemen on their decks from the reserve company sneaked into the village. The company commander in charge could see the Germans were preparing for another attack. He ordered his men not to fire until he gave the word.

Rising from their foxholes, the Germans stole forward, two whole companies, outnumbering the defenders three to one. Still the company commander did not give the order to fire. The Germans were on the outskirts of the village now. The tankers were getting very nervous. The German *panzerfaust* only had an effective range of 100 yards and the Germans, carrying the long steel weapon with its flowerpot-shaped hollow charge bulging from the end, were now within that range. Here, immobilized, engines turned off, they were sitting ducks. When was the infantry commander going to give the order to fire?

'*Fire!*'

That bellowed order, when it came, seemed to shock the defenders, but only for a moment. They opened up with everything they had. The blast of steel at that range was devastating. The first German company commander went down, dead before he hit the ground. With him another fifty of his men fell. It wasn't war, it was a massacre. The triumphant defenders, carried away by the unreasoning bloodlust of hot combat, fired and fired again. The Germans simply melted away. In the end the other company commander and thirty-five men surrendered. The rest fled. Dickweiler was safe.

By now it was dark. It was freezing cold too. The fighting was beginning to peter out. Both American and German, the infantry were looking to get undercover for the night. Most had fought all day without food or water. They were exhausted and hungry. A roof over one's head was vitally important.

Although the situation was very fluid and, at the top, the brass wouldn't really know what was going on at the front for another twenty-four hours, the fighting commanders were already implementing standard US tactics. Ever since the First World War it had been official US Army tactical policy to seal off a breakthrough by holding the shoulders of the enemy attack.

Helped by the German strategy which was to blast a hole into the American front – that celebrated 'Bulge', as Churchill was to name it – the Americans in the south were being pushed outwards where they would form the southern shoulder and hold it. To the north, where the 99th and 2nd Infantry Divisions of the US V Corps were doing the fighting, the same manoeuvre was taking place. Here would be formed the northern shoulder.

Indeed General Lauer, the commander of the green 99th Division, thought he was doing very well. Although one of his regiments had been forced to retreat, he believed that evening that he had held the enemy attack. General Robertson, the elderly commander of the veteran 2nd Division, which had been attacking through the 99th's positions when it had run straight into the German assault, thought differently.

In fact he was appalled and shocked when he entered Lauer's HQ in a Belgian villa at Butgenbach just behind the front. He entered the main room to find it packed with officers and enlisted men, all talking at once and, so it seemed, at the tops of their voices.

But his greatest surprise came when he spotted Lauer. The Commanding General of the 99th, which had already suffered serious losses this grim Saturday was seated at a grand piano playing away for all his worth, as if he hadn't a care in the world! He might well have been at some carefree party in a pre-war officers' club.

This, apparently, was what he always did in times of crisis. Robertson wondered how many crises he had faced. After all, this was the first time his division had been in action. Still he did not remark on the matter. Instead he said, raising his voice above the racket, 'Can't we go to your CP where we can talk?'

Lauer gave him his toothy smile and answered, '*This* is my CP.'

Robertson thought differently. To him the CP seemed like a madhouse and Lauer, with his piano-playing, seemed to be one of the prime inmates. He asked Lauer what he thought of the situation. Lauer replied that he had been attacked at several points, but he had the situation well in hand. With that he went back to his piano-playing and Robertson departed, shaking his head, and telling himself that Lauer and his division would be in for a few nasty shocks before this business was over.

Like General Lauer at his piano, some fifteen miles away at Butgenbach, Colonels Descheneaux and Cavender, commanding the 106th's 422nd and 423rd Regiments, were also quite pleased with themselves. They had been under some pressure admittedly. Auw had been lost, but Bleialf had been taken again. Casualties hadn't been too high. They had lost contact with the 14th Cavalry Group, but they assumed that General Jones back at his HQ in St Vith would soon rectify that situation. Indeed, just as darkness fell, Cavender at his CP radioed Jones: 'We'll hold our present positions until ordered differently'.

Now, as the fighting died away for the day, the officers of Cavender's 3rd Battalion crouched around the radio in the hissing white glare of the Coleman in the CP, listening to the BBC Home Service. They heard the dignified upper-class voice of the announcer (some said they still wore evening dress to read the 9 o'clock news even in wartime) say, 'The new German offensive has reached the Belgian border in three places.'

'Well,' one of the officers commented wearily, 'the folks back home seem to know more about it than we do.'

So the Golden Lions sat and waited and did nothing. It was a fatal decision.

Back at St Vith Jones was equally indecisive, although all indications outside were that something was going badly wrong at the front. Vehicles bearing the insignia of the 14th Cavalry Group were streaming through the town, as were trucks, artillery limbers, jeeps, armoured cars – anything on wheels.

There were enlisted men too, dirty and demoralized, trudging wearily up the hill that led into St Vith. And not only enlisted men. Private William MacDonald, a jeep driver with the 740th Field Artillery, which had been attached to the 2nd Division and which was now attached to the 106th, was so angry when he saw a colonel among the stragglers heading west that he pushed his way through them and roared at the blank-eyed officer, 'Why you're a goddam coward!' The colonel did not even seem to hear him.

Things were wrong, but Jones's morale was boosted by the news that a whole armoured combat command, the CCR of the 9th Armored Division, led by Brigadier General William Hoge, was being sent by Middleton to help him. Now at five-thirty Hoge, who had helped to build the Alcan Highway and whose division would one day capture the 'most famous bridge in the world' at Remagen, strode purposefully into Jones's HQ.

'You've heard about it?' Jones asked as the tall, dark-eyed officer saluted.

'I haven't heard anything,' Hoge answered in the abrupt manner which had made him many enemies and delayed his promotion. 'I was reconnoitring up in Monschau.' General Gerow – commander of the

US V Corps – 'told me my outfit was released and I was to report to you . . . I came straight on down.'

'It's bad,' Jones exclaimed, not realizing just how much Hoge abhorred any kind of emotionalism. 'They've hit my whole front around the Eifel. Two regiments are nearly cut off.'

'What shall I do?' Hoge asked.

'Move your combat command up here right away. I want you to attack towards Schönberg tomorrow morning. *Bring my regiments back!*'

Without comment General Hoge stamped out of Jones's office. The situation at 106th HQ was definitely bad, he thought. He then set about trying to find a phone or radio so that he could contact his command. While doing this he bumped into that spit-and-polish cavalryman Colonel Mark Devine, the commander of the missing 14th Cavalry Group.

'What the devil's happening up there, Colonel?' Hoge snapped.

But all he received in return was an incoherent mutter as Devine brushed by him and into Jones's office.

There were Jones and a Colonel Slayton, who had been assigned to Jones by Middleton in order to 'help get the division [the 106th] on its feet'.

Slayton thought that Jones was obviously shocked by Devine's appearance, but because Jones was new to combat himself he did not comment on the fact. As Slayton saw it, 'The man was completely demoralized by events' and had 'little knowledge of the location of his troops'.

After dressing Devine down for withdrawing a second time without orders and for leaving his troops in this crisis, instead of relieving him as Slayton thought Jones should have done, Jones ordered him back to his command. Unknown to any of those present, the 14th Cavalry Group was withdrawing again, with some of its units already clearing the Manderfeld–Schönberg–St Vith road and heading west. This meant the way was wide open for the complete encirclement of Jones's 422nd and 423rd Regiments.

Before Slayton could protest, an aide popped his head round the door and said urgently, 'Excuse me, General, it's the Corps Commander on the phone.'

Jones rose eagerly. It was the call he had been waiting for since late afternoon when he had called Middleton and requested permission to withdraw his regiments from the Snow Eifel. In the event this was going to be the most momentous event in Jones's life – and in those of some 8,000 'Golden Lions' who were going to suffer because of it. It is a telephone conversation that figures prominently in all the histories of the Battle of the Bulge. But no log was kept of it. All we know is General Middleton's version and that of an obscure, if self-important, junior officer in the civil affairs division.

Because both men suspected that the excellent German listening service (after the battle the Germans maintained they discovered much about American plans and intentions due to careless and excessive use of communications by the latter) might be eavesdropping, their language during this decisive telephone conversation was guarded and sometimes ambiguous.

Captain Hill (as he was then) was a civil affairs officer in Büllingen, where his task was to supervise the slaughter of the many cattle left behind by the farmers who had been evacuated from the area. But he also ran a telephone exchange located in the local post office, which had connections to both General Gerow, Commander of V Corps, located at Eupen, and General Middleton in Bastogne. Now, because all his operators had left, Hill put through the calls personally.

As he related the telephone conversation long after, during it the flap on the switchboard indicated that the 99th Division was calling. Hill, who had been listening to the conversation between Middleton and Jones, which he should not have, took the call. The 99th Division operator told him that he had a priority call from 'Dauntless Six (General Lauer) for 'Victor Six' (General Gerow, his Corps Commander). A harassed Hill told the unknown operator that the line was already occupied by two '6's on a priority call and that he would call the 99th operator as soon as Middleton and Jones were finished. Then, to his surprise, he discovered, 'When I plugged into General Jones's call, I discovered I had inadvertently broken the call.' Thus Hill's explanation of the tragic mistake that Saturday night. 'It was perhaps 15 years later that I deduced in reading one of the books on the "Bulge", that break caused a tragic and drastic misunderstanding.'

The call itself (according to Middleton) went like this.

'I'm worried about some of my people,' Jones said.

'I know,' Middleton answered, guessing that Jones was referring to his two regiments in the Eifel. 'How are they?'

'Not well. And very lonely.'

'I'm sending you a big friend. Workshop. It should reach you about 0700 hours tomorrow.'

Jones knew that 'workshop' was the code-name of the US 7th Armored Division, currently in Holland and under the command of the US 9th Army. Feeling much better at the news, Jones went on to say, 'Now about my people. Don't you think I should call them out?'

Later, during the inquiry into the conduct of the 106th and 14th Cavalry Group during the battle, Middleton maintained that he did not hear that crucial question. According to him, he asked a question of his own, 'You know how things are up there better than I do. Don't you think your troops should be withdrawn?'

Now it has always been stated that Jones didn't hear Middleton. He said, 'I want to know how it looks from where you are. Shall I wait? Is there time?'

There the conversation ended with Jones believing (according to the Middleton version) that he had to keep his two nearly trapped regiments in position. As for Middleton, he told a staff officer (so he said later) who had just entered his office, 'I just talked to Jones. I told him to pull his regiments off the Schnee Eifel.'

Two years later, however, Jones did not doubt one bit that he had been ordered to keep his troops in place. In the autumn of 1946 he told Stanley Frank, a journalist on the *Saturday Evening Post*, quite unequivocally that at 12.30 am on the *seventeenth* of December (i.e. one day later) Middleton sent him a message stating, 'Troops will be withdrawn from present positions only if positions become completely untenable. In no event will enemy be allowed to penetrate west of the Our which will be held at all costs.'

As Jones said 'laconically' to the journalist, 'In plain military language that means *stay till you're dead!*'

Now in Jones's St Vith HQ things started to move rapidly. Jones informed his adviser from VIII Corps, Slayton, and Colonel Craig, an artillery staff officer, 'Well, that's it. Middleton says I should leave them in. Get General Hoge.'

Craig went out to get Hoge. Now Jones told Slayton, 'But here's some good news. I'm getting the Seventh Armored. They'll be here early in the morning.'

Slayton was in a quandary. An armored division moved, at the best, at ten miles an hour. It would be impossible for the bulk of the

Seventh Armored to cover the 90 miles from the Maastricht area and reach St Vith early in the morning. Should he protest? 'I should have done so,' he admitted after the war, 'but that would have meant I should have to call the corps commander a liar. And colonels don't call corps commanders liars if they want to stay in the army.' So he said nothing.

Hoge re-entered the office. 'The Seventh Armored is coming,' Jones told him. 'They'll be here tomorrow morning at zero seven hundred hours.'

Jones strode across the office to the big wall map. He pointed to Schönberg directly behind the positions of the 422nd and 423rd. As he did so, he didn't know that already von Manteuffel had pinpointed it as the main objective of Hoffmann-Schonborn's 18th Volksgrenadier Division on the morrow. 'I'm going to have the Seventh attack Schönberg instead of you, Hoge. I want *you* to take Winterspelt – here.'

Thereupon Jones explained that his third regiment, Colonel Reid's 424th Infantry, had held the German attack all day, but in the village of Winterspelt a serious situation had arisen. Reed had used up all his reserve and his artillery had nearly used up all its ammunition. Hoge was therefore being switched from an attack in the north to an attack in the south to help Reid. Now everything in the north depended upon the early arrival of the Seventh Armored.

The Seventh Armored was alerted that evening 'to help out' against 'a little German counter-attack of three or four divisions'. In fact nineteen had been identified already. The alert came at a bad time. The Seventh had been in combat three months and a third of the men were in high spirits this Saturday evening because they had been told they were going on leave to Paris or Brussels. Another combat command had been alerted for a cavalrylike swoop on a German outpost. At the headquarters a group of officers, who had organized a 'little league' for Dutch children, were explaining the complexities of baseball to some of them. Thus it was that when a staff officer entered to say that the division was alerted for immediate movement, the news came, as Captain Merriam, 9th Army Intelligence officer, phrased it, 'like a bombshell'.

Immediately General Hasbrouck, the Divisional Commander, got down to work. The Seventh would move that night in two columns, one to the east and one to the west. (Unknown to Hasbrouck, both these march routes were directly in the path of *Kampfgruppe Peiper* of the 1st SS.

Leading the motorized march would be Brigadier-General Bruce Clarke, the commander of the 7th's Combat Command B. Hasbrouck's call alerting Clarke to his new task caught him at his HQ just in time. The General was packing for a seventy-two-hour leave in Paris. It hadn't been Clarke's idea to go. Hasbrouck had suggested it, for Clarke was suffering badly from piles, probably brought on by five months of almost uninterrupted combat.

Now Hasbrouck said, 'I'm afraid, Bruce, you can't go to Paris after all. The division has just got orders to move to Bastogne.'

'Bastogne!' Clarke exclaimed. 'That's practically a rest area. What are we going to do down there?'

'I have no idea,' Hasbrouck replied. 'General Simpson' – the commander of the 9th Army to which the 7th Armored belonged – 'told me to go down and report to Troy Middleton. You go on ahead and find out what the mission is. Maybe they're having a little trouble down there.' The phone went dead.

Hurriedly Clarke changed into combat gear, packed a few things into a battered old Mercedes which Hasbrouck had loaned him and set off for Bastogne, together with Major Owen Woodruff, a driver, and another driver in the follow-up jeep. This was the extent of the great relief force which General Jones was confidently expecting for seven o'clock the following morning.

While Clarke vanished into the dangerous darkness, for the Germans were breaking through everywhere now, Hasbrouck heard from VIII Corps that he was to go *not* to Bastogne, but to Vielsalm to the rear of the front. Half an hour later that was changed to St Vith.

Little did Bruce Clarke realize that this night was to become the turning point of his life. As he drove through the night, holding the gear shift in place next to the driver (it tended to slip back into neutral), he must have thought that the sudden call to Bastogne was just another of the routine alarms and excursions that he had encountered so often over the last months of combat. He could hardly realize that he would emerge from what was to come as a hero to some – the man who had set von Manteuffel's timetable back so badly that the Germans had really already lost the Battle of the Bulge, although the fighting went on for another five weeks. For others, in particular the many thousands of 'Golden Lions' who would soon disappear into German prisoner-of-war cages, Clarke would be the villian of the piece. Even after half a century they still accuse him of failing to come to their rescue and thus condemning them to months of misery and even death in the German camps.

Clarke was a big man, running a little to fat, with a craggy face and wavy brown hair. He had come from a poor family of many children, who had managed to have the army train him as an engineer. But when he had first gone into action on 31 July, 1944, he had done so in an armoured formation, Patton's favourite armoured division, the Fourth.

As soon as the Fourth, as part of Patton's 3rd Army, had begun its lightning drive across France, Patton visited Clarke's combat command and asked if he needed any help. Clarke, a blunt man, answered that he was working under supervisors who were accustomed to a two-miles-an-hour advance 'and I often run out of orders by ten thirty in the morning. What am I supposed to do in such cases?'

Patton's answer was typical of the man. 'Go east, Clarke,' he commanded.

Thereafter Clarke did so, advancing several hundred miles, something which didn't altogether endear him to his superiors. In the end Patton had warned him, 'Don't try to fight the whole war, Clarke!'

In October, 1944, when the Fourth had reached Eastern France, Patton had again visited Colonel Clarke and had surprised him with the words, 'Clarke, you are a damned nobody!'

Clarke stared down at him with astonishment. Smiling now, Patton had explained that the previous evening he had had dinner with General Marshall, head of the US Army. Patton had asked Marshall to promote Clarke, whereupon Marshall had asked if Clarke had ever served at Fort Benning, the advanced infantry school.

Patton had replied in the negative and Marshall had said, 'I don't know him.'

Now Patton said, 'Hell, Clarke if you had been an infantryman instead of an engineer and had served in Fort Benning, you would be a major-general by now.'

But Marshall must have checked on his file. For in November, 1944, Clarke had been given his first star and had been posted to the Seventh Armored. Clarke had hated to leave the 4th Armored and Patton's Third Army, but he was ambitious and wanted promotion.

This, then, was the man now driving through the night towards the battle and his date with destiny. He was ambitious, experienced and not a little ruthless, as we shall see. Soon several senior officers would have their reputations broken at St Vith, but not Clarke. St Vith would mean for him the start of the highest honours that his Army could bestow on him. He would be a man who advised presidents, licked a demoralized army into shape, trained the young officers who would fight America's wars in the 1990s. 'Clarke of St Vith' they would call him, the commander whose name was bound eternally to that small Belgian border town.* But on this icy Saturday night with the panzers roaming the roads and Skorzeny's killer commandos lurking everywhere, he was an obscure brigadier general driving to the sound of the guns.

For the Supreme Commander, this fateful Saturday was, at first, a day of celebration. He had received yet another foreign medal, had attended the wedding of his favourite orderly, Mickey, and later he would celebrate his fifth general's star. Duly that morning he attended the wedding of Mickey, whose aim in life was to become a bar owner, to a plump homely WAC sergeant, who had been a school-teacher in civilian life. Thereafter he drank a glass of champagne and in a high good mood returned to his HQ at Versailles outside Paris to attend to the only item of business for that Saturday afternoon.

It was an informal conference on the problem of obtaining sufficient riflemen for Bradley's divisions, sadly depleted this winter in the fighting in the Siegfried Line. Most divisions were at least five percent under strength, some were down as much as twenty percent. The question, which he discussed with his Chief-of-Staff, Bedell Smith, his G-2, General Strong, and Bradley among others, was where those reinforcements were to come from.

The conferences had begun at two that afternoon and, with the light getting steadily worse outside, it droned on slowly with few positive decisions being taken until the door to the rear opened. There stood Brigadier-General Betts. Betts was a normally calm, phlegmatic man. But Strong, his chief, noted that he now appeared to be 'rather shaken'. Strong excused himself and hurried to see what was the matter.

* Even when he was commander of the US Seventh Army, General Clarke would make a point of returning to St Vith to attend any veterans' reunion there. Once when there was a typhus epidemic there and all Americans were forbidden to enter the area, he disobeyed orders to go and attend a veterans' reunion.

Betts whispered something in the ear of the tall dark Scot. Strong frowned, asked a question and then returned to interrupt the conference with 'This morning the enemy counterattacked at five separate points across the First Army sector.'

Bradley reacted calmly enough. He was said to have stated that it was a 'spoiling attack'. 'If by coming through the Ardennes he can force us to pull Patton's troops out of the Saar and throw them against his counter-offensive, he'll get what he's after.' It was a remarkably quick assessment of what would happen nearly a week later. Too quick, perhaps, almost as if the plan had already been prepared.

According to what the US Army allowed the public to know after the event, Eisenhower said quite unequivocally, 'This is *not* a local attack, Brad. It isn't logical for the Germans to launch a local attack at our weakest point.' Again Eisenhower reacted remarkably promptly when for months now he had seemingly believed the predictions that the German Army was wasting away and that it would never again attack in the West.

Bedell Smith, a general troubled by an ulcer and with a temper as fierce as his red head, not a man given to gestures of affection, laid his hand on Bradley's shoulder and remarked, 'Well, Brad, you've been wishing for a counter-attack. Now it looks like you've got it.'

'A counter-attack, yes,' Bradley replied, 'but I'll be damned if I wanted one *this* big!'

It has often been stated in accounts of the Battle of the Bulge that Eisenhower reacted slowly on that first day of the great attack and that he had few reserves available to stem the German thrust. But before that afternoon was over two armoured divisions, the 7th in the north and 10th in the south, were ordered to march. In France two airborne divisions, the 101st and 82nd, were alerted to move to the VIII Corps area and in England, the 11th Armored, 17th Airborne and 75th Infantry Divisions were all commanded to speed up their preparations to move to France. Indirectly at his disposal Eisenhower had the British XXX Corps of nearly 100,000 men conveniently out of the line in the Belgium-Holland area. Further, the bulk of Patton's Third Army, nearly nine divisions, would soon become available. For a general who advocated a broad front strategy, with all his armies attacking all along the front, that Saturday Eisenhower had a remarkable number of divisions out of combat.

A coincidence? Or planned?

That night, with Strong now noticing that nineteen German divisions had been identified in the Ardennes, Eisenhower ate a remarkably fine dinner, prepared for him and his guests by his 'darkies', as he called his black mess waiters. A well-wisher had given him a bushel of oysters, which he adored. There were oysters on the half-shell as an entrée, followed by oysters stewed, with fried oysters to conclude the festive meal (Bradley ate scrambled eggs; he didn't like oysters). With the meal they drank vintage champagne. Thereafter there was scotch and bourbon and five rubbers of bridge which lasted till well after midnight. It seemed that a happy, smiling Ike hadn't a care in the world.

As Eisenhower and the top brass ate, Captain James Shomon of the graves registration company at Margraten heard of the great breakthrough on the BBC. Hastily he summoned Lieutenant Donovan and snapped; 'Ed, better get the company alerted straightaway. Put on a double guard. Send extra men to the cemetery and tell them to be on watch for paratroopers.'

Donovan doubled away into the freezing darkness, and Shomon went downstairs to meet the Burgomaster. Herr Ronckers, who had heard the news too, was very nervous. In his fractured English, he stuttered, 'De Boche iss tuff . . . Dey can still do much damage . . . This will be a hard Christmas for you Amerikans – and for us.'

Shomon nodded his agreement. He thought of the hundreds of dead young Americans who would soon be dumped in the burial fields outside the little Dutch village. Yes, he told himself, it *would* be a hard Christmas for the Americans.

DAY TWO:

Sunday, 17 December, 1944.

Weather: Overcast; cloudy; penetrating cold. Snow flurries turning to rain. Poor air observation, but some air reconnaissance in Holland, Luxembourg. Ground soft. Roads muddy and slick.

'They couldn't just abandon us in the line up on the ridge. We were Americans. Somebody ought to have come to rescue us.'

H. Kline, ex-423rd Infantry Regiment,
106th Division.

Bea Wain II started the first time. It was freezing cold outside, but the Sherman sprang to life without the slightest hesitation. To a delighted John Marshall of the Misfits, it was the 'sweetest sound I'd ever heard'. Cautiously the tank started to roll down the narrow valley road. Inside, the Misfits tensed. All night Germans had been passing what they thought was a knocked-out *Ami* tank and the four Americans knew that they were well behind German lines. They could run into trouble at any moment.

They were just approaching a lone house with a large '*pie*' in front (a heap of earth and straw which the local farmers used to store their root crops during the winter) when Marshall at the gun saw two Germans ahead. Alyea sang out, 'Get 'em!'

For some reason Marshall found himself unable to fire and Alyea yelled angrily, 'You just let two Kraut officers get away!'

Marshall, who had had the two Germans in his sights, said nothing, but he told himself grimly, 'Those Krauts were living on borrowed time'.

Cautiously the tank crawled nearer to the old stone house. Footprints were everywhere in the snow. The Misfits assumed there were Germans in the house. Suddenly a German soldier sprang up, hands raised, as if in surrender.

Marshall perked up. 'A German surrendering. It was a pleasant surprise. We must be winning.' Suddenly he looked behind him. The two officers he hadn't fired at were now crouching behind the '*pie*' with a couple of dozen other Germans. One of the Germans jumped up and pressed the trigger of his *panzerfaust*. Flame spurted from the back of the bazooka. A rocket, trailing fiery sparks, hurtled towards *Bea Wain II*.

The German had the whole side of the Sherman to aim at. But he missed!

Marshall pressed the machine gun, but the damned thing jammed.

Spencer reacted immediately. 'The 75mm's loaded,' he said simply. It was – with an armour-piercing, high-explosive shell. Marshall gulped. It was like trying to swat a fly with a sledgehammer. He pressed the foot pedal. The heavy gun boomed into life. The Germans flew to all sides, their blood staining the snow. All except the decoy. He was still standing there, hands raised; only his hands had been sheared off at the wrists.

Shells now started to fall about the tank. They pushed on, climbing the long incline in low gear until finally they broke free from the forest on to a broad straight road which ran the length of the ridge. John Alyea gave a little cheer. He knew that they were on Skyline Drive. They'd be bumping into their own troops soon.

He was right. Soon afterwards they came upon a bunch of engineers. They said the Germans were just behind. They were going to mine the road as soon as *Bea Wain II* had passed. They told the men to take the next road to the right. A group of infantry, plus two jeeps and a tank, had just gone in that direction, heading for Wiltz, where the 28th Division had its headquarters. But the Misfits weren't out of danger yet, not by a long chalk.

Six miles from where the Misfits were rolling through a rising fog trying to catch up with the infantry, Colonel Hurley Fuller, Commander of the 110th Infantry Regiment to which they belonged, knew he was about beaten. All morning bad news had been flooding in to his HQ at Clervaux. All along the Skyline Drive his battalions had been slowly forced back out of their fortified villages – Hosingen, Holtzhum, Marnach had all fallen.

Now even his own headquarters was wide open. The Germans were already in the lower town near the castle. Once he had seen a Tiger tank pass his own HQ. It was one of the flood of German armour bypassing the town, heading for 28th Division's headquarters at Wiltz to the south-west. Still the Colonel fought on with his provisional company of some 200 cooks, clerks, drivers and the like.

Unknown to Fuller, German signallers hidden in the local *pharmacie*, where the French writer Victor Hugo had once lived in exile, were directing fire on all the surviving US positions inside the town. What he did know, however, was that his own HQ in the Hotel Claravallis wouldn't survive much longer.

At three that afternoon he took a call from his 3rd Battalion. It's

C.O. pleaded, 'Give me authority to withdraw the men I've got left. I'll take them back to Wiltz.'

Fuller turned him down cold. 'The order still stands,' he snapped. '*Hold!*'

A few minutes later the distraught C.O. came back on the line. 'We're completely surrounded,' he cried. 'Send some relief.'

'There's no relief,' Fuller answered harshly. 'Take the tanks you've got and fight your way south to the 2nd Battalion.' The line went dead.

When dusk fell General Cota, in the rear at Wiltz, knew that his 28th Division was smashed. His 109th Infantry under Colonel Rudder had fallen back in the south to the positions of the hard-pressed 12th Infantry of the Fourth Division. To the north Colonel Reid's 112th Infantry was retreating towards the 106th around St Vith. As for Fuller's 110th, it seemed to have vanished altogether.

Fuller, whose regiment would be reduced in the next forty-eight hours from 3,000 men to 500, was not altogether finished. He had again managed to establish contact with General Cota's HQ and asked the latter's chief-of-staff whether he could speak to the General. He wanted to retire to the high ground beyond Clervaux. The staff officer said he couldn't disturb the General. He was at dinner. Before Fuller could blow his fuse, one of his own officers burst in crying, 'Colonel, six Kraut tanks coming down the street from the castle!'

'What's going on?' the staff officer asked.

'It's going to be the Alamo all over again. A Kraut tank has just laid one in my office. I'm getting out of here before they lay one in my lap!'

Machine-gun bullets splattered the length of the wall. The phone suddenly went dead. Fuller dodged out of the office. He bumped into his operations officer who yelled, 'Colonel, we're trapped!'

'Looks like it.'

'What the hell are we going to do?'

Fuller, who had never taken kindly to authority, forgot Cota's order. He shouted above the racket of the small arms battle, 'I'm going to try and get out.'

He grabbed his carbine and his coat. Already Germans were swarming into the hotel through the smoke. Wounded were everywhere; many were ready for surrender. Then a man cried, 'Colonel

Fuller, I've found a way out of the building. Do you want to take a chance?'

'Hell yes,' Fuller roared. 'Does anyone else want to go?'

A dozen voice showed their agreement.

From the floor above a voice said 'I'm blind. I'm blind in both eyes.' But he wanted to escape as well. Fuller told him to grab hold of his belt.

In single file the escapers crossed a narrow iron ladder to the cliff behind the hotel and made their way up the steep incline, the blind man hanging on to Fuller's belt. Behind them Clervaux burned. The 110th US Infantry Regiment, which could trace its history back to Civil War days, was finished.

At roughly the same time that John Marshall of the Misfits shot up the German ambush party, the 18th Volksgrenadier Division launched an all-out attack on Bleialf which they had lost the previous day. This time the scratch battalion of the 43rd which Colonel Cavender had sent to hold the place couldn't hold off the German attack and fell back. The Germans seized the opportunity immediately: Hoffmann-Schonborn, the 18th Volksgrenadier commander, sent in his armour. The half-tracks and self-propelled guns barrelled up past the church and started climbing up to what the GIs of the 106th called '88mm Corner'. Here one road led along the ridge line to Auw, while the other descended the valley to the Ihren Creek then began to climb again towards Schönberg in Belgium. The armour took the Schönberg road. From there it was only eleven kilometres to the key objective of von Manteuffel's 5th Panzer Army, St Vith.

The situation now seemed desperate to those of the Americans who knew what was happening, but the two regimental commanders, Colonels Cavender of the 423rd and Descheneaux of the 422nd, were not among them. The men of the 423rd either surrendered or backed off into the forests. The artillery, the most vulnerable element of the 106th, now without infantry protection, started pulling back. Some artillery-men simply abandoned their pieces. Others, such as Lieutenant Eric Fisher Wood and his crew made valiant attempts to save their gun. It would cost him his life, cut off in the woods for six long weeks, fighting a lone guerrilla battle against the Germans until they finally shot him down. By mid-afternoon, with one arm of the 18th Volksgrenadier coming through the positions abandoned by the 14th Cavalry and the other down the hill road to link up at

Schönberg, the 422nd and 423rd Regiments were cut off and surrounded.

The two commanders were strangely sanguine when they realized what had happened. At two o'clock that afternoon Descheneaux called Cavender and asked, 'What are we going to do?'

Cavender wasn't quite sure. He answered hesitantly, 'Jones says to withdraw from present positions if they become untenable.'

Descheneaux, at 35 the youngest full colonel in the US Army, frowned. 'Until Division tells me definitely to move, I'm staying right where I am.'

With new enthusiasm, Cavender said, 'So am I!'

Now he started to swing his battered battalions round in a tight defensive arc, facing west, south and east. Then he ordered a count of the casualties.

They were heavy. 'Two hundred and twenty-five killed, wounded or missing,' one of his officers reported. (During the same period the 422nd had suffered a mere forty casualties.) Before Cavender had time to comment on these losses, he was interrupted by 'Division, sir'.

He picked up the radio-phone. It was St Vith. He was given some very encouraging news indeed. 'We expect to clear out areas west of you this afternoon with reinforcements.' Further, the Colonel was told, 'Withdraw from present positions if they become untenable. Save all transport possible.'

Cavender smiled. It seemed a good omen that the force being sent to help them was the Seventh Armored Division. Which American kid wasn't familiar with those Western movies where the 'Seventh Cavalry' arrived just in the nick of time to prevent the wagon train being wiped out by the Indians?

At the same time Descheneaux also received good news. At two he heard from Division: 'Supplies to be dropped vicinity Schlausenbach tonight.' Transport planes from England were flying to the Continent to deliver vital food and ammunition. Not that he needed the latter too urgently. So far, unlike the 423rd, his regiment had not been involved in too much fighting. His own sector was very quiet, though he had only radio contact now with Cavender.

Indeed the mood was good in the 422nd positions. Staff Sergeant Petersen of the 422nd's mortar platoon remembered that 'the rumours were as wild as the imagination and fears of the teller of the tale made them. Rumours of parachute drops persisted.'

But at least they were not fighting and the only sound of battle came from their rear. To their front, deeper inside Germany, all was silent.

If there was any real panic that day in the sector held by the US Army's three greenest units in combat – the 99th, the 14th Cavalry and the 106th – it was in the rear echelon.

Down near Schönberg, Sergeant Jim Thorpe, the medic, his unit now flooded with wounded from the front, was horrified by the panic the attack caused the battalion's senior officers. They were 'bugging out', as he called it bitterly, on all sides. Abandoning the wounded, commandeering ambulances even, they fled west.

At the 47th Field Hospital in Butgenbach in the 2nd and 99th Divisional area, the medics, both male and female, smelled a rat when an ambulance from the 2nd Division rolled up carrying a superficially wounded man. 'What's this?' they asked. 'Don't you have a clearing station any more?'

The driver answered, 'Sorry, sir. We're pulling out right away and we haven't got an ambulance to take this man all the way to Malmédy.' With that the ambulance crew dumped the wounded man who had been their pretext to get out of the line and fled westwards. They were yet another part of the 'Big Bugout'.

Just outside St Vith Lt-Colonel Tom Riggs, C.O. of the 106th's 81st Combat Engineer Battalion, noted the panic too. 'Headquarters was jumpy,' and 'rumours were growing and difficult to dispute without the facts. Some service units, such as Corps Artillery, were starting to move to the rear without artillery. 'They were committing the artilleryman's cardinal sin – they were abandoning their guns!' The Engineer Officer, who was soon to become one of the heroes of the defence of St Vith, thought that 'A lot of people who shouldn't have were cracking up.'

Colonel Devine, who had already twice ordered his 14th Cavalry to withdraw without orders from above, now took it upon himself to leave his outfit and race to the headquarters of the 106th. With him he took his executive officer, Colonel Dugan, and his two senior majors; 'all his eggs in one basket,' as the historian of the 106th commented long afterwards.

Approaching the village of Recht on one of the backroads to St Vith, they spotted a group of men standing at the roadside. Dugan reacted first. He reached for his pistol and fired a burst. The driver swerved wildly. The car went into a skid and the passengers were flung into a ditch. If the men were really Germans, they didn't press their advantage. But Colonel Devine had had enough. Muttering something about 'checking with HQ', Devine turned over the 14th Cavalry to Dugan and set out for St Vith on foot. He arrived just as Brigadier General Clarke was conferring with General Jones. He burst into the latter's office crying, 'The Germans are right behind us. They've broken through in the north. My group is practically destroyed!'

Jones didn't know how to react. Clarke, who had seen much of war, was quicker off the mark. He said to Jones, 'Why don't you send the Colonel back to Bastogne? He could report the situation to General Middleton.'

Jones agreed and that was the last that was heard of Colonel Mark Devine in the Battle of Bulge.

Now the advanced units of the 7th Armored coming from Holland were beginning to bump into the columns of retreating vehicles. Progress was reduced to a mile an hour. Bumper to bumper, the retreating vehicles ranged from jeeps to huge prime movers towing 8-inch howitzers.

Major Don Boyer, another hero of the defence of St Vith, was with the advance party of Clarke's Command B. He fumed as his driver was forced to slow down to a walk. Just outside the village of Poteau to the rear of St Vith, the Seventh's column came to a halt. Voices were raised in anger. Horns honked impatiently. Drivers gunned their motors. Panic was in the air.

Boyer pushed forward. He spotted an officer with the yellow and blue lion patch of the 106th on his shoulder. 'Who are you?' he shouted above the racket.

The officer told him and Boyer asked, 'What's the score?'

'The Krauts – at least six panzer divisions – hit us yesterday,' the young officer said.

'And what are you doing about it?' Boyer asked, trying to fight back his rising anger.

'*Me*, I'm leaving!'

Boyer opened his mouth to argue with him, then changed his mind. He went back to his jeep. 'Move over, driver,' he ordered.

'What now, sir?'

Boyer showed him. He drove straight into the nearest field; it seemed as if that was the only way he was going to get to St Vith that day.

General Clarke, impatient for the arrival of his command, couldn't stand the depressing atmosphere of Jones's HQ any longer. He drove out to the centre of St Vith, where the road from Malmédy entered the *Hauptstrasse*. There he found his staff officer, Major Woodruff, standing by the road, defeated by the mass of retreating vehicles clogging the crossroads. Clarke, who had a short fuse, flared up immediately. 'What's happened, Woody?' he demanded, glaring at the convoy of artillerymen bugging out. 'How come you're letting this go on?'

'General, that lieutenant-colonel told me he was going to use the road. He'd shoot if I got in his way.'

Clarke flushed. He strode over to the artillery colonel. 'You get your tractors off this road so my tanks can get up. If there's any shooting done around here, *I'll* do it!'

The threat worked and Clarke directed the retreating artillery vehicles off the road, clearing it for the armour expected at any moment.

At that moment an undersized artillery colonel came up to the red-faced general who was waving his arms furiously at the artillery vehicles. 'General, I'm Roy Clay,' he introduced himself. 'I have a separate battalion of self-propelled 105's, the 275th Armored Field Artillery. We've got some ammunition left and we're ready to work.'

'God bless you, Clay,' Clarke exclaimed, beaming down at the little officer. 'You're all the artillery we've got. Head out to the ridge east of town and support those two engineer companies dug in there. Look for a tall engineer lieutenant colonel, Riggs.' The defence of St Vith had begun.

Clarke's 38th Armored Infantry Battalion had got stuck in the 'Great Jam' at Vielsalm, fifteen kilometres to the rear of St Vith. Its commander, Lt-Colonel William Fuller, detailed the company commander of his HQ company, Captain Carl Mattocks, to find out what was the cause of the delay.

Mattocks, a resourceful officer, who was to be one of the few officers in the US Army to win the British Military Cross, set out to discover the reason for the delay. Vielsalm was packed with fleeing civilians and vehicles of the 14th Cavalry. He worked his way to the head of the stalled 31st Tank Battalion where he met Boyer. Major Boyer was shouting at the leading Sherman tank commander, 'Run over any S.O.B. who tries to get in the way!' That worked. The 14th's vehicles edged to the side of the road and the Shermans started rolling again.

One fleeting artillery sergeant was so carried away that he dropped from his own vehicle, clambered on one of the tanks and shouted, 'I didn't join the army to run away. I wanna fight!' He raised a cheer among the 7th Armored men.

Mattocks, however, was in no mood for cheering. They were moving again. He'd better get back to his men. As he recorded later, 'I returned to my company and not a moment too soon as they had found some cognac and had a Belgian girl playing the piano for them.'

Now, with the 38th Armored Infantry following, the tanks started to roll again. In front of them was B Troop of the 87th Cavalry Reconnaissance Squadron commanded by one Captain Stewart. As they started to roll into St Vith at four that afternoon, Clarke fell in alongside Stewart's armoured car. His orders were the same as he had given to the little artillery colonel, Roy Clay: 'Keep going right down this road until you come to Lt-Colonel Riggs. Tell him you're attached to him. He'll tell you what to do.'

That Sunday the Top Brass seemed strangely unworried about the new situation in the Ardennes. The only positive step – at least it seemed positive to the Top Brass – was to order a total news blackout on what was happening. That day the *New York Times'* only story from the European battlefront was headlined, 'SEVENTH ARMY DRIVES DEEPER INTO REICH'. This was the US Seventh Army located in Alsace in France.

In Washington at the Pentagon General Marshall met with the Chief of War Department Operations, George Lincoln, and General John Hull, the representative of the joint chiefs of staff. Together they discussed the new situation in the Ardennes. There was some talk of trying to speed up the number of reinforcements from the States to Eisenhower. But Marshall vetoed the suggestion. He decreed 'We can't help Eisenhower except by not bothering him. No messages will got to the ETO* unless approved by me.'

---

* European Theatre of Operations.

In Versailles Eisenhower ate a late breakfast and chatted with General Bradley for a while before the latter left on the long journey back to his HQ in Luxembourg, which meant that the US Army Group Commander would be out of touch with events at the front for most of this crucial Sunday. Then Eisenhower settled down to write a few letters. One went to General Brehon Somervell. In it Eisenhower wrote, 'Yesterday morning the enemy launched a rather ambitious counter-attack out of the Luxembourg area which we have been holding very thinly. However, we have some armor which is now out of the line and resting. It is closing in on the threat from each flank. If things go well, we should not only stop the thrust, but should be able to profit from it.'

With an apparent crisis on his hands, with two of his frontline divisions already virtually smashed or cut off, it was a strangely calm letter, as if Eisenhower already had the situation well in hand. It was followed by another letter to Bradley and one to General Devers, the commander of the 6th Army Group in France. 'The enemy is making a major thrust through the Ardennes,' Eisenhower wrote. 'He still has reserves uncommitted. He may, therefore, use these reserves to increase the strength of his attack . . . It appears he will be prepared to employ the whole of his armored reserve to achieve success.'

How was it, now, that the Supreme Commander was suddenly aware that the Germans possessed significant reserves of armour? After weeks of taking the 'calculated risk' of holding the Ardennes with one weak corps, Eisenhower all at once knew that the enemy had a strong mobile force in reserve in the area. According to the official story, he was unable to predict the coming 'surprise' attack because Ultra had failed to produce the goods. The official account had it that over the months and weeks leading to the German counter-offensive, Ultra had been unable to give details of the assault divisions, whether they were armour or infantry or how many of them there were.

Yet suddenly Eisenhower is cognizant of the fact that this was a major attack and that the Germans still had plenty of armour in reserve. But this sudden knowledge did not dismay him. Indeed he would 'profit' from it.

It was almost as if Eisenhower was echoing Middleton's bold reply to him on 8 November when asked what he would do if he were attacked: 'It would be the best thing that could happen. I have

8. The face of the enemy: young SS troops captured during the battle.

9. Many German soldiers, however, were happy to be done with the fighting. Note the smile on the German POW's face standing against the shattered wall.

10. A lull in the fighting: a soldier reads the US Army newspaper *Stars and Stripes* while rations are cooked in the pup tents.

11. The 'Misfits' 707th Tank Battalion advancing through the Hurtgen Forest before they left for the Ardennes.

12. The stalled convoy of the 7th Armored Division on its way to St Vith, 17 December, 1944.

13. US engineers mine a road as the Germans advance.

14. The snow adds to the misery of fighting in such inhospitable terrain.

15. Soldiers in 'spook suits', made from Belgian housewives' best sheets, advance to the front.

nothing of value that I can't afford to lose between the front and the Meuse River.* If they come through we can trap them and cut their heads off, shortening the war by several months.'

Could it have been that Eisenhower was strangely untroubled that Sunday when his VIII Corps was falling apart by the hour because he was well aware of what was happening at the front and that he had already taken appropriate measures to deal with the emergency? Was it possible that the Supreme Commander had known what was to come for weeks, perhaps months, and had long made preparations for this eventuality? Was it possible that he had deliberately lured the Germans into attacking out of their fortifications and the young GIs of Middleton's VIII Corps had been the bait?

In late September, 1944, General George Catlett Marshall, Eisenhower's mentor and patron, was faced with an agonizing decision. Governor Tom Dewey, who was the Republican candidate for the office of President, was threatening to malign President Roosevelt by revealing all that he knew about 'MAGIC'. Magic was the codename for decoding operations run mainly from Arlington Hall, Virginia. Here, for four years, the experts had been reading most of the Japanese codes. Now Governor Dewey was ready to state publicly that Roosevelt, thanks to Magic, had known all along that Pearl Harbor was about to be attacked.

Marshall knew something that the ambitious former district attorney and now governor of New York State didn't: the same Magic code was *still* being used by the Japanese and if Dewey revealed everything he would destroy a war-winning Intelligence operation just as important as the Ultra op. being run from Bletchley Park for the British. What was he to do?

In the end, without knowledge of the President, he sent an emissary to Dewey to tell him. Dewey didn't believe him. He thought it was a whitewash job, designed to cover the President. Marshall tried again. On 27 September, 1944, three weeks after Hitler had made his decision to attack in the Ardennes, he sent Dewey another long letter explaining the position. In it he wrote: 'Now the point to the present dilemma is that we have gone ahead with this business

---

* Was it a coincidence that Bradley could reassure Eisenhower that he had no major supply dumps the Germans could capture in front of the Meuse, 'south of Liege and north of Verdun', ie the sector held by Middleton?

of deciphering their codes (Japanese) until we possess other codes, German as well as Japanese, but our main basis of information regarding Hitler's intentions in Europe is obtained from Baron Oshima's messages from Berlin reporting his interviews with Hitler and other officials to the Japanese Government. These are still in the codes involved in the Pearl Harbor events.'

Marshall went on to state: 'The conduct of General Eisenhower's campaign and of all the operations in the Pacific are closely related in conception and timing to the information we secretly obtain through these intercepted codes. They contribute greatly to the victory and tremendously to the saving of American lives.'

Even before he had finished reading the long letter, Dewey exclaimed, 'Well I'll be damned if I believe the Japs are still using those two codes!' By which he meant the ones used prior to Pearl Harbor.

Marshall's courier assured the former 'gangbuster' that this was the case and that one of the two codes 'was our life blood in intelligence'. Indeed, he stated, Churchill regarded this 'secret weapon' – the Ultra operation – as having really saved England back in the dark middle years of the war.

Dewey grunted and said, 'There is little in this letter that I don't already know. There is one point though. What in hell do Jap codes have to do with Eisenhower?'

As discreetly as he could, Colonel Clarke, Marshall's emissary, told the Governor something of the Bletchley Park operation and its value as a primary source of intelligence for Eisenhower. Clarke added that by 1944 the reading of the Japanese diplomatic cipher had become just as important for the Supreme Commander over in Paris. Indeed Eisenhower was one of the few recipients of 'Black Book' Ultra*. This 'Ultra within Ultra' was limited to a handful of top Americans, such as MacArthur in the Pacific and the President himself.

Now Dewey was impressed. He had a brief discussion with his adviser in the next room, then returned to Clarke. He said, 'Colonel, I do not believe that there are any questions I want to ask you nor do I care to have any discussions about the contents of this letter.'

* Back in the winter of 1944, Marshall had introduced a summary of all top Japanese intercepts which were bound in a black book, hence the name. In February, 1944, he started sending 'Black Book Ultra', as it was called by those in the know, to President Roosevelt.

Then the two shook hands and Dewey dismissed Clarke with 'Well I hope we meet again under more auspicious circumstances.'

They never did, but Dewey never mentioned that America had been able to crack the Japanese codes before Pearl Harbor and must have known of the coming 'surprise attack' on that 'Day of Infamy', 7 December, 1941. That disclosure might well have brought down President Roosevelt and won him the 1944 election. But he didn't and Roosevelt went on to win a fourth term in office.

Neither Marshall nor Dewey ever revealed either that they had been in touch with each other over the matter of Magic. When Marshall testified before the great Congressional Inquiry into the Pearl Harbor attack in 1945, he was pretty economical with the truth. The letter of 27 September, 1944, was never mentioned. Instead Marshall said, quite truthfully, that he had first met Dewey at President Roosevelt's funeral in April, 1945. Thereafter he had given Dewey access to the secrets of the codebreakers. Dewey, he maintained, had behaved with great consideration. Dewey, for his part, kept discreetly mum.

In December, 1940, one year before Pearl Harbor, the Japanese diplomat named in the secret letter as Eisenhower's main source of information on Hitler's intentions returned again to Berlin. He was the 54-year Baron Hiroshi Oshima, a soldier and an aristocrat. He had first served in Berlin in 1934 as the Japanese military attaché where he had made firm contacts with officers of the German *Reichswehr*, as it was then, and leading members of the National Socialist Party which had taken over the year before.

By 1939, when he had been recalled for a year to Tokyo, he had gained the Führer's ear as the leading representative of the third member of the 'Pact of Steel' (Germany, Italy and Japan), and a man whose political philosophy was very much akin to that of the Nazis. By the time Japan entered the war and had succeeded in defeating the Anglo-Americans in a series of spectacular victories virtually everywhere in the Far East, Hitler's respect for the dark-haired, diminutive Japanese diplomat had grown considerably.

The U.S. Signal Intelligence Service had broken the Japanese diplomatic code a few months before Oshima had returned to Germany in 1940. From that time onwards, right to the end of the war, Oshima would be the major source of Hitler's thinking and intentions. In his enciphered messages to Tokyo, the Japanese ambassador revealed many of Germany's intentions well in advance

– for insistance the invasion of Russia in 1941. In 1943 Oshima informed his masters in Tokyo that although the Allied 'bomber Barons' were causing heavy damage to Germany's cities, the raids by the British at night and by the Americans in the daytime were not affecting Germany's war production. Indeed as he reported to Tokyo in January, 1944, German output of essential weapons such as tanks and aircraft was actually rising.

In that spring, because the Japanese were interested in obtaining the new secret German jet fighters, Oshima took it upon himself to find out all about them. He did so with his usual energy and diligence, thus providing, unwittingly, the Western Allies with the speeds, ceiling capacities, rate of climb etc of these latest enemy wonder weapons.

For Eisenhower these Magic intercepts of Oshima's messages to Tokyo – and by now they were provided not only by Arlington in the States but also by Bletchley Hall – really became invaluable when the planning for the invasion reached its peak. Oshima revealed in the winter of 1943/44 priceless details about the Atlantic Wall. On 10 December, 1943, for instance, he radioed home a nine-page analysis of the defences in France. The report contained a clear picture of the fortifications, the number of German divisions and how they were rotated, plus an analysis of the German command structure.

A week later, he sent an account of the varying depths of the defence zones at danger points like Dieppe, Boulogne, Le Havre, etc, even noting the individual siting of German machine guns. For Eisenhower it must have been like manna from heaven, especially when on the eve of the Invasion Oshima made it clear, after a personal meeting with Hitler, that the Führer did not suspect that the Allies were going to land in Normandy. It must have made that supposedly agonizing decision to send in the invading force on 6 June, 1944 a lot easier for Eisenhower.

For two months thereafter Oshima kept fairly silent. Thus it was with a great deal of anticipation that both Bletchley and Arlington Hall read the Japanese diplomat's request for an audience with the Führer in late August. That audience was granted on 4 September. By this time Eisenhower's victorious armies had chased the beaten *Wehrmacht* right across France and Belgium and were now nearing the German frontier. Victory was in the air. Hitler was almost defeated. Within the week the first elements of the US 5th Armored and Middleton's old 4th Infantry Divisions would cross into the

Reich from Luxembourg. Had the Führer still got anything left up his sleeve to stave off the inevitable? Or would he tell the Jap he was going to throw in the towel?

Finally the decode came through on 5 September. In a message marked 'Extremely Urgent', Oshima signalled Tokyo that he had 'left for High Command HQ on the 3rd,' exactly five years to the day since Britain and France had gone to war with Germany. There at Hitler's East Prussian Headquarters, he 'had an interview with Foreign Minister Ribbentrop and then one with Chancellor Hitler on the 4th.' On the 5th he returned to Berlin, from whence 'I am writing a gist of the interviews separately.'

If the Allied listeners had expected that on this fifth anniversary of the outbreak of the war Hitler would confess he had had enough they were in for a great surprise. Frankly, Hitler outlined the difficulties he had faced since 20 July when his own generals had tried to assassinate him. The plotters had now been taken care of. The German Army had been forced to make a fighting retreat back to the Reich itself. Now, however, most of the retreating divisions were behind the protection of the *Westwall* and the line was to be stabilized by launching a counter-attack with forces being massed south-east of Nancy.

The news that Germany was in a position to attack, even at this eleventh hour, must have made the officers who were assessing Oshima's information blink. But now they were in for an even greater surprise. Hitler also planned a large-scale offensive in the West. Oshima summarized Hitler's words thus: 'It was his intention, as soon as the new army of more than a million men now being organized was ready, to combine them with units to be withdrawn from the front in every area and, waiting upon the replenishment of the air forces which is now in progress, to take the offensive in the West on a large scale.' Hitler expected that this build-up would take place under the cover of rainy weather in September and October when the Allies would not be able to make full use of their superior air power. Thus the large-scale attack in the West would take place 'after the beginning of November'.

That was the last interview Hitler ever gave the Japanese ambassador, but for Allied Intelligence it should have been the most decisive. For it was the very first indication that, within weeks, Hitler would involve America in its greatest battle of the 20th century.

*

On the evening of 18 September the German Fifth Panzer Army, commanded by a new general from the Eastern Front, von Manteuffel, attacked Patton's Third Army at Luneville, just north of Nancy. For a day or so it was touch-and-go, especially in the sector held by Colonel Bruce Clarke, then still a member of the 4th Armored Division. But Clarke fought off the attack and would live to battle with von Manteuffel again. By 29 September the little German commander had had enough. The attack by the German Fifth Army was called off. But the American drive to the east had been stopped, as Hitler had wanted, and Patton concentrated on trying to capture Metz which would take him until the first week of December.

But the attack had shown that Baron Oshima's information was correct. Now a flow of messages from Berlin to Tokyo was intercepted at Bletchley and Arlington. All dealt directly or indirectly with the great counter-offensive. The codebreakers learned that Hitler attached high hopes to this offensive, with the recapture of Antwerp as its main objective. Antwerp, the great supply port, had to be re-taken before the Allies could clear the mined, blocked channel to the port and pour in troops and material. Such troops would be thrown in to stop Hitler's offensive if that clearance was achieved. Hence, it was imperative to start the offensive as soon as the bad weather period began.

The Allied codebreakers knew that the rainfall in the Ardennes-Eifel and Eastern France normally doubled in November. So November had to be the month when Germany would attack. Oshima confirmed this when he signalled Tokyo that Hitler had ordered the counter-offensive must be launched no later than the last week of November.

On the 16th of that month Oshima sent two messages to Japan. In the first he gave a detailed account of his meeting with Hitler's Foreign Minister von Ribbentrop at Sonnenberg, sixty miles east of Berlin. During the conversation Oshima reminded Ribbentrop that in September Hitler had promised an offensive in the west. According to the Führer, it would be launched 'after the beginning of November'. Now it was already the second week of that month. Had the Führer changed his plans?

Von Ribbentrop was evasive. He wouldn't give details of the timing. He said Germany might attack in the west. On the other hand, the great attack could be in the east.

Oshima mentioned the great Ludendorff offensive of March,

1918, which had sent the British Army reeling back in France in almost total disarray. However, the ambassador observed, some historians thought that that offensive had hastened Germany's defeat. Would it not be 'a wise plan for Germany to fight a war of attrition?'

'Absolutely not!' von Ribbentrop snorted. 'The Chancellor believes we cannot win the war by defence alone and has reiterated his intention of taking the offensive to the bitter end.'

Oshima came away from that meeting unconvinced. He signalled Tokyo that Ribbentrop's remark was 'one of the instances in which truth from the mouth of a liar reaches the highest pinnacle of deceptiveness.' Later that day he changed his mind. He signalled that 'we may take at face value' the intention of the German leadership to attack, for 'a Germany whose battle lines have contracted virtually to the old territory of Germany . . . will have no choice but to open a road of blood in one direction or another.' In his opinion, that 'road of blood' would lead westwards.

In all, between 16 August and 15 December, 1944, Oshima sent twenty-eight messages to Tokyo dealing with the coming German counter-offensive. In eighteen of these messages he implies that Germany intended resuming the offensive as soon as possible. In eight he states that a large-scale attack is planned for late 1944; and in two he is confident that a large-scale attack would soon begin and mentions the Aachen area.

Why didn't Eisenhower act upon this top-secret source of information? His chief, General Marshall, had written in his secret letter to Governor Dewey, 'The conduct of General Eisenhower's campaign . . . [is] closely related in conception and timing to the information we secretly obtain through these intercepted codes. They contribute greatly to the victory and tremendously to the saving of American lives, both in the conduct of current operations and in looking towards the early termination of the war.' Ever since he had been appointed Supreme Commander in Europe and had been initiated into the Ultra Magic secret, Eisenhower had made these intercepts, which let him know Hitler's intention, almost as soon as Hitler's subordinates did, the basis of his plans and strategy. When he returned to the States after Germany's defeat, one of the first official visits he made as the new US Chief-of-Staff was to Arlington Hall Station. At that time he told General Vandenberg, his Assistant Chief-of-Staff, that he wished to extend his personal thanks to those 'individuals who had produced information on the German fortifications,' which he felt was 'vital to the success of the Allied invasion in June, 1944'. He also told one of the officials at Arlington that he wanted to express 'his gratitude for the information from the Japanese diplomatic intercepts which had been provided to him'.

If, then, the Supreme Commander had always based his strategy in part on the information obtained from Oshima, why had he not been alerted to the threat of the counter-attack as soon as he read the 'Black Book Ultra'? After all, Eisenhower had had confirmation of what Oshima had learned of Hitler's intentions when that predicted counter-attack near Nancy took place two weeks later.

Was it gross carelessness on Eisenhower's part? In his defence after the battle, it was argued that, due to his 'broad front strategy', he couldn't cover the whole front adequately. That winter the front covered five hundred miles. With sixty-five divisions at his disposal, each division would have been responsible for just over seven miles. But you don't win wars by defence. Therefore divisions had to be concentrated in the assault areas. The result was that areas like the Ardennes had to be thinly defended. Here each of the three infantry divisions in the line had to defend twenty miles.

It was also argued in Eisenhower's defence that, even though he knew the Germans were going to attack – he admitted that himself in a confidential memo to Secretary of State for War Patterson, in December, 1945 – he did not know *exactly* where. But that's not true. He did.

Although Ultra was not picking up signals from the three land armies soon to be launched into the attack in the Ardennes, it *was* deciphering other German signals. These signals were connected with the movement of troops into the Eifel and the necessity of air cover to protect the troop transports.

Throughout November and December the boffins at Bletchley were reading the *Reichsbahn* code and that of the *Luftwaffe*. During this period some 800 troop trains crossed the Rhine, heading for the front. Each time a train moved from the eastern bank of the Rhine, heading westwards, Model's Army Group B asked for fighter cover.

In the main the Rhine proved a bottleneck, with trains being limited to certain crossing points, namely Cologne, Bonn-Remagen, Koblenz, Bingen and Mainz, funneling the mass of the traffic through those cities. From there the traffic would continue to the main railheads of Euskirchen, Gerolstein, Wittlich, Kyllburg and Bitburg.

Apart from certain exceptions, Ultra was not able to identify those divisions passing westwards, though the boffins knew that the highest priority was being given to armour. On 12 November Bletchley picked up a *Reichsbahn* signal from Kassel stating that 2nd SS Panzer Division was thirty-six hours behind schedule, the Panzer Lehr twenty-four hours and the 12th SS Panzer twelve hours. However, they could identify pretty accurately the stations where these divisions were being unloaded. They were all south-west of Cologne, ie facing the area held, in part, by Middleton's corps.

By late November Bletchley was deciphering *Luftwaffe* signals from Model's HQ asking for aerial reconnaissance. The spots to be surveyed were the Eupen-Malmédy area and the Prüm-Houffalize.

By 29 November there were daily requests for the *Luftwaffe*'s high-speed Arado 234 jets from *Abteilung Sperling* to recce the Meuse from Liège in the north to Givet in the south. The pilots were told to look out for specific items. Were the *Amis* bringing up reinforcements? Where were the American tank concentrations and supply dumps? It was now 'a matter of the greatest urgency', thus the Bletchley decode, to photograph some of the Meuse crossings and the road junction at Ciney in Belgium (the most westerly point reached later by von Manteuffel's 5th Panzer).

Finally a big conference of fighter squadron commanders was recorded as being held on the evening of 5 December at Ulmen air base in the Eifel. Later, decodes showed that the Germans had managed to assemble 300 fighters of the Middle Rhine Command, the largest noted at the front for months, especially when Germany's hard-pressed cities to the north were crying out for air cover to protect them against the 'Anglo-American air gangsters'.

So by the end of November Ultra had recorded what section of the front the bulk of the German troops were heading for; the fact that much of the troop traffic was armoured; and that, for the Germans, it was a matter of urgency to discover if the Americans had been strengthening the defences of the River Meuse below Liège.

Troops detraining on the general line Gerolstein-Bitburg – Eifel place names which were appearing all the time in Army Group B's requests for air cover – were within ten to fifteen miles from the line held by Middleton's VIII Corps. But their presence there was explained by top-level US Intelligence men as follows: The area was centrally located. From the Eifel area, the troops could be switched to either the Saar, in case of a breakthrough by Patton there, or to the Aachen area to meet any attack by Hodges' 1st Army. That explanation lacked one thing. The Eifel did *not* have the roads to north and south for such transfers of troops in an emergency. Nor did the Eifel have the requisite railways.

The obvious conclusion which should have been drawn from the *Reichsbahn* and *Luftwaffe* decodes, plus those decodes dealing with the reconnaissance of the Meuse crossing points, was this: Middleton was going to be attacked and the armour being brought up into this supposedly quiet sector would be used to drive for the River Meuse.

Apologists for Eisenhower's lack of decision, when presented with the Ultra intelligence, would maintain that he didn't know where that armour was. But he did. For he possessed yet another intelligence-gathering source, one of the very latest kind, whose activities have, in part, remained secret to this day: Air Vice-Marshal E. B. Addison's Number 100 Group of the Royal Air Force.

Number 100 Group became operational in mid-1944, flying from bases in Norfolk, with its headquarters at Bylaugh Hall. It was composed of night-fighters, some quite obsolete, bombers, again many obsolete, plus a new batch of sixty N-17 Flying Fortresses just arrived from the United States. With this motley collection of planes and men only partially trained in the job they were going to do, it didn't seem a very promising unit. Yet Addison, a slim regular RAF officer, was eager to prepare his men and machines for operations. For the technology they would use was at that time the most advanced in the world.

In particular, the newly arrived 'Forts', which were being worked on in Scotland night and day under conditions of the greatest secrecy, were going to be in the forefront of the 100th Group's activities. Up at Prestwick mufflers were being welded on to the exhaust pipes to screen the exhaust flames; for these 'Forts' were going to fly at night, unlike those of the US 8th Army Air Corps which flew by day. Inside the planes, jamming gear was built into the bomb-bays, scanners were installed, and the planes' noses suddenly sprouted the bulbous blisters of the H2S scanner. The big bombers were crammed with the latest electronic technology.

This varied equipment could be use to 'blind' the gunners manning radar-controlled flak guns, mislead enemy night fighter controllers, jam aerial signals between enemy night fighter formations and, above all, 'read' the ground below. This was done by the H2S radar set. The set broadcast a radar signal from a scanner under the fuselage. It received back a signal on a cathode ray tube.

By carefully adjusting the set the operator could pick up, for instance, built-up areas which could be checked with Mercator charts to identify the object being viewed. In some cases, objects, if they were big enough, and especially if they were close to a large body of water, could be identified up to a distance of fifty miles.

Right throughout October and November, 1944, the 100th Group was active in the Rhineland, assisting Bomber Command in its attacks on the Rhenish towns and the Ruhr. Cologne was bombed repeatedly, as were Düren, Jülich and half-a-dozen other places west of the Rhine; and all the time the H2S radar operators were reporting large concentrations of vehicles throughout the Eifel.

These sightings were backed up by reconnaissance sweeps carried out by the USAF 67th Tactical Reconnaissance Group, which supported Hodges' 1st Army. Although the American airmen encountered a bad weather period from 17 November onwards, which lasted twenty-nine days, they still managed to fly numerous missions over the Eifel between Cologne and Trier on the Moselle. On 19 November, for instance, the pilots spotted heavy rail traffic around Gerolstein, Mayen and Bitburg, the very areas where the Fifth Panzer Army was assembling for its attack on Middleton's VIII Corps. Road movement was heavy too. Truck convoys were spotted heading south from Trier and Gerolstein. Fifty haystacks, which were obviously camouflaged tanks, were spotted outside Prüm.

Six days later twenty railway flatcars were noted heading for Münstereifel, laden with Tiger tanks. More were spotted at Wenger-rohr, the marshalling yards just outside Wittlich. Two days later all sorts of vehicles, including halftracks and tanks, were noticed throughout roads in the Eifel. Dumps of supplies, probably petrol and ammunition, were also noted on the sides of the roads every-where in the area. If this was the 'ghost front' where nothing had happened since the previous September, why suddenly all this activity and clear evidence that thousands of enemy soldiers, together with armour, were moving into the area? You don't use armour in defence!

As the official history of the US Army Air Corps* states: 'These

---

* Craven and Cate: *The Army Air Forces in WWII* Vol III. Office of Air Force History, Washington, 1983.

German moves became the subject of much speculation in the intelligence reports of 12th Army Group, SHAEF, First Army and, though to a lesser extent, of the Third Army.'

Why, then, with all this information at his disposal, from both the codes and aerial observation, didn't Eisenhower do something? For example, a deep-ranging patrol, say around Losheim or Echternach, would have speedily confirmed that major German forces were preparing for the offensive.*

By mid-November it was amply clear where the German blow was going to fall – on Middleton's VIII Corps. And it was equally clear that Middleton's three divisions holding sixty miles of front were going to be decimated in the process. After all they would soon be attacked by *three* armies. Why didn't Eisenhower reinforce those divisions, or place substantial armour reserves to their rear? He had spare armour enough to do so. For most of the fighting done that month was carried out by the US Army's hard-pressed infantry divisions. Why was the Supreme Commander so willing, or so it seemed, to sacrifice the lives of so many young Americans, without making an attempt to prevent the tragedy which was soon to come?

By December, 1944, Eisenhower's armies had been battering themselves against the Siegfried Line for three months and getting nowhere. Losses were high and most of his infantry divisions were up to only eighty percent of their official strength. In the Hurtgen Forest alone an average of one infantry division every two weeks went in, to be withdrawn two weeks later, decimated.

The bolder spirits at higher headquarters maintained that the Allies were winning this bloody battle of attrition. In fact it was Germany which was winning. In September a German *levée en masse* had raised a dozen new divisions for the Western Front. At the same time, German arms production was the highest of the war. In contrast the Allies were finding it tremendously difficult to fill the gaps in the decimated infantry divisions. Montgomery would cannabilize two of his infantry divisions to find replacements. In London, Churchill was considering calling up a quarter of a million 45-year olds for infantry duty, while Bradley was making a five per cent *levée* on rear echelon personnel for the same purpose. Soon in

---

* Before the 'surprise' attack, German patrols roamed far and wide behind the US front. They kidnapped US officers, checked out US positions and even slept with local women behind the US lines. In one case, known to the author, a Belgian SS soldier actually came home on leave to his native village of Schönberg!

an army that had been strictly segregated for decades, Eisenhower would be asking for volunteers from black quartermaster companies to serve as infantrymen.

How was Eisenhower to break the impasse and crack the Siegfried Line?

That autumn there must have seemed to an increasingly desperate Eisenhower one sure way of making the Germans do battle in ground of his own choice, where he could make full use of his superiority in armour and airpower. That was to lure them out of their Siegfried Line fortifications and commit them to one decisive battle, in which they would use up all their remaining strength and reserves in the West. But how?

German Intelligence knew the strengths of the US Army. Of Bradley's three armies, his 1st and 9th were strongest in the north in the Aachen area. Bradley's 3rd Army was strongest in the south, in the general area of the Saar. Montgomery's 2nd British Army was of little interest to German planners, whose objective was the port of Antwerp, because the way through them to Antwerp would be the longest route. In short, the quickest and most efficient approach to Antwerp, despite the rugged terrain, would be where the 1st and 3rd US Armies linked up – through Middleton's weak VIII Corps.

On 7 December, 1944, Eisenhower, Bradley and Montgomery met at the Dutch city of Maastricht to plan future operations on the Western Front. They agreed that the all-out offensive should start in early 1945. Meanwhile, pressure should continue to be exerted on the enemy. Only nine days before the Germans attacked in the Bulge, Eisenhower's armies were to be shown to be engaged in active operations on other fronts, while the 'ghost front' in the Eifel-Ardennes, where nothing ever happened, was still held by three weak US divisions – a very tempting target for a massive break-through by three whole German armies.

But how many actual Allied divisions were committed to battle so that they wouldn't be available to help stave off the German attack when it came on 16 December? At the Maastricht conference Montgomery had stated that he wanted to 'tidy up his front' in Holland. In the event he cancelled the 'tidying-up' operation on account of bad weather. 'Operation Veritable', his next major attack, planned for December, was postponed until January. In essence all his divisions, with the exception of a few small units, were engaged in static warfare. Montgomery's most powerful corps, the 100,000-

man strong XXX Corps commanded by General Horrocks, which Montgomery would switch to the Meuse line in Belgium when the balloon went up, was neatly placed in reserve in Belgium and Holland.

In Hodges' US 1st Army, Eisenhower's largest, only Gerow's V Corps was in combat. But of that Corps' four infantry divisions and two armoured combat commands, only parts of two infantry divisions, the 78th and 2nd, were actually in action when the Germans counter-attacked. Its neighbour, Simpson's 9th Army, was totally on the defensive.

To the south, both Patton's corps of his Third Army were engaged in operations. In fact, however, only three of his infantry divisions were actually in combat. All four of Patton's armoured divisions were 'resting and refitting'. Hence the speed with which he would attack into the 'Bulge' when the call came.

Nowhere on that long Allied front was there a single Allied armoured division engaged in combat. All fourteen of them were out of the line. Why? Because it was the armoured divisions which Eisenhower would need to respond rapidly to the German 'surprise' attack. Chance? Or planned?

By nightfall that Sunday it was clear to the unwitting victims, the bait that Eisenhower had used to lure the Germans out of the Siegfried line, that they were in serious trouble. In St Vith, to which the 7th Armored Division had been sent, apparently with the task of rescuing the two 106th Infantry's regiments trapped in the hills, the first priority now was to defend the town. A whole German corps was assembling ready for an attack on the place which was von Manteuffel's first priority. As the first units arrived, Clarke hurried them to the Prumerberg just outside St Vith, where, on both sides of the road that led to Schönberg, Lt-Colonel Riggs was setting up a blocking position. It was very 'spotty', as Captain Carl Mattocks of the 38th Armored Infantry thought when he first saw the position, with 'at least five hundred yards [undefended] between [his own] A and B Companies'. But it was the best Clarke and Riggs could do.

While Clarke, the most junior general officer at 106th HQ, was working feverishly to set up the defence of St Vith, with elements of his own 7th Armored, Hoge's 9th Armored and remnants of the 14th Cavalry, now reduced to the strength of a squadron, his commander, General Hasbrouck arrived. Hasbrouck ordered that the attack in the direction of the two trapped regiments should be postponed till the morning of the 18th. He said that Clarke didn't yet have sufficient armour to attack. He would have to wait till the rest of the Seventh's Combat Command B arrived.

Clarke agreed. After all he had been a brigadier general for only nine days. Yet he was passing on orders to a major general (Jones) and a brigadier general (Hoge) who had years of seniority to him. If Hasbrouck thought the counter-attack should be postponed, so be it. He was the boss. So the fate of the 8,000-odd men trapped in the Eifel hills was sealed. The 7th Armored would never be given another chance of rescuing them. From now Clarke's men would be fighting for their lives.

Less than ten miles away that Sunday as darkness fell, in addition to the two infantry regiments trapped on the wooded heights, there were the elements of two artillery battalions, medics, engineers and what was left of Company C, 820th Tank Destroyer Battalion. These had been formed into two defensive groups: Colonel Descheneaux's on one side of the Bleialf-Schönberg road, with its centre south of the village of Schlausenbach; Colonel Cavender's on the high ground around the hamlet of Oberlascheid.

These green young Americans, who had unwittingly served Eisenhower's purpose and were no longer needed, were now confined to an area of six by four and a half miles. The road network was now in German hands. There were tracks within the 106th positions, but they weren't really suitable for vehicles. Mostly they were steep logging trails with a surface that soon turned to mud.

The trapped men had plenty of rifle ammunition and there was still a basic load for the mortars. Available too was one day's supply of K-rations. But there was a shortage of surgical supplies to care for the couple of hundred casualties the two regiments had been unable to evacuate before the Germans had closed in on them.

All in all, the position of the two regiments was not too desperate. They had food, water, ammunition and transportation. Their problem was that they were green and lacking in energetic leadership. For the two infantry colonels were inexperienced and preferred to wait for orders rather than make their own decisions.

As yet, however, none of the thousands of young soldiers trapped in the freezing hills realized that they had been selected as victims. They still believed that the US Army would not abandon them. Rescue was surely on the way.

That night it seemed as if they might be proved right. At his St Vith HQ, spurred to new efforts by the arrival of the 7th Armored's first units, Jones sent his first real order since his division had been attacked two days before. It read: 'Panzer regtl CT on Elmerscheid-Schönberg-St Vith Rd, head near St Vith.* Our mission is to destroy by fire from dug-in positions S. of Schönberg-St Vith rd. Ammo, food and water will be dropped. When mission accomplished move to area St Vith-Wallerode-Weppler. Organize and move to W.' At last the 442nd and 423rd had a concrete mission. They were to root out the Germans on the Amelscheid-Schönberg road, who barred their withdrawal, and then proceed to the new line being formed by Lt-Colonel Riggs on the Prümerberg. There was still hope.

But there wasn't really. The victims were not going to escape their ordained fate. The Misfits had failed to find the infantry the engineers had told them about. Instead they found themselves in a village filled with GIs 'from every branch of the service imaginable', either stragglers or bugging out. They halted *Bea Wain II* and, leaving Spencer to stand guard, in case any other tankers decided to run off with their Sherman, set off to do a little foraging.

They found a house with a sign on the door, 'Off Limits to Enlisted Personnel. Officers' Club.' Immediately, as John Marshall recalled with glee many years later, 'we knew we'd hit paydirt'. They pushed open the door and started looting the assorted goodies they found there – butter, jam, milk, cheese etc. There was even whisky, but for some reason they didn't take that.

But they weren't fated to eat the first food they had seen since the previous day. Suddenly, in the light of the candles they had lit, they were confronted by Jack Brennan from their own company. His tank was stalled on a wall below. Could they help? The Misfits could. But hardly had they started the recovery operation when the Germans switched on searchlights. Startled and not a little frightened, the Misfits looked upwards. Sixty feet above them they could see the bellies and protruding guns of German tanks.

John Marshall yelled, 'Let's get out of here.'

Mac the Invisible Shield drawled, 'What for? They haven't done anything yet. Besides I can see what I'm doing now.'

So they continued, but their luck wouldn't hold out much longer.

---

* Jones meant Amelscheid, which is a hamlet just inside Belgium at the top of the two roads leading down to Schönberg.

Not far away Captain Hurley Fuller felt the same. He had lost the blind man, plus several of the others who had fled from Clervaux with him. Now he and four companions were making their way through rough country in pitch darkness, heading in a generally westerly direction. Now and again the night was illuminated by the explosion of a shell. A couple of times they saw tracer spurting through the darkness.

Fuller was twice the age of the men with him and he knew he couldn't keep up with them much longer. But he knew that without him they were lost. None of them could read a compass and without a compass they'd soon be wandering around in circles in this rugged countryside, known locally as the 'Luxembourg Switzerland.'

During that long night of staggering ever westwards, Fuller must have thought bitterly how fate was against him. Here he was, after a lifetime in the Army, still a colonel. He had failed in Normandy and had been relieved of his command. Middleton had given him his second chance. Now he had failed again. He had lost his regiment. He was finished. Little did he know that by the morrow his 110th Infantry Regiment would have its third commander since the offensive had started. But by then he would be a German prisoner-of-war and his military career would be over for good.

Thirty miles from where Fuller and his four companions wandered through the night, the one-eyed machine-gunner, Pfc Harry Martin of the Golden Lions's 424th Regiment, was also lost. During that long day his nightmare had come true. A plane had come diving out of the clouds, its machine guns chattering angrily. But it had turned out to be an American fighter-bomber and had veered away. But his situation was serious. The company had been ordered to withdraw. In single file they had crept from their positions. Somehow Harry Martin and four companions got lost. They wandered on, having no idea where they were or where they were going. Not only that, they had acquired a German prisoner. Several times they had told the German, who spoke a little English, to go away. But always he smiled and said in broken English, 'I go with you.' Now he trotted after them 'like a happy puppy-dog'.

That Sunday hundreds of Eisenhower's victims were trying to save themselves. Puzzled, fearful and confused, they were trying to make it back to their own lines. Others from the 28th and 99th Infantry Divisions were already in German captivity. Miserable, hungry and defeated, they were being herded back to the German cages in Prüm and Gerolstein by their triumphant young captors. There were the wounded too, huddled in ditches or in wrecked barns to the rear, often abandoned by the medics.

Of course there weren't only victims. All along that shattered front there were men who wanted to fight, were going to fight, were fighting. But even they would ask themselves in the years to come why had it all happened. That winter they had been told by those in authority that victory was just round the corner. They might even be home for Christmas. The Krauts were finished.

Now the Krauts were attacking! The US Army was on the run. *Why?*

It was a question that none of the military historians, movie makers, or biographers would ever be able to answer satisfactorily. A trap had been set, the bait had been placed inside it and the predators had stalked up and taken it. They were the bait.

That night Hasso von Manteuffel arrived in the newly captured village of Schönberg. The place was a shambles. Troops and trucks clogged the roads everywhere. The makeshift hospital near the church was packed with German and American wounded. Surgeons were operating round the clock. Sawn-off arms and legs were piled by the back door. There was blood everywhere.

The little General took it all in his stride. He had seen it all before in Russia, and worse. What worried him that evening was the fact that Hoffmann-Schonborn's 18th Volksgrenadier Division had not pushed strongly enough towards St Vith. He had intended seizing the town on the first day of his attack. Now, on the second, it was still in American hands.

Von Manteuffel made his way down the cobbled street. There he bumped into another general officer almost as small as himself. It was Field-Marshal Model who commanded Army Group B, to which the Fifth Panzer Army belonged. As always the Field Marshal, who affected a monocle and wore coats with fur collars, liked to be up front with his troops. He had come to view the situation in Schönberg personally.

Von Manteuffel had fallen out with Model in Russia. But now the Field-Marshal was friendly enough. He said he, too, was not satisfied with the progress of the 18th Volksgrenadier Division. He intended to speed things up a bit. 'I'm letting you use the Führer Begleit Brigade,' he said. This was the Führer Escort Brigade, made up of troops who had once guarded Hitler. It was an elite unit, commanded by Major-General Otto Remer who had helped to put down the plot against Hitler the previous July and had been promoted as a consequence.

Von Manteuffel hesitated a moment. He wanted the brigade for an attack further west.

'You are not in agreement?' Model asked.

'Not really.'

In silence they walked on. The noise of the battle was dying down. In the distance, of course, was the ever-present rumble of the guns, which the two generals, who had been in constant action since 1939, no longer even heard. But the small-arms fire had ceased. For a few moments they watched the flares hissing into the night sky over St Vith, bathing all below in their eerie light. Then von Manteuffel said, 'I'll turn off here, *Herr Generalfeldmarschall.* Good night.' They shook hands.

'Good luck tomorrow,' Model said.

'Thank you,' von Manteuffel replied as he vanished into the shadows.

The last of the flares died out on the horizon. It was nearly midnight. That terrible Sunday was almost over. Silence descended upon the battlefield.

DAY THREE:

Monday, 18 December, 1944.

Weather: Improved. Aircraft can operate in support of troops. Warmer temperatures lead to thaw, which confines tanks to roads.

'There's been a complete breakthrough, kid. The thing could cost us the works. Their armour is pouring in. They're taking no prisoners.'

Ernest Hemingway.

Mary Welsh, Hemingway's new mistress, loved collecting celebrities that winter in Paris. Operating from the Ritz Hotel, she loved being invited to the constant parties held in the capital by the Top Brass. On the evening of 16 December, while Hemingway and General 'Red' O'Hare, of Bradley's staff, went off to see 'a girlie show' at the Lido, she hurried to a dinner being given by General 'Tooey' Spaatz of the Army Air Corps.

Social climber that she was, Mary Welsh was also a reporter – and curious. Now as they worked their way through several courses, she was puzzled by the constant stream of aides with anxious looks on their faces who kept coming to whisper something in the general's ear.

Something very serious was happening, she told herself. She knew that 'I must get out of the way as smoothly and quickly as possible', So, as soon as dinner was over, she excused herself. Spaatz did not attempt to hold her back. Instead he offered his car to take her to the Ritz. Then he did something strange. He insisted that, in addition to the driver, she should have an escort of an armed soldier. Now Mary Welsh knew the balloon had gone up somewhere.

The scene at the Ritz confirmed her forebodings. The lobby was in a turmoil. High-ranking officers were leaving in a hurry. Suddenly there were armed soldiers everywhere. Hemingway came home, slightly drunk. He fell into bed and his kid brother Leicester, who shared the room with him, recalled him saying, 'There's been a complete breakthrough, kid. This thing could cost us the works. Their armour is pouring in. They're taking no prisoners.'

On the following morning Hemingway telephoned General 'Tubby' Barton, the commander of his 'favourite division', the Fourth, in Luxembourg. He explained he was sick and in the process of going home. 'But,' as Barton explained afterwards, 'he wanted to know if there was a show going on which would be worth coming up for. For security reasons I could not give the facts over the telephone, so I told him in substance that it was a pretty hot show and to come on up.'

As the man who had been voted 'America's most popular novelist' that year, Hemingway had plenty of clout. Not only could he telephone generals whose commands were in active contact with the enemy, he could also beg favours. He asked General O'Hare for transport and the latter, although he must have had many other pressing problems that Sunday morning, obliged.

This time, carried away by the great flap, Hemingway packed a pistol. That autumn he had been threatened with a court-martial for carrying weapons, which were forbidden to war correspondents. Now he didn't care. He told his brother, 'General Red O'Hare is sending a jeep over for me. Load these clips. Wipe every cartridge clean. The Germans have infiltrated guys in GI uniforms.'

Now, as Mary helped him into the two fleece-lined jackets he was to wear for the trip, they speculated on what might happen. Mary remembered how she had seen French government officials outside the Quai d'Orsay burning papers before fleeing the capital back in May, 1940. Was this going to be another complete German breakthrough followed by another Dunkirk?

Hemingway seemed to have been taken by the same idea. Just before he left in the jeep, he handed Mary 'a canvas sack full of papers with instructions to burn them if she were forced to flee Paris'. Why Hemingway thought his personal papers would be of any interest to a German intelligence officer he never explained. Perhaps he had greater delusions of grandeur than usual.

He clambered into the jeep. The driver thrust home first gear. The policeman opposite, now with an old-fashioned rifle slung over his shoulder, saluted and they were off to the front. Hemingway was on his way to his final battle. This was the last hurrah.

In the event, when he arrived at Tubby Barton's CP on Monday morning, he found that the latter's 22nd Regiment, to which he had attached himself twice before, was not in action. Barton told him that Colonel Chance's 12th Regiment was 'carrying the ball' for the 4th Division. Barton asked Hemingway to ensure that 'Bob (Chance) and his outfit' received 'a good publicity play'.

The request soured Hemingway's mood. He had come to Luxembourg hoping to find himself in the midst of a great battle. Instead he was expected to be a publicist for an obscure colonel. He decided to take to his bed and be sick. This he did for the next seventy-two hours, rising only to drink the wine cellar empty in the absence of the owner of the house in which he was billeted. He took a childish delight in refilling the empty wine bottles with his own urine, labelling the bottles 'Schloss Hemingstein 1944'. The joke, however, backfired when he went into the wine cellar in the dark, opened a bottle and took a swig from it.

By the time he got up again the danger to the southern shoulder of the Bulge would be over. All that Monday, as Hemingway lay in bed some six or seven miles behind the front, Chance's 12th Regiment slogged it out with the Bavarians of the 212th *Volksgrenadierdivision*.

At the hat factory in Echternach, the American survivors of a company overrun by the Germans on 16 December still held out. Indeed the German divisional commander, General Sensfuss, was wounded leading an attack on the 132 stubborn GIs. It was no different in the surrounded villages of Dickweiler and Osweiler where the men of the 12th Infantry held out against all the Germans could throw at them.

That Monday morning, with the aid of the first Shermans from Patton's Third Army, the 12th counter-attacked in an attempt to relieve their comrades holding out in the Parc Hotel. Ten tanks of the 70th Tank Battalion, each Sherman carrying five riflemen, rumbled through the wooded trails to the outskirts of the village of Bergdorf where the hotel was situated. Above the besieged hotel they could see the Stars and Stripes waving proudly.

But Sensfuss's tough Bavarians were not prepared to let the trapped GIs escape that easily. They were waiting for the advancing Americans with their *Panzerfausts*. Rockets hissed through the air. The first tank was hit and rumbled to a halt. The riflemen flung themselves to the ground. A lethal small-arms battle began. The trapped men would have to remain trapped for another day.

All that day the fighting continued. In one case, Barton threw in a whole company for a counter-attack. It lost all its officers save one second lieutenant. His 2nd Battalion reported that it was down to half its strength. Tanks supporting the infantry turned and withdrew without orders. But the southern shoulder was holding. The German Seventh Army was going to make no further progress in Luxembourg.

*

In the north too the shoulder was holding, though only just. The 99th was still pulling back under pressure. But it and its companion division, the 2nd Infantry, had definite positions to fall back on – the Elsenborn Ridge, where General Lauer of the 99th had his HQ in Camp Elsenborn. There the two divisions would be joined by the 'Big Red One', the US Army's premier infantry division. The 1st Infantry Division had fired the first shots of the US Army in both the First and Second World Wars. It had fought in North Africa, Sicily, Italy and right throughout the campaign in Europe. It had been badly hit in the Hurtgen and most of its rifle companies were down to 100 men. But it did have a tremendous fighting reputation and Generals Lauer and Robertson were much cheered when they heard the news.

But still, as the generals tried to regroup on the key defensive feature, the fighting was nip-and-tuck. All that Monday German armour from the 6th SS Panzer Army struck the American defenders repeatedly. One battalion lost 400 of its 600 men in the fighting. Others suffered similar losses as the SS Panthers tried time and again to break through their positions.

Urged on by the Army Commander, Sepp Dietrich, the boys of the Hitler Youth Division, mostly new to combat, attacked with all the fervour and youthful self-sacrifice which had been drilled into them in the Hitler Youth. But it was their experienced, combat-wise officers (who included von Ribbentrop's son) and NCOs who took the casualties. In the Hitler Youth Division, the officers and NCOs led from the front and suffered accordingly.

In the 2nd Battalion of the Hitler Youth's 25th Regiment, all the officers, with the exception of the adjutant, were killed or wounded by midday that morning. Still they pushed on, unaware that the Americans were buying time with their lives. The longer they could hold the SS as they moved back to those prepared positions on the Elsenborn Ridge, the easier it would be for the defenders later. The northern shoulder would hold against anything and everything that Sepp Dietrich's 6th SS Panzer Army would throw at it.

The centre of what had been the VIII Corps line was a disaster. The Misfits had started this Monday with an attack on a Tiger tank. It had not been a success. The puny 36 tons of *Bea Wain II* faced up to the 68 of the Tiger. Marshall got off the first shot. The armour-piercing shell hissed straight for the Tiger and the shell struck home.

Instantly Spencer cried '*Loaded*!' Marshall fired again. Once more he hit the metal monster in exactly the same spot. To no effect. 'I might just as well throw an orange at the tank; it did no damage.' Hurriedly they scuttled away for safety, before the Tiger's massive 88mm gun opened up on them.

Now the Misfits were running into fleeing 110th Infantry soldiers on all sides. They were all trying to reach what they thought was the safety of divisional headquarters at Wiltz. They kept running up to the tank and begging the Misfits to fire on a barn, shed or house which lay to the front. By this means they hoped they could get back without running into a German ambush. John Marshall noted that 'many of them did not have guns'. It wasn't something that he approved of.

Later that day, after leaving the roads and crossing the fields for safety, they spotted what looked like a line of moving tree stumps – and the stumps were coming right at them!

It was a company of Germans wearing camouflaged capes. They would run bent for sixty feet or so, and drop to the ground. If nothing happened, they'd move out, followed by the next line of 'stumps' coming out of the woods behind.

Mac ordered Spencer to load white phosphorus into the 75mm. Marshall winced. It was a terrible shell. It seemed 'to explode in slow motion as if it was a gigantic fluffy lump of talcum powder showering down on the victim. It doesn't burn; it eats through the clothing and continues when it reaches the body.' After the war a German told him that 'a splotch the size of a dime landing on your wrist would be the size of a half dollar when it comes out on the other side.'

Marshall never found out if his statement was correct. They fired their load of seven phosphorus shells, leaving the German 'stumps' 'some crawling, some rolling over and over again', many who 'never moved again', and fled.

But their long odyssey was coming to an end. About one o'clock that Monday afternoon *Bea Wain II* was rolling under a bridge at the side of a river when a shell slammed against the side of the tank. The impact knocked it off the road and into the water, sealing the turret hatch shut.

Water started to pour in. Soon it was reaching their chests. Marshall shouted to Spencer, 'Of all the things we've been through and we end up drowning!' Then he stopped short. Someone was hammering on the outside of the tank. It was Alyea. His hatch was open. But they had to be quick. There were Krauts only yards away. They would have to duck below the water, wriggle around and twist sideways out of the driver's hatch. Marshall said, 'I'll go first and see if it can be done.'

Mac the Invisible Shield didn't agree. He said, 'If you get jammed between the driver's seat and the basket none of us will ever get out. Let's see if we can push the seat forward with our feet to make more room.'

It was no use. They had to do it Marshall's way and they made it. Now they crouched in a ditch, shivering and soaked. They discussed surrendering. Marshall then suggested splitting up. The other three disagreed. Marshall kept on insisting. Suddenly his three comrades got up and started moving off, leaving him there. But luck was on Marshall's side. He was discovered by a sergeant of the 707th. He was given dry clothes and some bread and butter. Then 'something happened which was pretty unbelievable'.

A command car pulled up outside the house where he was wolfing down the bread. Four high-ranking officers stepped out, followed by a 'real General'.

'The stars on his helmet were smudged as were his pearl pistol grips. The stars on his shoulders were of cloth,' Marshall remembered years later, 'and he had silly looking boots.'

It was 'Blood and Guts' Patton of course, who looked at Marshall in disgust, before turning to the sergeant who had rescued him. 'Where's your tank, Sergeant?' he asked.

Sergeant Faught replied, 'That's it, sir,' pointing to his burning Sherman. 'We ran out of gas and ammo.'

Patton said, 'If we get you gas and ammo, do you think we can stop them?'

Manfully the NCO answered, 'We've been trying, sir.'

Marshall noted that, all the time Patton was speaking, the Lt-Colonel with him was recording his remarks on a clipboard.

Suddenly a shell exploded nearby and Patton decided he had seen enough. He walked back to the command car where another colonel was already holding the door open for him. That was the last Marshall saw of him. Later he recalled, 'I didn't impress Patton, but then he didn't do anything for me either.'

But what was Patton doing that day on the US 1st Army front? He was supposed to be conducting a battle of his own in the Saar from his headquarters in Nancy, some hundred miles to the south.

Earlier he had attended a conference with Bradley at his HQ in the Hotel Alfa in Luxembourg City. There, Bradley had informed him of the situation in Middleton's VIII Corps sector and asked Patton what he could do to help. Patton had replied, 'Brad, my three best divisions are the 4th Armored, the 80th and the 26th. I'll halt the 4th Armored right away and concentrate it at Longwy, beginning tonight. I'll start the 80th on Luxembourg tomorrow morning and I'll alert the 26th to stand by and be ready to move on a day's notice.'

It was all too pat. As Colonel Robert Allen, Patton's Chief of Combat Intelligence, wrote about Bradley's supposed 'calculated risk' in Middleton's VIII Corps sector: 'The only thing "calculated" about the risk was its unbelievable and indefensible provocativeness. It provoked surprise! *Begged for it!*'

Back in November Patton had already been telling his staff that Middleton's inactivity might tempt the Germans into attacking him. At a meeting on 12 December he told his staff in so many words that he regarded an enemy breakthrough in the 1st Army area as a distinct possibility. He actually instructed two of his key staff officers, General Gay and Colonel Maddox, to make 'a study of what the Third Army would do if called upon to counter-attack such a breakthrough'.

Forward planning? Foresight? Clairvoyance? Hardly. Patton was in the plan all along. On the night of the 15–16 December he told his Chief of Intelligence, Colonel Koch, 'If they attack us, I'm ready for them. But I'm inclined to think the party will be up north. VIII Corps has been sitting still – a sure invitation to trouble.'

Then he had turned to Gay and Maddox and asked how they were coming on with the study he had ordered them to make four days before. They told him, and Patton became more specific: 'I want you gentlemen to start making plans for pulling the Third Army out of its eastward attack, change the direction ninety degrees, moving to Luxembourg and attacking north.'

A remarkable feat of intuition! Without a single shot having been fired in the Ardennes, General Patton was ordering his army to cease its attack in the Saar and prepare for a drive north to meet a German Army which had disappeared from the Allied order-of-battle of enemy troops nearly two months before!

The following morning he sent his mistress and niece Jean Gordon off to what he thought was the safety of Paris and waited for what was to come.

On that Monday Patton's supposed arch rival and another prima donna, Field-Marshal Montgomery, the commander of the British 21st Army Group, was also making rapid decisions. Although he was not under attack either, on the previous day he had alerted the 51st Highland Division for an early move. Now he moved his Guards Armoured Division and two infantry divisions, the 43rd and 53rd, switching them to west of the River Meuse. Like Patton's moves, his were *apparently* made without the prior approval of the Allied Land Forces Commander, General Eisenhower.

By that afternoon Manteuffel's Fifth Panzer Army had cut a twelve-mile breach in Middleton's defences and had three armoured divisions racing towards the Meuse. But already the first troops of the Household Cavalry were approaching the other side of the Meuse, just in case they broke through to the river.

General Horrocks, who was in charge of Montgomery's XXX Corps, was delighted with his new assignment. Later he said: 'They [the Germans] were playing into our hands. Instead of the Allies having to launch their attacks across flooded rivers like the Roer and then stand up to sharp enemy counter-attacks from armoured divisions, the Germans had come to us and stuck their armoured heads into our noose. With any luck we might destroy a large part of their last available armoured divisions.' General Eisenhower could not have described his own plan any better.

As Horrocks journeyed to the Meuse from Brussels, he was 'quite cheerful'. His Corps would take up its long-stop position quite close to Waterloo, and he 'had a momentary hope that it might fall to the lot of Horrocks to fight the second battle of Waterloo.' In fact, he crossed the Meuse to see General 'Lightning Joe' Collins, commander of the US 7th Corps positioned there, and said, 'Let them come. We will be delighted to deal with them.'

Collins grinned and answered, 'I can't do that, General, but it's mighty comforting to know you are there.'

So the shoulders were holding and now the British were moving up to seal off the Meuse, just in case. Things were falling into place. But nothing could now save the 106th Infantry Division's trapped regiments.

*

Colonel Cavender received General Jones's message of the previous day at seven thirty that morning. He and his men, camping out in freezing temperatures for the second day, weren't particularly happy. Half the night they had been unable to sleep. Men simply stayed awake waiting for the promised re-supply. But it didn't come. The trapped men didn't know that the British airfields had been 'socked in' for most of the night. Besides, Jones's request for air re-supply had not gone any further than 1st Army Headquarters. 1st Army HQ was in a state of total confusion and soon its staff officers would be fleeing for their lives. Nobody had time for Jones.

Cavender and his staff prepared a rough-and-ready plan. As he saw it the two trapped regiments should advance almost parallel to the road that led from Bleialf to Schönberg. Each battalion of the six concerned would move in line abreast, contact between the 423rd and the 422nd being maintained by a single small patrol.

It was Cavender's intention to by-pass Schönberg which was well defended and attack the Germans on the road that led from there to St Vith. It was a hasty plan and not very good. The terrain was tough. It would be difficult to use vehicles and right in the middle of the approach march the attackers would be faced with Ihrenbach, which marked the border between Germany and Belgium. In normal circumstances one could spit over the little creek, but now it was swollen and the only bridge the Americans could use had been blown. It was no wonder that when Colonel Descheneaux received the plan over the radio-phone he bowed his head and said to his intelligence sergeant, Sergeant Loewenguth, 'Oh my poor men. They'll be cut to pieces!'

Now the orders were given out. Heavy equipment was destroyed. The service companies destroyed their trucks. They poured petrol over them and set them on fire. Anti-tank guns had their firing pins destroyed. Gunners exploded shells in bigger guns. The wounded were given over to the care of those who had volunteered to stay behind.

Pfc Charles Stenger was one medic who didn't volunteer. He had his hands full already. He had just taken care of an infantryman who had gone berserk. Now he pushed off with the rest, well aware of just how useless he was as a medic. (One day he would become a vice-president of Chrysler.) Now, as he followed his battalion, mortar bombs began to fall on the column. Someone screamed 'Medic!' His first reaction was, 'You son of a bitch. Now I've got to get up.' But he rose to his feet and tried to help the wounded man, who insisted he had been wounded in the leg, when actually he had been hit in the eye. He pulled out his morphine syringe to kill the wounded man's pain. To his disgust he found it had frozen up.

Colonel Deschenaux took the lead of his 422nd Regiment. His mood of despair had vanished.

'You're crazy, Colonel,' his Operations Officer gasped as they started up another steep incline, 'You're going to get yourself killed.'

The young Regimental Commander shook his head. 'I've got to be sure we're going in the right direction.'

The assembly area for the 422nd in the coming attack on the German tank regiment that Jones had thought yesterday was holding Schönberg was only four miles away. But, as the morning wore on, the weary infantrymen were making slow progress over the difficult terrain. Gas masks went first.* Then came the overcoats. Then the clumsy rubber overshoes. 'We abandoned everything,' Captain Roberts of D Company recalled, 'except our weapons and ammunition. There was no straggling. Stops were made every few minutes as the advance guard searched every inch of the terrain. No shots were fired in the vicinity of the column where I was.'

By now they were lost. As Lieutenant Walker of the 422nd's H Company recalled, Colonel Descheneaux asked his S-3, Colonel Scales, 'Where the hell are we?' But Scales didn't know. For the 422nd was lost. All around Walker, the men grumbled about 'all this running and no fighting'.

Once however they came close to one of the German-held roads and spotted some of the enemy. The order was given to 'fix bayonets'. But nothing came of that chilling order so rarely heard in modern warfare.

In the end there were no shots fired at most of the 422nd that Monday. Colonel Descheneaux ended his first day in combat with his hands as bloodless as they had been when he had set off at dawn. He saw no Germans. Nor did he fire his personal weapon.

By midday the strain was beginning to tell. Men started to wander off. Some got lost, not always accidentally. Pfc Malinowski remembered many years later, 'It was all confusion. Men began to bug out. I think they just wanted to get over with it. My guess is that they

---

* Fifty years later the author was still finding those gas masks and overshoes as he followed the trail of that doomed march.

16. Survivors of the 28th Division who managed to get back to their own lines, now totally exhausted.

17. A soldier from 7th Armored Division being treated for a wound inflicted by a sniper in the 'fortified goose egg'.

18. US flak guns manning a 'meat chopper' on the southern shoulder of the Bulge.

19. Men of the 99th 'Checkerboard' Division captured by the Germans on the second day of the offensive.

20. General Bruce Clarke who later commanded NATO troops in Europe.

21. Major Boyer, one of the heroes of St Vith, who spent the rest of the war as a prisoner.

22. Field Marshal Model, Commander of the German Army Group B, which carried out the attack.

23. General Hasso von Manteuffel, Commander of the 5th Panzer Army, with General Bruce Clarke in 1966.

24. General Eisenhower,
the Supreme Commander,
with King George VI.
Behind the King is General
Bradley.

25. General Matthew Ridgway, who did not want to evacuate Clarke's
men, decorates a soldier. Behind Ridgway is General Montgomery,
whose insistence on their evacuation saved 22,000 American lives.

simply deserted and surrendered to the Krauts who they knew were on the roads.'

Some of the 422nd officers began to say out loud that it had been foolish ever to set out. They should have stayed in their well-established bunkers in the Siegfried Line and waited until someone came to rescue them. By late afternoon, with darkness falling fast, the 422nd Infantry Regiment was effectively lost. And about beaten.

Cavender's men had also destroyed their heavy equipment. Those of the wounded who couldn't walk, or didn't want to, were left behind at the regimental collecting station. Then the 423rd set off with Lt-Colonel Puett's 3rd Battalion in the lead. One hour later they ran into the enemy.

Cautiously a weapon carrier from the Battalion emerged on to the Bleialf-Schönberg road. The driver hit the brakes. The Germans had erected a roadblock, covered by an enormous 88mm cannon. They reacted first. The 88mm thundered into action and the shell slammed into the carrier. At that close range the impact was so great that the carrier was blown right on its back, its front crumpled like a peeled banana. Two dazed soldiers crawled out of the smoking wreckage. But they soon gathered their wits, grabbed the carrier's undamaged 50 calibre machine gun and turned it on the German gun crew. The Germans didn't wait for another burst. They fled, leaving the two surprised young Americans in possession of their well-prepared position.

About the same time Corporals Dienstbach and Watters fell into German hands. The enemy didn't hesitate. They stuck the two prisoners on the hood of a captured US jeep and, keeping them covered with machine pistols, they headed down the road to the 423rd. They were using them as human shields. But the two captives reacted correctly. The jeep had almost reached the riflemen when the two corporals yelled in unison, '*Germans!*' With that they flung themselves into the snow.

The Americans didn't hesitate either. The German jeep driver took a burst of machine gun fire in the chest. He slumped over his wheel. The jeep careered off the road and smashed into a ditch. The rest of the attackers surrendered very tamely.

Staff Sergeant Petersen, his mortar gone now, was plodding on with the rest of the Battalion when the section was joined by three black artillerymen. They were carrying Thompson sub-machine guns, 'great weapons at close range'. Although Petersen's men weren't used to serving with blacks, they accepted them for their weapons. Suddenly some Germans came out of the trees to the front. The section dropped as one. As Petersen recalled afterwards, 'One gray-coated German managed to come out of the trees close to my left side. I was lying on the right side of a tree trunk for protection and could not swing my carbine to get a shot. The burp of a Thompson cut him down.' One of the black artillerymen had fired and probably saved Petersen's life. As he recalled, 'Any racial prejudice I may have felt left me forever then.'

But the advance was taking its toll. Charles Stenger, bogged down with the rest of his section near the Ihrenbach creek, knew he had to do something for the wounded. Some of them were in a very bad way, especially those shot in the stomach. They'd die if he didn't do something. Desperately he sought for something white. In the end the only thing he could find was a bandage. He tied it to the end of a stick and rose to his feet, praying that the enemy wouldn't fire at him.

He was lucky. He was spotted by a German officer, who ordered his men to help recover the *Ami* wounded. In all fourteen wounded men were brought in and taken to the nearest German aid post. Stenger said to the German Officer, 'Well thank you. I'm going back now.' It was a bluff.

The German said, 'You can't do that.'

Stenger said, 'I'm a combat medic and we are under the Geneva Convention. We are not combative.'

But the German officer now turned the tables on the American very neatly. He said, 'Then why don't you stay and take care of your comrades.'

Stenger gave in. He had been trapped. Yet another Golden Lion was now fated to spend the rest of the war behind barbed wire. The toll of the victims was mounting.

By mid-morning, when Colonel Puett's battalion was beginning to run into serious opposition, Colonel Cavender received his last but one message from Division. Jones stated that 'Big Friend', the 7th Armored Division, would be unable to come to the rescue of the doomed regiments. They'd have to attack Schönberg with what they had. Cavender passed on the message to Descheneaux and then ordered Colonel Klinck's 3rd Battalion to move to Puett's right and help him in the attack.

Klinck did as ordered. He pushed forward, advanced across the Ihrenbach, climbed the hill into Belgium and dug in above Schönberg. There the 3rd lost contact with Cavender's 423rd and Descheneaux's 422nd. Cavender called a quick conference. At it there were Colonel Kelly of the 589th Artillery, Colonel Craig of the 1st Battalion, which was now ordered to help Puett, and Colonel Nagle, Cavender's executive officer.

Then the German artillery opened up. To Kelly it 'sounded like every tree in the forest had been simultaneously blasted from its roots.'

Nagle went down, wounded in the back. Craig was struck in several places and mortally wounded. His executive officer, Major Moon, was ordered to take command of the 1st Battalion and lead it to the aid of Puett's 2nd.

But now, with their colonel dead, the 1st lost heart. The psychological moment had passed. The two battalions, the 1st and 2nd, started to go to ground. Exhausted by the terrain and the harsh weather, the infantry slumped to the snow, not enough strength left to even dig a shallow foxhole. Their only desire was to close their eyes and ears and blot out the misery and death around them.

Perhaps Cavender was feeling the same. He said to one of his soldiers, pointing at the bullet hole that had gone through the windscreen of his jeep, 'I wish that had happened to me.' Already he had suffered 300 casualties, including sixteen officers – and in this kind of fighting he couldn't afford to lose any more. For it was the officers who were leading from the front and keeping the men going.

That afternoon Colonel Brook of General Jones's staff had sent his own message to Cavender. It read: 'Attack Schönberg, do maximum damage there to the enemy. This mission is of the greatest importance to the nation. Good luck. Brook.'

The words would have been farcical if the situation on the heights had not been so tragic.

The first indication to Colonel Fred Warren, commander of the Seventh Armored Division's CCR, newly arrived on the St Vith perimeter, that he was already outflanked was brought by a lone soldier who staggered into his CP. He was bareheaded, bleeding from a face wound and was almost incoherent. But he was from the 7th and not a straggler from the 14th Cavalry or 106th.

Warren sat him down. Quietly he listened while the man told his tale. It wasn't long and was slightly confused, but it told the Colonel all he needed to know. The man was the driver of the 7th Armored's Chief-of-Staff, Colonel Matthews. He told how the Colonel's car had been ambushed on the road leading into St Vith from the northeast. The Colonel had been killed. He had escaped to find the area alive with German troops, all of them wearing the crooked silver runes of the SS. Now Colonel Warren knew that the SS had driven westwards and outflanked him.

He sent the driver to General Clarke's HQ in St Vith to ask for infantry reinforcements; he'd need them. At the same time he ordered his 17th Tank Battalion under Lt-Colonel Wemple up the road into the village of Recht. He was to find out what was going on, but he was not to get engaged in a fight with German infantry. Unprotected tanks were ideal targets for infantry armed with the *panzerfaust*. One blow struck anywhere near the Sherman's highly flammable petrol engine and it burst into flames. No wonder the British called the Sherman the 'Ronson'.

So Wemple went off into the unknown.

At St Vith Clarke already knew what was coming. His HQ in the school was being flooded with alarming messages from the rough-and-ready defensive line he had formed the previous day. '*Enemy penetration at Hünningen . . . Infantry – tank attack coming in at Wallerode . . . German column on the Schönberg road.*' On three sides, north, south and east, von Manteuffel was making strong probing attacks on the *Ami* perimeter, attempting to find a weak spot where he could throw in his armour.

Clarke, who had had no more than an hour's sleep the previous night, already knew he was being attacked by a whole corps from von Manteuffel's Fifth Panzer Army and that the 1st SS Division, the 'Adolf Hitler Bodyguard', was getting into position to attack, with perhaps more armour from the 6th SS Panzer Army to follow. He was heavily outnumbered by the enemy and would continue to be so, although in the end his command included, not only his own division, but Hoge's 9th Armored Combat Command, Jones's 424th Regiment and Cota's 112th Regiment, plus an assorted mix of smaller units. Von Manteuffel was determined to take St Vith. He'd continue to build up his attacking force until he did.

'Cox's Army'*, as Riggs called his mixed force of engineers and

---

* The author has been unable to find out the reason for this name and at the time of writing Colonel Riggs was too sick to be bothered.

armoured infantry of the 106th and 7th Armored defending the Prümerberg, had been under attack most of that morning. Time after time he had beaten off the German probes. Once he had sent out a tank destroyer platoon, so new to combat that its three guns didn't have aiming sights. It was not surprising that the entire platoon disappeared in their first attack, never to come back. Captured or surrendered, no one ever found out.

But the mixed force, which also included the 106th's cooks and bandsmen, kept throwing back the Germans coming up the road from Schönberg. One of Captain Mattocks' officers came up to him crying his heart out. Mattocks sent him back to his men with a stern warning. The C.O. of the 28th Armored Infantry, Colonel Fuller, was observed by the battalion surgeon, Dr Josepf Jehl, 'popping pills'. He reported this to General Clarke. Clarke had him medically evacuated for 'combat fatigue'. Mattocks thought it was wrong. But men were beginning to crack.

He ordered that at nightfall that Monday officers would command all platoons to see that there were no desertions. Riggs decided to do the same. He had seen just too many abandoned foxholes as the assorted bunch which made up 'Cox's Army' slipped off to the rear. Every hour he walked his men's positions.

But the great majority slugged it out with the Germans, surviving on the one can of marmite (a self-heating soup invented by the British) they received that day and their own bitter humour. Going up to visit his men, Captain Mattocks was alerted by a sudden burst of heavy machine-gun fire from one of his sections. He ran through the snow to find out what was the cause. A 'Sad Sack' of a German soldier had apparently wandered onto the battlefield unaware of what was going on. When he spotted the *Amis*, he had dashed to hide in a house some 100 yards to the defenders' front. Suddenly, as Mattocks was being told what had happened, he made a run to escape from the house. Mattocks borrowed an M-I from the rifleman, took aim and fired. The running German flung his arms up and flopped to the ground. Mattocks was not going to take any chances. He emptied a whole clip into the inert body. Then he handed the weapon back to the rifleman. The latter looked at the Captain and grunted: 'Guess I'll have to clean that goddam thing now.' Mattocks grinned. The reply was, he thought, typical of the dour humour of his veterans.

*

That afternoon, however, 'Cox's' started to come under severe pressure. Panthers began to rumble up to the 38th's foremost positions. Mattocks received a call from one of his platoon leaders, Lieutenant Bob Moranda: 'Rusty, it looks as if I'm going on an extended vacation. Over and out.' Moranda's next five months would be spent behind German wire.

By midday it was clear to Clarke that St Vith was under major attack. At Poteau, to his rear, a massive tank battle was beginning. It would last for seventy-two hours and become the greatest in US military history*. Villagers at Recht, where the 1st SS had set up base, remembered twenty or more tanks going into action every night for the next four days and coming back at dawn laden with casualties.

Now as the last of the 424th Regiment pulled back wearily into the perimeter and, from the top of his headquarters building, Clarke could actually see German troops advancing on St Vith from the direction of Steinebruck, he ordered his headquarters moved. He would pull back to the hamlet of Crombach on the pre-1919 German-Belgian border.

But he still had the problem of General Jones on his hands. What was he to do with him? Clarke found him 'strangely listless', concerned only by the fate of his own son, who was an officer in one of the trapped regiments. Once, when one of his staff officers had remarked that General Jones always carried a few hand grenades in the front of his Packard, the Divisional Commander had said quite seriously, 'Welton, the Krauts will never get me alive.' Jones didn't seem to care whether he lived or died.

Now Clarke wondered if Jones was going to stay on in St Vith to the bitter end. The only thing that still seemed to interest him was whether the Army Air Corps would still stage an air-drop to his trapped regiments. When, at a quarter to three that Monday afternoon, there was still no news from Middleton about that drop, Jones gave in. He accepted Clarke's advice to drive back to Vielsalm and set up his headquarters next to that of General Hasbrouck of the Seventh Armored.

Clarke was in charge now, as Jones drove away, slumped in the back of the Packard, grenades still unused in their tray. He was

* Not in terms of the number of tanks involved but in the length of the engagement.

about finished. He had spent a whole lifetime preparing for this and he had failed.

The mood at Supreme Headquarters that morning was confident and optimistic, though according to Eisenhower's secretary-lover Kay Summersby, 'the more pessimistic staff members' were beginning to predict 'a drive on Paris itself, plus a blitz through to the huge supply centre at Liège and the key port of Antwerp'.

Eisenhower, on the other hand, was worried only that the Germans wouldn't penetrate *deeply* enough. That morning he attended a conference of his key staff officers. General Bedell Smith, his Chief-of-Staff, later said that 'our greatest concern at this time was that we had overestimated the Germans' determination. We were afraid that they might be discouraged too soon and order a withdrawal before we were in a position to inflict maximum destruction. If the Germans could not drive in a salient deep enough to offer us the opportunity we now sought for a decisive counter-attack, it might be desirable to encourage them by pulling back our own troops.'

The Supreme Commander reassured the staff officers that there was 'no need for a mousetrap'. The advance was still moving, though at what must have been a pitifully slow rate.

No mention was made, of course, of the suffering being endured by the men of Middleton's VIII Corps who had been use as the cheese to bait that 'mousetrap'.

During the course of the afternoon, however, the mood of confidence seemed to ebb away. General Juin of the French Army, with a group of his officers, visited the headquarters. He appeared to be surprised that everyone was working normally, typists busy at their machines, telephones ringing, staff officers striding about purposefully. General Juin, who had only gone over to the Allies in 1942 when they had landed in North Africa – till then he had dutifully served Vichy France and the German 'Control Commission' in North Africa – remarked to Generals Strong and Bedell Smith, 'What! You are not packing?'

The remark was reported to Eisenhower who convened another meeting of his staff. This was described by Kay Summersby as 'very tense'. It was followed that evening by Eisenhower's decision to travel on the morrow to Verdun, where he ordered Bradley, Patton and Devers, commanding the 6th Army Group in France, to meet him. At this meeting his strategy was laid down for containing the enemy and preparing for the great counter-attack.

Now Eisenhower started, or so it appeared, to worry. Apparently unaware that Montgomery had already begun moving troops to guard the west bank of the Meuse and the bridges across it, the Supreme Commander contacted General Lee, commander of his rear section, Comz Z, and ordered him to organize troops – drivers, cooks, clerks, anybody – to guard those bridges. He sent personal representatives to the Comz Z area to pick out men who could fight and send them to the front. He made an offer, too, to men in military prisons. Any man who would take a rifle and go in combat would receive a free pardon and be released from the stockade at once. He ordered Lee to issue a circular to his predominantly black service troops, appealing for any who would volunteer to fight as riflemen. He promised them that in a strictly segregated US Army, they would be assigned to outfits, 'without regard to color or race'.

When General Leven Allen, Bradley's Chief-of-Staff, read these various messages to Lee and his boss, in particular the need 'to organize service units' to defend the Meuse bridges, he snarled, 'What the devil do they think we're doing, *starting back for the beaches?*'

Nightfall brought no hope for Clarke, busy moving his HQ to Crombach. Officers coming up from Middleton's HQ in Bastogne reported that there were virtually no troops in the hinterland. Middleton himself was preparing to move his headquarters over the Meuse to Neufchâteau. His perimeter was functioning, but proper wireless communications between the varied infantry, armoured and engineering outfits that manned it was difficult. Messages sometimes had to pass through four or five different units before they reached the ones for which they were intended. Maintaining command and issuing orders was therefore difficult and time-consuming.

At Poteau a fierce battle was raging. Outgunned as they were, the American Shermans of Clarke's 7th Armored fought back bravely. Solid armour-piercing shot flew back and forth in white burrs. If a shell penetrated, then shards of metal flew everywhere. If a Sherman's gas tank was hit, ninety gallons would go up instantly and the shells clipped to the inside of the tank would explode.

Back at his HQ, the general looked grimly at his situation map in the white light of the Coleman lanterns. It was covered with a rash of blue and red crayon marks. New ones were added all the time. From what he could make out, Clarke thought he had control of the three roads to the west. But the roads to the south were up in the air. To the east, the road system was under heavy German attack. The situation was not good. On the morrow, he knew, it would be worse.

At the Luxembourg city of Wiltz, some thirty-odd miles to the south, what was left of the battered 110th Regiment was also preparing to make its last stand. Some time that day its original commander, Colonel Hurley Fuller, had been captured. When news reached Wiltz that he had, one of the sergeants who knew him well snorted, 'The Krauts'll be sorry they took Hurley!'

In his place General Cota of the 28th Division appointed another veteran to command the 110th, the third in two days. He was Colonel Daniel Strickler, a wavy-haired, part-time soldier. In his long career he held every rank from private to general. He had volunteered to fight in Mexico in 1916, had fought in the trenches in the First World War and, in the Second had fought right across Europe with the 28th. Between the wars he had built up a successful law practice.

Now Cota ordered him to hold onto Wiltz for as long as possible. Like St Vith, Wiltz barred the roads to the west and the Meuse. When Strickler thought he could defend the place no longer he had permission to withdraw to Bastogne. In the event, when he did decide he could hold out no longer, his regiment existed no more and Bastogne was surrounded.

After giving out his orders General 'Dutch' Cota departed westwards, leaving Strickler to view his command.

It wasn't much now. It was a provisional battalion made up of headquarters personnel, MPs, drivers and the like. Now this 'battalion' was digging in outside the town as hundreds of civilians were trudging westwards.

It was a bitter sight for the men of the 28th Division. Three months before the Division had liberated Wiltz from the Nazis. Now the Germans were coming back and those who stayed behind knew they faced the rule of terror imposed by the Gestapo once again.

But Strickler had no time for such considerations. He was too busy mustering his resources. His artillery was particularly weak. It comprised eleven armoured vehicles from the Misfits' 707th Battalion, six of which were crippled, plus some anti-aircraft guns and six towed anti-tank guns. Later that day he was cheered up somewhat when General Middleton sent him a 600-strong engineer unit, the 44th Combat Engineers. He sent them out to various spots on the perimeter.

But that afternoon the German command had no intention of attacking Wiltz; they wanted to by-pass the place. The objective of General Lucht, commanding the corps which had originally attacked the 110th Regiment, was the key road-and-rail centre of Wiltz. Wiltz could be by-passed.

But the German Corps Commander hadn't reckoned with the young paras of Colonel Heilmann's 5th Parachute Division, 'the Green Devils'. Heilmann, a veteran paratrooper and an original 'Green Devil' who had held Monte Cassino in Italy against all the Allies could throw against his mountain fortress, now commanded a shadow of his old formation. After Italy and Normandy there were few of his veterans left.

The 5th Parachute Division was a parachute division in name only; only a handful of its members had done a jump. Now the Division was made up of men from the *Luftwaffe*, who had a few days' infantry training at the most. The same was true of their officers, right up to regimental commanders. They were former pilots or chairborne warriors from Goering's Air Force Ministry in Berlin. They were brave, but they lacked the ability to command men in ground warfare.

Now these men were hungry and freezing. Their aim this Monday was to take inhabited places in which they could find shelter and warmth, and above all loot! Already they had been amazed at the stuff the *Amis* had left behind in their retreat from the River Sauer – chocolate which they had not seen in months, cartons of cigarettes made of 'real Virginia tobacco' and not the stinking black weed they smoked, all sorts of delicious foods in cans, including a kind of bean in tomato sauce. Now the hungry young paratroopers were out of Heilmann's control. They had heard that Wiltz was the headquarters of an *Ami* division. There could be no better place to loot than that.

In the snowbound woods above Schönberg, the two trapped regiments of the 106th Division also prepared for one last desperate fight. Some semblance of order had now been made. Contact had been established between the two regiments once more. Colonel Klinck's had been found, and although the Germans still periodically pounded the woods with artillery and mortar fire, they had ceased attacking into the trees.

But the men were mostly tired, hungry and apprehensive. As Sergeant Peterson recalled after the war, 'The quiet was oppressive after the intensity of the battle*. In the fading afternoon, every man stared at the tree-covered hills and waited.'

They were running out of ammunition too. The brown canvas ammunition containers they carried were now limp. The dark green metal ammo boxes which should have been full of white-webbed machine gun belts were empty. Here and there a soldier still had a grenade clipped to his equipment, but most of them were down to a dozen or so bullets.

Food was low as well. Those who had the energy scratched around the battlefield, looking for abandoned ration cans or searched their own equipment in case they might have overlooked a piece of candy or a ration biscuit.

Colonel Brook's final message to the 423rd, with its bombastic 'this mission is of gravest importance to the nation', annoyed most of Colonel Cavender's officers as he read it to them that night. Besides, how could they fight if they didn't have the ammunition or supplies?

Cavender was beyond caring about such matters. His main concern was his regiment. What was he going to do? He went over to where his staff officers were waiting. From the direction of the Regimental Aid Post, there came a miserable whimpering. An angry medic snapped, 'Knock it off, willya! Do you want the Krauts to hear?' Cavender winced. The sound reminded him of the wounded. Was he going to have to leave them behind once again?

Now he told his officers that, as Puett's 2nd Battalion had seen the heaviest fighting on the previous day, he would concentrate on Klinck's Third. They were dug in on the other side of the Ihrenbach stream, on the heights overlooking Schönberg. 'All right, gentlemen,' Cavender, said, 'we'll support the 3rd Battalion's attack tomorrow morning.'

---

* Testimony to that intensity can still be found in those woods. They are full of shrapnel. Even fifty years on, one can't go far without finding a rusting shard of metal that once was a bomb or shell.

The notepads came out. His officers began to scribble down the regimental commander's orders. Weary runners started to move through the trees to the various outfits concerned. Weary NCOs pulled themselves together and began rounding up their men. A voice complained peevishly, 'I ain't got no more ammo.' An NCO snarled in return, 'Use your side arm!'

Slowly the weary men began to move out. In the darkness they collided with each other, but they were too tired even to curse each other. Pfc Malinoski saw a man slip in the mud and roll down the hillside. No one went to fetch him. He lay there, drained of all strength. The others plodded by him unfeelingly. The Golden Lions were moving up for their final attack.

On the roads surrounding the 'Pocket' the young grenadiers waited at their posts. They stamped their feet in the freezing cold, glad of their felt overshoes. Some smoked forbidden cigarettes in their cupped hands. Now and again they cocked their heads to the wind, trying to catch the faintest sound. There was none. There was nothing at all.

There weren't many of them. The 293rd Infantry Regiment, perhaps 2,000 strong, a single battalion of field guns and the newly arrived 669th *Ost-Battalion*, made up of ex-Red Army POWs officered by Germans. Most of von Manteuffel's command was up around St Vith, which had been by-passed by both the Fifth and Sixth Panzer Armies. But they were confident. They controlled the roads. Soon the *Amis* would have to come out of the woods. It was either that or starve to death in the freezing forest. When they did, the waiting grenadiers knew, it would be the end of the *Amis*. They were trapped to the rear of a whole German Army. Their nearest comrades were eleven kilometres away and they were fighting for their lives. The *Amis* hadn't the slightest chance of escaping what Fate had ordained for them.

DAY FOUR:

Tuesday, 19 December 1944

Weather: Misty and fog. No aerial activity.

'It's either root hog – or die! Shoot the works. If those Hun bastards want war in the raw, that's the way we'll give it to them!'

General Patton, 19 December.

In the morning mist Cavender's 423rd Regiment huddled behind the saddle of Hill 536. Down below, just visible, was Schönberg. The weary infantrymen rubbed their red-rimmed eyes and stared at it. This was their objective.

Swiftly Cavender reviewed his dispositions. He was with Klinck's 3rd Battalion on the hillside closest to the Belgian village. To the right on the reverse side of the slope was Puett's 2nd Battalion, while the 1st Battalion, now commanded by Major Moon, was to the rear. He didn't particularly like the set-up but the sky was beginning to clear a little and he still hoped for that long-promised airdrop.

At nine Colonel Cavender called a conference of officers. He told them: 'We will attack at ten hundred hours in columns of battalions.' He pointed to Colonel Klinck. 'You are in the best shape. You'll carry the burden of the attack.'

Klinck nodded. His Battalion would come down the steep logging trail from Hill 536 to where the road descending into Schönberg made a ninety degree turn. It could be that the enemy would be in the cluster of whitewashed houses to the right next to the Catholic grotto. With luck his Battalion would be able to rush them. Then it was only a matter of yards to the centre of Schönberg. Klinck told himself that they would be finished climbing, at least. From now onwards it would be all downhill.

Cavender, precise and formal, perhaps even a little old-fashioned, right to the end, looked at his watch and began to co-ordinate the time. But he didn't get very far.

Abruptly the morning stillness was torn apart by an unholy howl. Shells shrieked out of the sky. The officers stiffened. 'Look out!' someone cried and they flung themselves down. Fist-sized lumps of shrapnel scythed through the trees. The lone German field artillery battalion along the Bleialf-Schönberg road had begun pounding Hill 536.

The German grenadiers began attacking under the cover of their barrage. Without difficulty they overran the 590th Field Artillery, gunners without guns. They came up from their rear, firing wildly from the hip, yelling like men demented. The American artillerymen started to raise their hands in surrender. In a matter of minutes Cavender's rear was cut off. Now there was only one way for him to go – *forward*!

But for a while Cavender had other problems than the surrender of the artillerymen to his rear. The short artillery bombardment had seemingly demoralized his regimental staff. Now they had gone to ground and refused to move out.

'*Move out!*' an enraged NCO yelled at the frightened men. But they refused. They clung stubbornly to whatever cover they could find. Cavender berated them, as did Colonel Nagle, his wounded executive officer. To no avail.

Just then a very large black sergeant stalked through the trees with a tommy gun tucked underneath his arm. It was as if he were going for a morning stroll. He seemed totally unconcerned by what was going on all about him.

'Colonel, suh,' he said in a rich Southern accent, 'You seem all alone here. I'm from the 333rd Field Artillery. Anything you want me to do?'

Colonel Nagle nodded to the cowering men, 'Get this platoon organized, Sergeant,' he said gratefully. 'Move north, covering our flank.'

Klinck's 3rd Battalion moved out smartly. They stumbled down the steep logging trail. Captain Huyatt's company was in the lead. They hit the road and hurried down round the next bend. There, pointing straight at them, was an 88mm cannon, covered by a twin-barrelled 40mm flak gun being used in the ground role! The Germans opened up immediately. Huyatt yelled to his men to take cover, but the road was bordered by a deep ditch and then a drop. So the trapped infantrymen lay on the road or the smaller ditch to their right. Above the racket Huyatt now heard the rusty clatter of tank tracks. He raised his head. There was no mistaking it. It was a Sherman. He turned to the men around him. '*It's one of ours!*' The Seventh Armored was coming to their help at last.

The next moment the Sherman fired. Shrapnel cut the air above their heads. The tank had been captured by the enemy. An instant later it rattled by and the fire from the 40mm cannon started to slacken. But there was a new danger now. In the sudden silence, Huyatt could hear the sound of Germans moving through the trees above him. He reacted immediately. Taking half the company with him, he panted back up the logging trail. The Germans pulled back and the exhausted men of Huyatt's company slumped into the foxholes they had dug on Hill 536 the previous night and took stock of their situation. It was bad. There were about thirty riflemen left, plus fifteen armed with a BAR, a US automatic which dated back to the First World War. They were cut off from the rest of the 3rd Battalion and were down to one clip of ammunition per man.

One hour later, at eleven thirty that Tuesday morning, the Germans attacked Huyatt's survivors from all sides. The battered Americans held out for only ten minutes before their ammunition ran out. There was nothing they could do now. Men started to rise, holding their arms up in surrender. Others took off their helmets. By now the Germans recognized this strange *Ami* custom which signified defeat. The Germans ceased firing and concentrated on looting their new prisoners.

Not far away Klinck's other companies had been just as unsuccessful. None of them had carried their objective, although they had tried hard enough. An hour after Huyatt surrendered, Colonel Klinck ordered his companies to withdraw and begin digging a defensive perimeter. It was the last they would dig as American soldiers.

Gloomily Sergeant Petersen took stock of the situation. 'How the hell did we get here?' he asked himself. 'We spent over two years training and now we're probably going to die because someone has failed to get ammunition to us.'

As he fumed on that battletorn hill that Tuesday afternoon Petersen could not know who exactly had betrayed them. But he had other problems on his mind. News was coming in that 'our 2nd Battalion was lost somewhere and the 1st Battalion was completely wiped out.'

The news was nearly right, but not quite. Under Major Moon, the 1st Battalion had set off downhill. The lead company did well, in spite of initial losses. It made the road, with Schönberg, their objective, less than 200 yards away. Then, like Huyatt's company, they ran into concentrated fire from German flak guns used in a ground role. The attack halted. Men fell dead and wounded. Desperately the platoon leaders tried to rally their men, but no one was prepared to face that solid wall of fire. Tanks started to come out of the trees. The 3rd's B Company was unable to move either backwards or forwards, so it stayed where it was and fought back until, as the historian of the Golden Lions states, it was 'eliminated'.

Colonel Puett's 2nd Battalion had borne the brunt of the previous day's fighting. Still the 2nd did its best that Tuesday. The Battalion came out from the wooded heights east of Schönberg, where the road runs to Andler. Now runners were reporting to Puett that there were Germans about four hundred yards to the Battalion's right – and there weren't supposed to be Germans there.

Before Colonel Puett could investigate, firing broke out. Eager to take revenge for yesterday's defeats, Puett's riflemen were pouring it on and the yells of pain told them they were hitting their targets. Suddenly a bare-headed soldier ran out from the forest. Raising his hands, he yelled '*Don't shoot!*'

The man was wearing the same uniform as themselves. They had been firing at Colonel Descheneaux's men of the 422nd.

At about the same time as Captain Huyatt was withdrawing what was left of his company up the logging trail, eighty miles away the Eisenhower convoy was approaching the town of Verdun. The armour-plated staff car, escorted by two score of MPs carrying sub-machine guns, rolled by the railway station and turned right up the narrow road that led to Caserne Maginot. Above them towered the heights where the greatest battle in Western European history had been fought, in which a certain *Gefreiter* Hitler had been wounded. The convoy drove through the iron gates, the MPs dropped from their jeeps, tommy guns at the ready, to form a protective circle as the Supreme Commander, accompanied by Generals Strong and Bedell Smith, limped into the barracks named after the gigantic Sergeant Maginot who had lost his leg at Verdun and as war minister had saddled France with the great white elephant named after him.

The Top Brass assembled in a squad room heated by a single pot-bellied stove. None of those who were present that Tuesday morning are still alive, but General Strong, Eisenhower's British Chief-of-Intelligence, remembered the atmosphere as 'tense, with the handful of Britons present not very confident of the Americans' ability to handle the crisis. Stories of great bravery on the part of individuals and units did not change their opinion.'

Strong gave the Top Brass a quick rundown on the Intelligence situation and then Eisenhower rose to say, 'The present situation is to be regarded as one of opportunity and not one of disaster.'

Patton reacted as Eisenhower had expected him to: 'Hell, let's have the guts to let the sons-of-bitches go all the way to Paris. Then we'll really cut 'em off and show 'em up!'

The ice was broken. Bradley smiled and Eisenhower, grinning, said that his strategy was based on a 'counter-attack on the southern flank'. His exposé finished, the Supreme Commander turned again to Patton and said, 'George I want you to go to Luxembourg and take charge of the battle, making a strong counter-attack with at least six divisions.'

'Yessir,' Patton replied promptly.

'When can you start?'

'As soon as you are through with me.'

'What do you mean?'

According to Strong, this remark caused 'some laughter around the table, especially from the British officers present'. To most of them it seemed a typical 'Blood an' Guts' reaction. But they didn't know that Patton had been planning his attack north *four* days before the battle had begun and *seven* days before this conference. Nor did they stop to wonder why Eisenhower was going over Bradley's head and giving orders *directly* to one of the latter's army commanders. But they were not in a position to perceive the real significance of this 'historic conference', as it would be seen after the war. The Germans were supposed to be beaten. Now they were attacking deep into the heart of an American army with some twenty-odd divisions. Only a few of them knew how it had all been arranged.

Undoubtedly Patton was delighted with the role he was soon to play. That day, as he set up his new command post in Luxembourg City next to Bradley's, he issued his first order of the day. It read: 'Everyone in this army must understand that we are not fighting this battle in any half-cocked manner. It's either root hog – or die! Shoot the works. If those Hun bastards want war in the raw, then that's the way we'll give it to them!'

He was so delighted that he failed to ask why his objective was Bastogne – *at the point* of the German offensive, instead of *at its base*! He also seemed to have overlooked the fact that, so far, there was going to be no US 1st Army counter-attack from the north to link up with his 3rd Army. Even the dullest student of military history knew that a two-pincer attack into the base of the salient is the surest way of doing the greatest damage to the enemy. But Patton did not ask those questions.

A little while later another senior general failed to ask the Supreme Commander another crucial question. He was General Jacob Devers, commander of the Sixth Army Group in France. Eisenhower didn't rate Devers very highly. In his evaluation of the officers under his command, Eisenhower once wrote that Devers 'was often inaccurate in statements and evaluations. He has not, so far, produced among the seniors of the American organization here a feeling of trust and confidence.' It was said that Eisenhower had not sacked Devers only because he hated firing lieutenant-generals.

Now, just before he left the Verdun conference, Eisenhower had a word with Devers. He told him that he should anticipate an attack on his Seventh Army under General Patch. When and if this happened he had to give ground 'slowly on his northern flank, even if he had to move completely back to the Vosges'.

An hour before, Eisenhower had explained that he had been let down by Ultra. That organization had failed to produce the intelligence which would have allowed him to predict the German counter-attack in the Ardennes. Yet here, on the 19th, Eisenhower was telling him to expect a German attack which, in effect, would come *twelve* days later, on 1 January, 1945. So accurate was Eisenhower's information that Devers was told – and passed the information on to Patch – that on 27 December 'a hostile attack on your flank west of Bitche may force you to give up ground from your main position. To meet such a possibility it is necessary that your west flank be protected by a reserve battle position.'

Two days later General Alexander Patch, the Seventh Army Commander, could tell his two corps commanders that they should expect an eight-division German attack in Alsace in the early hours of New Year's Day.

But Devers neglected to ask the Supreme Commander one vital question: where had Eisenhower obtained this intelligence? Ultra had failed on 16 December. Yet now, three days later, it was operating at peak efficiency, giving detailed information of the German intentions. Why were the Germans using Enigma once more when they could still be using safe land lines? After all, the German assault force was on German territory where land lines could easily be used. Or did Eisenhower have some other source of information about the enemy's intentions? Devers never asked.

General David Belchem, Montgomery's Chief-of-Operations, had received 'some slender indications of a possible enemy action of some kind in the Ardennes during early December'. But 'our US Allies [were] so sure of continued inactivity there that we disregarded them.' Now, however, the British, and in particular Field-Marshal Montgomery, were becoming alarmed at what was happening in the Ardennes.

All kinds of rumours were flourishing at British HQ. It was said that only five US military policemen were guarding the vital bridge over the Meuse at Namur. At Liège, also on the Meuse, the crossings were patrolled by black US service troops. They had shot three Germans dressed in US uniform trying to get across. They'd also shot two innocent Belgian civilians.

Without Eisenhower's permission – or knowledge – all sorts of emergency measures were being taken this Tuesday. A British anti-tank regiment embarking for home at Zeebrugge was stopped fifty minutes before the ship was due to sail. The disappointed gunners were soon on their way back to the front. A tank brigade resting nearby at the Belgian holiday resort of Knokke, after handing in their battered tanks and waiting for new ones, were ordered to grab their old ones and proceed to the Meuse.

That day when Belchem called Montgomery to let him know what was going on to the rear, the Field-Marshal said, 'Put road blocks around Brussels. If any German armoured cars do get into the city, get yourself a Boyes anti-tank rifle and stalk them with any of your chaps you can muster.'

Later Belchem concluded that Monty had been pulling his leg. The Boyes anti-tank rifle hadn't been used by the British Army since 1940. But Montgomery was a worried man that day. He had heard that Patton was moving north to the attack. But would he be in time to stop the Germans reaching the Meuse? Hodges was holding the northern shoulder. But what was he doing about attacking the German flank as Patton was doing on the southern shoulder? Most worrying of all, however, was that he, as an army group commander, had had 'no orders or requests of any sort' from Eisenhower. What was going on at Supreme Headquarters?

*

That Tuesday afternon confusion seemed to reign everywhere. At Vielsalm, where General Jones had set up his CP near Hasbrouck's (though he had precious little to command now), the two generals did not know very much about what was going on in the St Vith 'Horseshoe', as Clarke's defensive perimeter was now being called. They had heard that the 424th Infantry Regiment and the 9th Armored's Combat Command B were under heavy attack. They were also running out of food and ammunition. But who was responsible for those two commands?

Middleton's last words to Hasbrouck had been, 'You and Jones carry on up there'. Hasbrouck had interpreted that as meaning that he and Jones were in joint command of the horseshoe. But Hasbrouck was worried about Jones's ability to command. At times he seemed numb and apathetic, stricken by the fate of his son with the trapped regiments. Then there were moments when he was wildly over-optimistic, seemingly unaware of the gravity of the situation.

Still worrying about the situation in the Vielsalm command set-up, Hasbrouck was disturbed by the arrival of an exhausted infantry colonel in his schoolroom office. The newcomer introduced himself as Colonel Gustin Nelson of the 112th Infantry Regiment, belonging to the 28th Division.

'What are you doing way up here?' Hasbrouck asked in astonishment. 'And where the hell's the rest of your division?'

Nelson shrugged. 'Don't ask me, General. I only found out where *I* was this morning when I ran into one of your patrols.' He explained that he had lost contact with his division and had been wandering about the countryside all the previous day. He hadn't suffered too many casualties, but the men of his regiment were tired and very hungry.

Hasbrouck wasn't particularly concerned about the state of the new arrival's men. They were bodies and he needed every man capable of holding a rifle in the horseshoe. He telephoned Jones straight away and suggested that the 112th Infantry should be attached to the 106th and put in to plug a gap in the horseshoe between the 424th and CCB. It didn't seem strange that he, a brigadier general, was giving an order to a major general. Nor did it, apparently, to Jones. He received the offer gratefully. As Hasbrouck wrote after the war, 'I never knew who was in my command. I just did everything I thought necessary. The command status was more or less an assumption.'

It appeared that something was going wrong with the Eisenhower scheme. Things were becoming confused. Nothing was going to plan, save that the two 'shoulders' were being held. But on that Tuesday one thing *was* certain. The victims were still dying.

About the same time as Colonel Nelson left Hasbrouck's office, Major Moon, the new commander of Descheneaux's 1st Battalion, surveyed the road that led from Auw, through the valley, over the River Our and on to Schönberg. It appeared to be deserted. No Germans in sight. There were plenty of forest trails running up the heights, so if enemy artillery spotted them, they could dodge into the woods. He made up his mind. 'Move out!' he ordered.

C Company broke cover and headed for the road. They didn't get far. Five German tanks came out of the trees and started firing high explosive at once. Some of the Americans hesitated. The first platoon, however, doubled across the road and disappeared into the woods.

Now the 1st Battalion began to bog down. Colonel Descheneaux came up and tried to co-ordinate the crossing of the road but he didn't have much luck. More Germans appeared on the right flank and started firing. The Golden Lions hugged the ground. As one survivor recalled, 'Another tank pulled in behind us and began to fire at the other end. The slaughter at the end of the valley by the road was bad.'

Still, they were brave men and they fought back. A bazooka team rushed to tackle the new tank but they were shot down as soon as they broke cover. Another team took up the challenge, but as one of them remembered, 'We loaded and got ready to fire, but when I saw several of our men walking toward the tanks with their hands up, I knew it was useless to fire because I was sure we would kill those men. We broke up our weapons and surrendered. There were two hundred and fifty in this group'.*

Major Moon, however, was in no mood to surrender. He rose to his feet and, with his staff and a few other brave men, he dashed back the way they had come. Minutes later the rest of his Battalion began to surrender. Pfc Mario Garbin, a medic, was one of Moon's

---

* There is still clear evidence that they did break them up. The author's wife found (1993) a walkie-talkie, dated 1944, in a ditch on that road. It had been broken in two.

group. Later that day they found a strange little haven of peace in the midst of the mayhem. It was a battalion motor pool: They had blocked the track leading to their position with their trucks to stop the German tanks moving in on them. They'd been there for three days without having been attacked.

Garbin put the drivers in the picture – the Division was surrounded and had been unable to break out. The drivers suggested they should join them. 'So we dug into the frozen ground, cut down trees and made foxholes that held two or three guys and built four layers of logs over them because we thought they'd be firing tree bursts.' And there they would wait, their only form of combat firing at the buzz bombs 'on their way to England'.

Colonel Scales' 2nd Battalion of the 422nd had stopped their advance when they heard the German tanks firing at the 1st. Scales went back to his mortar platoon and ordered the men to destroy their weapons. Lieutenant Walker, in charge, refused. At that instant heavy small arms firing broke out. Major Ouellette, the Battalion's Executive Officer, was wounded in a freakish way. A bullet glanced off his collar insignia and creased his neck. He carried on, as did the rest.

For now they had spotted vehicles crowded bumper to bumper on the Andler-Schönberg road. Immediately the rumour spread that this was the long-expected relief force of vehicles from the 423rd. When tanks appeared, the men cried, 'It's the armoured breakthrough. They're coming to pull us out!'

They were wrong. For the men manning the tanks wore the black uniform of the German *Panzerwaffe* and the men of Remer's Führer Escort Brigade now started to shell the Golden Lions. At once the Battalion started to fall apart; but some, like Walker and his comrades of the heavy weapons platoon, were determined to fight on.

Staff-Sergeant Almond of Walker's H Company rolled a hundred yards down a hillside. Standing in full view of the enemy, he mowed down the crew of a Spandau machine gun. Miraculously he remained unwounded. The squad machine gun kept on firing until it was 'shot out from under them'. With the one remaining mortar, a group of corporals and privates scored three hits with eleven rounds at 2,000 yards range, knocking out two German self-propelled guns and crippling the third.

By now Walker had been hit in the left arm and shoulder. Shaken and bleeding, he ordered the remaining heavy weapons destroyed and the wounded men evacuated. All about him scores of men were discarding weapons and ammunition. It was apparent that he was the only officer in the area. Men crowded around him urging surrender, but Walker 'could not do that and face my own sergeants'. Instead he led a column of men into the pine woods and, as the firing died away and he had chance to rest, he managed to count his new command. There were 199 men from fifteen different companies.

Two hours later he found the 'lost' motor pool, which was now commanded by Majors Moon and Ouellette. Only then did he allow a doctor to tend to his wounds.

Behind, what was left of the 2nd Battalion began to surrender. 'Red' Prendergast was one of them. He remembered afterwards, '[How] the sun was going down, about three thirty. A flag of truce came and a German officer came. He said in perfect English to our colonel, "You've been up here for quite a while and you haven't fired a shot since noon. We strongly suspect you don't have ammunition. If you don't come down in twenty minutes, none of you are coming down."

'The colonel considered for a few moments, then ordered, "All right, everybody destroy your weapons".'

Prendergast was disgusted. 'All I had was this beautiful .45 that I'd been treasuring. I took it apart and threw it in the snow.'

The Germans were furious with him for having dispensed with the Colt. They wanted it as a souvenir. But they didn't hurt the big soldier. Instead they looted him and the rest of everything they could find. As punishment, however, they took off his overshoes and ripped them up. Fifty years on he is still suffering from frostbite. 'From October to May I don't feel like I have any toes at all. Once you've got it, you've always got it.'

Colonel Thompson's 3rd Battalion of the 422nd was luckier than its two sister battalions. The Third found an unexpected gap in the German cordon. In single file the riflemen moved through the woods down towards the road that led from Andler to Schönberg.

After some time the leading platoon spotted some shadowy figures up ahead near a log hut. It was misty and they could not make them out, but they reasoned that the men could only be Germans. So they started firing. The shadowy figures began to return their fire. It was only after several men had been hit that they concluded they were firing at their own people. They were men of Colonel Puett's 2nd Battalion of the 423rd Infantry.

That tragic accident about put an end to Colonel Thompson's advance. Now the woods started to fill with leaderless, confused and demoralized Golden Lions. But Staff-Sergeant Petersen felt his company could still fight. But they had no ammunition and they were burdened by the wounded. 'Help from the air or the ground would not come. We were alone and abandoned on the hill.'

While Peterson sat there reflecting on their fate, scouts were sent out to try and find an escape route. There was none. The Germans were in full control of all the tracks leading out of the woods. The 422nd was packed into an area of two square miles. The Golden Lions were sitting targets. The Germans could fire at them at will and the Regiment began to take more and more casualties.

In mid-afternoon two gunners whose position had been overrun staggered into Descheneaux's perimeter. They reported that Cavender's 423rd was about a thousand yards away. It too was in a bad state, and they were talking about surrender.

Descheneaux called a conference of his officers in a trench which served him as a CP. The conference was interrupted for a while when the officers heard the rattle of tank tracks below. Had the Seventh Armored come to rescue them at last? The hope was soon dashed. The tanks were Panthers from Remer's Brigade.

Colonel Kelly said later, 'We had nothing – no food, medicines or blankets. The latter items were worst because there was a steady stream of wounded from the gully to our west and without dressings or blankets there was nothing we could do except let them lie in their gore and shiver. I put my coat over one. When it was all over, I felt like a heel going back for it, but he didn't need it any more. The situation was hopeless.'

It was against this background that Descheneaux was forced to make his decision. He said, 'I don't believe in fighting for glory if it doesn't accomplish anything. It looks as if we'll have to pack it in.'

Colonel Kelly heard what he said. Later he recalled, 'The situation was hopeless. But some of us were in favour of holding out until dark and attempting to get out in small parties. I thought that had been decided upon. Now Kelly said to the C.O., 'Desch, you can't surrender.'

'No?' Descheneaux said bitterly, looking at the mounting pile of dead and wounded next to his command post.

Kelly shut up. He knew it was no use now. Later he said, 'If his command post hadn't been the regimental aid station he could have stood it a little while longer. He had been right up with the leading elements in the attack that morning.'

The Colonel saw the look of contempt in the eyes of some of his officers. He knew what they were thinking, so he said, 'As far as I am concerned, I'm going to save the lives of as many as I can. And I don't give a damn if I am court-martialled!'

A thousand yards away Colonel Cavender was about to make the same decision. Colonel Kelly said of him, 'Cavender was reluctant to take command without an order. Now he would have to take command without orders and make that overwhelming decision. He knew that the decision would mean the end of his military career.* West Point had no place in its curriculum for what he was about to do.'

As it began to grow dark Colonel Cavender called a conference of his officers. He told them, 'There's no ammunition left. We're down to a clip per man.'

Most of the officers guessed what he was going to say next. Yet still they tensed, not wanting to hear those fatal words. 'I was a G.I. in World War One,' Cavender continued, 'and I want to see things from their stand-point. No man in this outfit has eaten all day and we haven't had water since early morning.' Cavender paused and then let them have it. '*Now what's your attitude to surrendering?*'

His answer was a shocked silence.

As Colonel Nagle went down the hill with a soldier who spoke German to surrender, the order was given to break up the weapons and transport. Jeeps were rendered useless by exploding a small TNT charge next to the engine block. Firing pins were pulled out of rifles and smashed against rocks. The recoil springs of pistols were tossed away.

As the Germans started to move up, the Golden Lions were told to move to designated areas. 'Unarmed, and without their trappings,' Staff Sergeant Petersen thought, 'the young soldiers looked bare and

---

* It didn't. He served on till 1953. Colonel Cavender is still alive and in his 90s.

vulnerable. Everyone appeared whipped. Some looked dazed and were led by their comrades. The quiet movement of so many men was eerie. Their footsteps were muffled by the carpet of pine needles. The whole affair took on the ghostly quality of an old silent movie.'

Now the luckless prisoners saw their captors for the first time. Some appeared drunk. Others screamed at the prisoners. Most were too busy looting the Americans of cigarettes, watches and fountain pens. For the first time these young Americans were being humiliated by men they had referred to contemptuously as 'Krauts'. They had to stand there and take it as smelly German *Landsers* rifled through their pockets, tugged at their rings, whipped off their wristwatches.

Petersen and some of his platoon were detailed to carry a huge German officer to the clearing station in Schönberg. He had suffered an appalling wound to his stomach and was dying. They pushed their way through the miserable prisoners and the triumphant Germans. They were passed by a German officer sitting in a baby blue MG, which was being drawn by a horse. Petersen thought that officer had style. Yet he asked himself how an army which had so little gasoline could beat the highly mechanized American Army?

The clearing station at Schönberg, so hastily evacuated by Sergeant Thorpe's 330th Medical Battalion two days before, was a shambles. The wounded were crowded everywhere. Nurses in white rubber aprons moved back and forth, their aprons splattered in blood.

Petersen was glad to get out of the place. Now he set off on that long bitter march which would take him to Prum and the cages beyond. As he did so he was seized by a sudden fury at the smug looks on the faces of his captors. At the same time he desperately wanted to believe he still was an American soldier. He pleaded: 'Forgive me for whatever I did wrong. Tell me and I'll fix it. Please, please don't leave me.' With whom he pleaded he did not quite know. Perhaps it was God.

Lieutenant Alan Jones, the son of the divisional commander, simply couldn't believe the Golden Lions were surrendering. He stared at the men wandering around in confusion. He had formed the stragglers into a makeshift company that morning. Now they were stragglers again. Just then a negro artilleryman carrying a tommy gun came up. 'We haven't even started fighting, Lieutenant,' he said. 'Let's go and kill some Germans!'

138

But that wasn't to be. Already the triumphant young German grenadiers were swarming through the trees, out for loot. Jones raised his hands in surrender. Son of the Commanding General, he too joined the great mass of prisoners. They were all sorts – generals' sons, the grandson of Buffalo Bill Cody, the future science fiction novelist Kurt Vonnegut, future university professors. For the next six months they would simply be '*kriegies*'.*

Not all the Golden Lions surrendered tamely. Scores of brave, desperate men refused to carry out the Colonels' orders. Captain Murray, Sergeant Rifleman and Private Dickens of the 423rd sneaked away before the Germans came. They avoided the Germans till after dark; then they set off for St Vith. Next day they were back in the line again with the Seventh Armored.

A Company of the 423rd which had been cut off from the rest that afternoon also decided to make its way to St Vith. Guided by a Lieutenant Lang of the Regiment's Intelligence and Reconnaissance Platoon, they got under way. But they were spotted and shelled. They decided to split into smaller groups. But Ivan Lang still kept picking up stragglers. Somehow he managed to bring nearly seventy men back to the St Vith perimeter. There Clarke had them placed in the basement of his schoolhouse HQ. They were fed and allowed to sleep. Next day they were told they were going back in the line and Clarke noted that 'their enthusiasm was high'.

As we have seen, back in late November, Bradley, probably with Eisenhower's approval, had ordered General Middleton to 'simulate the movement of additional units ... in order to draw enemy divisions to his front'. But the Germans were not fooled. It would, however, have been militarily useful to have discovered what the Germans had done in response to the movement of these 'new American divisions' to the Eifel/Ardennes front. A sure way to do this would have been to send out patrols across the Our and Sauer to find out. The 'Ghost Front' was very porous. German soldiers and local civilians were moving back and forth all the time that November. So why hadn't Middleton ordered patrols? The answer is clear. He didn't want evidence circulating at lower levels that the Germans were massing three armies in the Eifel. The alarm signals would have

* Name taken from the German for POW *Kriegsgefangene(r)*.

started ringing and the great plan been endangered. Naturally Intelligence were routinely giving warnings about the dangers of a German attack in the Eifel-Ardennes, but fighting soldiers knew that Intelligence officers were 'nervous Nellies', always seeing dangers where there were none. To cover themselves, the Top Brass allowed Eisenhower's Chief-of-Intelligence to warn Bradley in the first week of December that the Germans might attack in the Ardennes. Later Strong reported that he had seen Bradley 'for about three-quarters of an hour and he told me he was aware of the danger but that he had earmarked certain divisions to move into the Ardennes area should the enemy attack there'.

After the war Eisenhower also agreed that Strong had warned him that an attack might come through the Ardennes in any period of bad weather which might keep Allied air grounded. He went on record as stating back in the autumn of 1944 that he might face a 'nasty little Kasserine' in that area.

Now, as Eisenhower journeyed back from the Verdun conference, he must have realized that he was facing a *damned great Kasserine*, that first battle of the US Army in the West which had shattered a whole American corps and had nearly cost him his first command. Two of his divisions, the 106th and 28th, had melted away and the 7th Armored was fighting for its life. The Germans were advancing with 600,000 men at a much faster rate than he had ever imagined when he had first baited the trap with VIII Corps. Hodges, the 1st Army Commander, had been forced to flee his HQ at Spa, with the Germans already on the heights above the town. To the south Bradley was cut off from his 1st and 9th Armies, which hadn't heard from their commander for two days. The spearhead of the German drive was already a mere fifteen miles from the River Meuse and Patton's counter-attack into the Bulge was days away yet. What was he to do?

During the war Eisenhower was always portrayed as the plain-dealing, plain-speaking democratic soldier. He avoided the fancy uniforms that some of his generals were addicted to and it was said that he preferred speaking to private soldiers rather than generals. But, as one cynic remarked, 'Ike has never put on those silk drawers of his for years without the help of servants.' At Supreme Head-quarters he was surrounded by 5,000 staff and hangers on. He had a mistress-secretary. He had a public relations man, Commander Butcher, whose principal job was to sell 'Ike' to the Press. He was consulted by prime ministers and presidents. Politicians and civic leaders were in and out of his office all the time.

In 1944 Eisenhower was the 20th century link in that chain of American military leaders, from George Washington through Andrew Jackson to Ulysses S. Grant, who had won the nation's highest office on account of their wartime successes. Twice Patton moaned about him to his staff that 'Ike is bitten by the Presidential bug and he is *yellow*', and 'How can anyone expect any backbone in a man who is already running for President?'

Now Eisenhower had shown some fortitude, had taken the great risk of sacrificing his own soldiers, in order to make the Germans come out and fight. But the German attack was getting out of hand. It wasn't developing the way he had imagined. By the time he reached his HQ at Versailles, where he would be virtually imprisoned in his office for the next few days (because Intelligence thought the Germans were trying to assassinate him), he must have realized he had made a great mistake – one that could cost him the presidency that, if Patton is to be believed, he was already actively preparing for.

Patton, who in 1944 was seemingly at odds with the whole world, habitually called Field-Marshal Montgomery the 'little fart', or sometimes 'the little limey fart'. But Montgomery was a very determined 'little fart', who had a high sense of his own importance. Now, on this grey Tuesday with his young liaison officers, British, American and Canadian, sending him ever gloomier news from the Ardennes, he decided it was time to act.

He signalled to his boss in London, Field-Marshal Sir Alan Brooke, Chief of the Imperial General Staff, 'The American forces have been cut in half and the Germans can reach the Meuse at Namur without any opposition. The Command set-up has always been very faulty and now is quite futile, with Bradley at Luxembourg and the front cut in two. I have told Whiteley* that Ike ought to place me in operational control of all troops on the northern half of the front. I consider he should be given a direct order by someone to do so.'

Brooke did not like the idea much and signalled back: 'I think you should be careful about what you say to Eisenhower himself on the subject of Command set-up as it may do more harm than good, especially as he is now probably very worried over the whole

* Assistant Chief of Operations at Eisenhower's HQ.

situation. It is a different thing, however, to make suggestions to Whiteley as you have done and these may well bear fruit.'

The events of that Tuesday night are confused. General Belchem, Montgomery's chief-of-staff, writes 'Late on the night of December 19, General Jock Whiteley rang me from Supreme HQ [where he was the senior British Army Liaison Officer] to tell me that Eisenhower had made up his mind to hand over command of the First US Army to Montgomery. He mentioned the long debate which had led to this decision and that Ike's Chief-of-Staff Bedell Smith had been in favour of the change. In spite of the obvious political repercussions, I called up Montgomery and warned him of what was afoot.'

Kay Summersby, Eisenhower's confidante, who was there, says: 'While there [at the Verdun conference] General Ike realized General Bradley, with his communications cut in shreds and his headquarters in the awkward position at Luxembourg, would have difficulty commanding troops on both sides of the German breakthrough. This is when he made the controversial split of command, giving Field-Marshal Montgomery direction of all forces to the north. General Ike returned to Versailles that evening, weary from the rough trip, but happier now that command problems were straightened out.'

These, then, are the two schools of thought which have been followed by chroniclers of the Battle ever since: either Montgomery proposed himself or Eisenhower did. Whichever school one accepts, it was clear that Eisenhower was rapidly losing his nerve – and his temper. When he phoned Bradley to inform him that Montgomery was now getting his 1st and 9th Armies, Bradley said aghast, 'By God, Ike, I cannot be responsible to the American people. If you do this, I resign.'

In return Eisenhower snorted, 'Brad, I – not you – am responsible to the American people. Your resignation, therefore, means nothing.'

There was a pause. Then Bradley protested again, but without threats this time. Eisenhower cut him short, with 'Well, Brad, those are my orders.'

Montgomery was in. Now he would shape the battle to come. Whatever Eisenhower had planned would not take place. The 106th and 28th Divisions had been sacrificed for nothing.

'The victims' knew nothing of the military politics. That night the weary beaten men of the 106th Division were worried about other

26. US soldiers shoot one of the many Germans found in US uniform.

27. The author Ernest Hemingway came up on 20 December, 1944, to view the battle, but spent most of the time in bed, having overindulged in stolen wine. He is seen here flanked by General Barton and Colonel Chance.

28. The survivors go home
after the battle.

29. The recently evacuated Siegfried Line positions above Echternach, seven storeys deep.

30. 'Skyline Drive', the most famous highway in Europe, on the third week of December, 1944.

31. The 7th Armored Division Sherman tank memorial at Vielsalm.

32. The monument above St Vith recently erected on the orders of President Clinton to commemorate the Engineers' defence of the ridge.

things than the decision being made in Paris. Hundreds of the new *kriegies* were housed in the churchyard at Bleialf, with their own dead snowy mounds in the gutters outside. Others packed Schönberg. At Kessler's wooden *Tanzsaal* (Dance Hall), SS officers were questioning more senior officers. Official photographers snapped Blacks and Whites together to show the people in the *Reich* what a rotten racial mix the *Amis* were.

Others were already marching back to the railheads at Prum and Gerolstein, where soon they might be killed by their own air forces.

As they laboured wearily up and down the slushy roads, their mood grew progressively blacker. On all sides there were numerous signs of a great American defeat – abandoned trucks, wrecked jeeps, shattered anti-tank guns – and the dead.

As ever more German reinforcements headed westwards, the filthy columns of *kriegies* were forced into the ditches or fields to wait until the victors had passed. But weariness and apathy soon banished their anger. Like tame sheep they let themselves be ordered back on the roads to begin their march once more.

In the midst of the mob, Colonel Descheneaux marched alone and unrecognized. We do not know his feelings, for he did not survive long enough after the war to rationalize his emotions; the tuberculosis he picked up in the *Oflag* would soon kill him. But that afternoon he suffered perhaps the greatest insult of his military career. One of his soldiers recognized him and said, 'I've got a message for you, Colonel.'

Descheneaux had looked at the private dully. 'What?' he asked.

By way of response the soldier had stuck out his tongue at the tall officer and given him the Bronx cheer.*

* Raspberry in English-English.

DAY FIVE:

Wednesday, 20 December, 1944

Weather: Thick fog, limited visibility. In higher elevations, ground frozen, lower areas thawing. Ardennes roads muddy and slippery.

'*Even* generals wet their knickers.'

British Army Saying.

Out inspecting the perimeter this Wednesday morning, General Bruce Clarke, the mainspring of the horseshoe defence line, was arrested – by his own MPs!

He kept repeating, 'I'm General Bruce Clarke of CCB!'

'Like hell!' his captors sneered. 'You're one of Skorzeny's men.' They meant the special agents working for *Obersturmbannführer Skorzeny*. They were supposed to be everywhere behind the lines this day, spying, sabotaging, slaying high-ranking Allied officers. 'We were told to watch out for a Kraut wearing the uniform of a one-star general.'

Despite Clarke's protests, the MPs hustled him off to a nearby house and locked him inside. (One of the MPs had the gall to ask for his autograph.) Now they were sure they had captured a Skorzeny agent. Only a Kraut would have insisted the Chicago Cubs were in the American League. There he remained for five hours until he was finally identified and released.

Pfc Mike Klimick of the 87th Recon knew they'd got the wrong man. He'd seen Clarke before and recognized him. But there was nothing he could do. They were 'changing the password all the time' and the only one he knew was 'Mickey-Minnie' and he was sure that was out of date. If he interfered, they'd probably lock him up too.

Besides, he had problems of his own on this freezingly cold morning. The inside of his Staghound armoured car was like an ice-box. The inner steel wall was one sheet of ice and he had put on every stitch of clothing he possessed in a vain attempt to keep warm.

He wasn't alone. All along the perimeter the infantrymen and the armoured troopers were finding the biting cold as hard to fight as the Germans. By day their uniforms got wet and at night they froze, making their lives miserable. As Lieutenant Walter Pennino, a platoon leader with the 7th Armored's 48th Armored Infantry Battalion, recalled long afterwards, 'You either had frostbite or trenchfoot in the end. For frostbite they gave you the Purple Heart. For trenchfoot you got a reprimand. It was a hell of a life.'

It was. To the rear of the perimeter the supply men had been issued with grenades and axes to destroy their vehicles if Skorzeny's men attempted to capture them. In the line the wounded remained where they were; there was no means of evacuating them. One ambulance sent back with wounded by Pennino returned filled with SS men dressed in US uniform. 'The Germans didn't do much damage. They were killed, but the passengers suffered the same fate.'

K-rations, which didn't freeze so easily, were exhausted. The remaining C-rations froze hard in their cans. Men trying to eat the frozen mush got severe stomach cramp. But no one dared attempt to heat the cans. The trees were full of German snipers. Fire would attract their attention immediately.

On this day von Manteuffel, three days behind his schedule, made an all-out attack on the St Vith perimeter. At first light he threw in the Führer Escort Brigade. Under the personal leadership of that fanatical Nazi, Otto Remer, the Brigade's Panthers broke through the American perimeter near the village of Hünningen. Scattering the GIs left and right, not bothering about prisoners or loot, the German tanks scuttled up the snowy slope, pressing deeper into the American flank.

On the reverse side of the slope, 90mm tank destroyers of the 814th Tank Destroyer Battalion were waiting for them, their crews tense, eyes strained to catch the first glimpse of the advancing Germans. They knew that the ones who got off the first shots might well be the victors in the coming battle.

The first wave of Panthers breasted the slope. The American gunners didn't hesitate. The heavy cannon crashed into action. Solid shot and armour-piercing shells hissed towards the Germans. Here and there they bounced off the steep glacis plates of the Panthers like glowing golfballs. But there was also a hollow boom as metal penetrated metal. The first Panther lurched to a halt. Another followed. Smoke started to pour from its engine. In a matter of minutes the jubilant American gunners had knocked out four of the first wave of attackers. That was too much for the second wave. They turned tail and fled.

Furious at being stalled so early, Remer sacked the battalion commander. But he did not press home his attack. He stayed the assault of his armoured infantry until more tanks came up to support the infantrymen.

Further east General Hoffmann-Schonborn, commander of the 18th Volksgrenadier Division which had beaten the 106th Division, led the attack of his 295th Regiment personally. He had to. Von Manteuffel was breathing down his neck. His objective this Wednesday was the railway station at St Vith. He needed it to transport supplies and troops for the push to the Meuse.

The grenadiers started to advance on the position held by the mixed force of 81st Engineers and the Seventh's 38th Armored Infantry. For Captain Carl Mattocks it turned out to be 'the busiest fifteen minutes of my life'. He could see the grenadiers swarming everywhere and hear their sergeants barking out orders. There seemed to be hundreds of them. Just then his new C.O., Major McDaniels, came on the radio and directed him, using a reference to a popular wartime song, 'to get on the Chattanooga Choo-Choo and head West.'

Mattocks needed no urging. He gathered his small headquarters group together and started working his way south to the assault guns positions on Hill 495. He told the gunners that the Germans were on their way. 'With a great deal of reluctance,' he ordered them to spike their guns and follow him.

Now the little bunch of Americans worked their way through the Germans, grateful for the mist. They skirted the road that led down to St Vith and successfully managed to contact 'Battle Police' posted by Clarke to guide stragglers. The Police directed them to a new defensive position east of Crombach.

Mattocks accepted a drink and then asked where the C.O. was. First Sergeant Alvie Davis gave him a look of disgust. 'In the basement, sir,' he replied.

Mattocks went down the steps where he found the C.O. His nerve had gone and he wanted to surrender. Mattocks refused. He had other things to do. The Germans up top were already blasting away with tank guns at the C.P., but he was still prepared to fight on.

So also was Colonel Riggs. But they could hear the Germans quite clearly now – they were that close – and his 'Cox's Army' was about finished. 'The only hope we had left,' Riggs related long afterwards, 'was to break into small groups, travel by night and try to infiltrate out of there.'

Riggs discarded his badges of rank and left with seven men. The

Germans were everywhere, but he was confident that they could make it. And they almost did. But they ran into a platoon of Germans who opened fire with their mortars. A fragment of a shell hit Riggs on the back of his head and the impact knocked him out. When he came to, he found himself a prisoner. Afterwards he said, 'I guess that was the lowest I ever felt in my life. I had hardly eaten or slept during the fighting at St Vith. I just felt beaten to the ground'.*

But although Hoffmann-Schonborn's grenadiers broke through 'Cox's Army', they got little further. They were spotted by the Seventh's artillery. For the American gunners they offered 'a wonderful target'. The Germans were milling around the hilltop village of Wallerode and now the gunners 'threw everything at Wallerode but the shoes on their feet', as a participant recorded.

Within thirty minutes the German attack had fizzled out. The 295th Regiment withdrew badly shaken, its commander wounded. Hoffmann-Schonborn was not to capture the railway station at St Vith that day.

That one-eyed machine-gunner with the over-active imagination had spent the night in a foxhole with two buddies on the Belgian side of the River Our. Plagued by the memories of that first day when the Germans had come charging at the positions of the 424th Regiment, Harry Martin had slept little. He was glad when dawn came. Someone had told him that Hitler wanted all the Americans out of the Fatherland. Now they were in Belgium and Harry Martin told his buddies that 'maybe Hitler would leave us alone'.

That morning they heard that a spy had been shot in the nearby village of Burg-Reuland. That didn't cheer Harry and his buddies up particularly. Perhaps they weren't safe in Belgium after all? Martin's nerves started to act up once more. The men guarding the Our had orders to fire one shot each if they spotted any Germans attempting to cross it and 'then run like hell'.

Some time that morning a rifle shot rang out to their right. Harry and his two buddies, Williams and Yannucci, didn't wait to see what

---

* But not for good. Colonel Riggs would escape once more, work his way to the Russian lines and fight for ten days with them before being sent to Italy. Here he insisted on being sent back to the fighting, otherwise he'd turn into a 'basket case'. The authorities allowed him to return, although it was against US Army policy. In March, 1945, he rejoined his old outfit.

was happening. They raised their rifles and fired and then they were up out of their freezing foxhole and 'running like hell'. They kept running for about fifteen minutes until one of the company officers stopped them. He told them it had been a false alarm and ordered them back to their foxhole. Feeling a little foolish they trudged back the way they had come. Later, as they crouched shivering in their hole at the side of the river, Yannucci said, 'There's been a casualty.'

The other two stared at him. Harry Martin asked, 'Who?'

Sourly Yannucci answered, 'My condom.' I just shot the hell out of it.' He explained, 'I put a condom over the end of my rifle to keep the dampness out and I forgot to take it off when I fired the rifle.'

Harry Martin laughed for the first time in five days. 'Don't worry about it,' he said. 'I'm sure this is the only way you'll use one of them up here.'

He was right.

But there was precious little to laugh about on this grey foggy day. When a fuming Bruce Clarke was finally released by his captors and arrived at his new CP in a *Gasthaus* in the village of Neuendorf, south-west of St Vith, the news that met him was not good.

Ammunition and food were running low. Clarke ordered that ammunition rations should be cut to one third. He told his artillery commanders, 'Use artillery only if the situation looks critical.' Then he ordered rations cut.

By now Clarke knew from prisoners that he was facing three *Volksgrenadier* divisions, the 2nd Panzer Grenadier Regiment of the 1st SS, plus parts of the 2nd and 116th Panzer Divisions, and Remer's Führer Escort Brigade. Pitted against his mixed bunch of some 20,000 men holding a perimeter of thirty-two miles, there were three infantry divisions, parts of three tank divisions, with another armoured division, the 9th SS, on its way. He was outnumbered by at least three to one.

Help was on the way, he knew, in the shape of the 82nd Airborne Division of General Ridgway's XVIII Airborne Corps, to which the St Vith's defenders now belonged. But on the 20th the nearest airborne units were thirteen miles away. Could they reach him before the Germans launched a decisive attack on the perimeter? Somehow he felt they wouldn't. But he told no one his gloomy thoughts. Going outside his CP, he spotted a sergeant trailing his feet, his hands black from powder burns.

'How are things going?' Clarke asked. 'Rough?'

'Yeah,' the NCO said tersely.

'Well things are looking up,' Clarke tried to encourage him. 'General Patton is driving up from the south.'

The sergeant's unshaven face broke into a grin, 'Well now,' he said, 'that makes a different story. If old Georgie is coming we've got it made.' He saluted quickly and went off.

Clarke knew George Patton. He had served under him for nearly a year. But again he wondered, just as he had done with the 82nd Airborne, whether even 'Ole Blood an' Guts' could make it in time.

Montgomery, dressed in a camouflaged smock and red beret, complete with the silver winged badge of the 'Red Devils', appeared in the town square at Bilsen at eleven. He went into the caravan of a local brigadier, briefed General Dempsey, commander of his 2nd Army, what the new task was, then stepped out into the square packed with troops. Smiling and alert, he told the soldiers to gather round him.

Brigadier H. Essame of the 43rd Infantry Division who was there thought 'his manner was paternal and unhurried. He radiated confidence.' About noon he left in his jeep. Monty was on his way to the new battle.

He was in his element. The Yanks had made a mess of things. He had been saying for months that they would. They had insisted in spreading their troops in 'penny packets' all along the Western Front. It was all part of Ike's 'Broadfront strategy'. But you didn't win wars by spreading your divisions all over the place. You concentrated. Then you struck the decisive blow. Every student of military history knew that. '*The fustest with the mostest*,' Mosley had described it aptly if somewhat inelegantly in the American Civil War. No matter. He was in charge now. He'd 'tidy up the battlefield' and eventually, in his own time 'see off the Hun'. After all he now had twenty American divisions under his command.

At about one o'clock that Wednesday Monty strode into Hodges' new headquarters at Chaudfontaine. His first words to Hodges and his staff were, 'Well, gentlemen, I gather that a difficult situation has arisen. Now tell me the form.'

Hodges obliged and, according to Belchem, 'It was obvious to us that his communications system was in disarray and the most serious of his worries was that two of his divisions appeared to have been surrounded and captured or destroyed by the enemy.'

Montgomery listened attentively, then asked if he could be alone with Belchem. Hodges gave him a spare room in the hut. The first thing that Montgomery said to Belchem was that the two missing US Divisions 'could not have been overwhelmed in such a short time'. He was going to send his scouts to find them and 'if successful, to explain the situation and to request the commanders concerned to withdraw westwards to positions where they could link up with other US divisions.'

Montgomery had been left for dead on the battlefield as a young officer in 1914. Throughout that war he hated generals who threw their men into battle regardless of the casualties. Ever since 1942, when he had gone out to Africa to take command of the Eighth Army, he had always been mindful of his soldiers, trying to keep casualties to a minimum. Now his first concern was the men of the 106th and 28th Divisions. So far no American general, from Eisenhower through Bradley right down to Middleton, had shown one bit of interest in the welfare of the men who had taken the brunt of the fighting. Nor would they ever do afterwards. The GIs of the 106th and 28th had been expendable. They had played their role and that was that.

After discussing the situation with Belchem, Montgomery returned to the conference. He told the Americans that he knew the Germans would attempt to cross the Meuse south of Liège. He felt that an immediate American counter-attack in the north was out of the question. 'I propose,' he continued, 'that you assemble a corps north-west of Marche for a counter-attack. But first we must sort out the battlefield, tidy up the lines.' He concluded: 'The primary job is to pull everyone out of the great St Vith pocket.'

Hodges didn't like that. American commanders never liked the idea of giving up ground for which they had fought. So the fate of the men defending the perimeter at St Vith hung in the balance. Hodges maintained that the St Vith salient would be a valuable bridgehead for the northern counter-attack. Montgomery argued that, as Belchem put it, 'sporadic counter-attacks hastily mounted would be of no avail in the conditions obtaining.' First there would have to be a continuous front. Second there would be the need to concentrate a reserve corps behind it 'in order to plan and execute a co-ordinated counter-attack in conjunction with Patton's Third Army.'

It was about then that an exhausted colonel was ushered into the conference. On his shoulder he bore the triangular patch of the Seventh Armored. He was Lt-Colonel Fred Schroeder, General Hasbrouck's chemical warfare officer. With him he brought a letter from Hasbrouck which he handed to Hodges. The latter read it hastily and then said, 'Gentlemen, I think you'll find this news from St Vith interesting.' He read aloud:

'Dear Bill [Hoge]: I am out of touch with VIII Corps and understand XVIII Airborne Corps is coming in. My division is defending the line St Vith-Poteau inclusive. CCB, 9th Armored Division [Hoge], the 424th Infantry Regiment [Reid] and 112th Regiment of the 28th Division [Nelson] are on my right and hold from St Vith (exclusive) to Holdingen. Both infantry regiments are in bad shape. My right flank is wide open except for some reconnaissance elements, TDs and stragglers we have collected into defense teams at road centers as far back as Cheram inclusive. Two German divisions, 112th Panzer and 560 Volksgrenadier, are just starting to attack north-west with their right on Gouvy. I can delay them the rest of today but will be cut off by tomorrow. VIII Corps had ordered me to hold and I will do so, but need help. An attack from Bastogne to the north-east will relieve the situation and, in turn, cut the bastards off in the rear. I also need plenty of air support. Am out of contact with VIII Corps so am sending this to you. Understand 82nd Airborne Division is coming up to my north and the north flank is not critical.

Bob Hasbrouck.'

Now Hodges said, 'In the light of this new information, Ridgway's XVIII Corps will have to keep driving forward toward St Vith to Hasbrouck's relief.'

Montgomery conceded the point. 'I agree,' he said, 'that the chaps in St Vith must be helped.' But it had to be done his way. Ridgway should continue to attack to open an escape route for the Seventh Armored. Once that had been done, the line of defence had to be shortened drastically. 'After all, gentlemen,' he concluded, 'you can't win the big victory without a tidy show.'

Montgomery had no intention of wasting any further American lives for the sake of prestige. Men were too precious. He'd let the US Top Brass have their way for a little longer, then he would act. No wonder Bruce Clarke admired Montgomery to the end of his life. As his son noted: 'Dad once drew up a list of generals involved with the period 16–24 December, 1944, and gave them *yes* or *no* ratings, depending on his view of how effectively they had dealt with the situations they had confronted at this time. *Yes* ratings went to Montgomery, Hasbrouck and Hoge. *No* ratings went to Hodges, Ridgway, Middleton and Jones.'

At Neufchâteau no one briefed the Field-Marshal on the situation of the 28th Division or the situation at Wiltz. So the man who had fought Pancho Villa in Mexico back in 1916, Colonel Daniel Strickler, the last commander of the 28th's 110th Infantry Regiment, had to make his own decisions. For him no help came from higher headquarters. Neither General Cota nor General Middleton were concerned. Strickler had to fend for himself.

By now Wiltz was surrounded and by-passed. Troops on either flank had been pushed back by the 'Green Devils'. Already the paras were on the heights above the blazing city. Strickler could do nothing about it. His command seemed to have melted away. There were still odd pockets of the provisional battalion that had been assigned to him for the defence of Wiltz holding out. But mostly his men had withdrawn in the direction of Bastogne with or without orders.

Now he decided that it was time for him to abandon his command post. He tore the situation map off the wall, pulled from it the piece detailing the area around Bastogne and set fire to the rest. As an afterthought he grabbed a compass. It was going to prove very useful in the days to come. Then, with a Major Plitt and his driver, Corporal Robert Martin, he set off in his jeep.

Martin steered the jeep through the battle-littered streets and they cleared the dying town. Then a mortar bomb hit the cobbled road to their front. The jeep skidded and ploughed into the ditch. For a while the three men tried to get it out, but to no avail. It wouldn't budge. Strickler cocked his ear to the thunder of the guns. They were German and they were not firing at Wiltz, but towards Bastogne. He explained that that meant Bastogne was under attack, but with luck and care they could make it on foot.

John Marshall of the Misfits was already there. For him it was 'a picture of frenzied confusion. Thousands of men, some sick or wounded, some dying, some falling into groups to go into battle.

Countless trucks, jeeps, tanks and vehicles of every description: some manned, many abandoned. It was the scene of a great calamity.'

Marshall bulled his way through the confusion. He found a house behind the church and opened the door. 'The place was packed with people. They gave me a chair and in moments I was given bread and chunks of cheese and American coffee. There were quite a few women present, several nicely dressed and wearing high heels. One of them, quite attractive I thought, asked in fractured English, "Boche comin"?'

Years later Marshall recalled, 'I was dirty, smelly and unshaven, but I was an American soldier. These people, warm, clean and fed, were looking for assurance.' Although the artillery thundered outside and the night sky was red with the explosion of shells, 'I lied and said, "No, they're not coming."'

Then he went out, back to the war.

There were many American soldiers like Marshall that night. They had lost their leaders. They knew nothing of the 'big picture.' They were little men caught up in the turmoil of a great battle. But they did their best, kept their heads and prepared, if necessary, to fight and die for their country.

The Germans had found the last battered remains of the 106th on that hillside, miles behind enemy lines, that morning. At first the Germans did nothing but play music through loudspeakers, broken by invitations to surrender.

Mario Garbin remembered the Germans shouting through the series of loudspeakers they had strung up in the trees around the US position: 'Hey fellows, what the hell you wanna stay up there and freeze your ass off for? Hell, you're up to your ass in water.'

They were right. The Americans' foxholes were ankle-deep in mud and melted snow.

Then the loudspeakers would bellow, 'Hey, fellas, why don't you come on over? We've got hot food, hot dogs and good stuff? Come on in for a hot shower and clean sheets.'

As Garbin recalled years later. 'That really broke us up. We hadn't seen sheets since we left the US and we sure as hell knew they didn't have any.'

But the invitations, the taunts and the music began to have an effect. Major Fridline, the 423rd's regimental surgeon, who had done such yeoman work with casualties over the last few days, recalled seeing a soldier sitting in a ditch, tears streaming down his dirty cheeks, yelling every few moments in the direction of the loudspeakers, 'Blow it out, you German son of a bitch!'

'There wasn't much we could do about it,' one survivor recalled. 'It just made us awful mad. It sounded as if the bastards were all around us.'

The Germans were, and they were getting closer. But they were second-line troops. They were not prepared to make a frontal attack or suffer too many casualties. They left it to the men of the *Propagandakompanie* – their psychological warfare troops – to talk the *Amis* into surrender.

But they had not broken the trapped men's resistance altogether. Staff Sergeant Thomas of Lieutenant Walker's H Company rounded up a few volunteers. They crept up to a little hill where the German sound truck had been set up. Thomas lobbed a grenade at it and it reared up on its back axle, flames spurting from the interior. Then, as the historian of the 106th records, 'Berlin Betty's playful references to the joys of playing baseball in a POW camp ended.'

Shortly after noon Sergeant Thomas went out again. He had spotted a German recon car coming from Schönberg with a white flag attached to its cab. Thomas came back with a German officer and a medic from the 423rd who had been captured earlier. They asked for permission to use the roadnet dominated by the trapped men in order to evacuate German and American wounded.

Majors Moon and Ouellette agreed. They would order their men not to open fire. But at the same time they sent Lieutenant Houghton back with the German medic to check that the enemy were not using the ambulances (mostly captured US ones) to transport troops.

After darkness had fallen Houghton returned to say that the Germans had artillery trained on the hill and infantry were preparing to attack. Moon looked worried, but said nothing.

A little later Garbin was on duty on the perimeter defences when out of the woods 'walked an SS sergeant, black uniform, death's head insignia, highly polished boots and all. He was the epitome of military courtesy, saluting and so forth.'*

After introducing himself the NCO 'began his pitch'. He said, 'I'm

---

* Allied soldiers often confused the black uniform of German armoured troops with that of the peacetime SS.

157

authorized to guarantee you protection under the Geneva Convention if you surrender now. If you decide not to surrender, that's okay too. But I want you to know that we've advanced ten miles past your position already, and when we've got time we're going to come back and clean you up. Then we won't ask you to surrender. We'll just get rid of you. We won't want to be bothered.'

That was the 'sour'. Now the German tried the 'sweet' technique. 'Fellows, let me tell you something. I was a prisoner twice of you Americans and you guys really treated me right. I appreciated that. This isn't a trick. If you don't agree to come out, you're dead. Think hard and take good advice. Come out honourably.'

Garbin and his officer took the English-speaking German to Major Moon. Garbin thought that 'this guy's speech was just another one of their psychological ploys.' But 'he must have made one hell of an impression on our commanding officer.'

Garbin was right. After conferring with the other officers he decided to surrender, though the indomitable Walker, wounded as he was, was in favour of holding out for another couple of days just in case the promised airdrop might come.

Moon agreed to surrender under certain conditions. He wanted time to prepare his men for the ordeal to come. As Walker recalled, 'We took a chance to give our men time to get some sleep, gather what food they could, scrounge some extra clothing from all the bags in the area, and for those who felt they could a chance to escape. Many attempted, as evidenced by small arms fire all night long, save to the east.'

Garbin felt that the men took the news they were soon to surrender quite well, except 'this one guy who had come to us after fleeing from Poland and joining the US Army. He had lost his mother and sisters to atrocities. He was raging. He couldn't believe we were going to surrender. He just went crazy. He tried to kill Moon. Finally we had to knock him to the ground and tie him up.'

So they slept, passing away their last night as free men for a long time. Here and there individual men crept away chancing their luck. One man who had fought the Germans in the First World War and then in Italy in the Second declared, 'No Kraut is gonna get me.' He slipped away. No one ever saw him again. The last organized American resistance in the German Eifel was about to come to an end.

*

Twelve miles away from where the exhausted men now slept, the ubiquitous Major Don Boyer, 'the unsung hero of the battle for St Vith', as Captain Mattocks called him, was checking his little command before he turned in for an hour's sleep. He crept from foxhole to foxhole in the freezing darkness. Although he did his best to be cheerful and encourage his men, he could see that they were almost at the end of their tether. They were hungry and exhausted. Ammunition was low and virtually every one was suffering to some degree from the effects of frostbite.

'We're in a tough spot,' he told one man who was all by himself in a foxhole on outpost duty among the shattered trees, 'and I feel you should know it. We're like a thumb sticking in Fritz's throat.'

The man's reply is not recorded. Perhaps he was one of those many who would be killed on the following day. But Boyer was right. They were sticking down 'Fritz's throat', and one Fritz in particular, Hasso von Manteuffel, was determined they wouldn't do so much longer. On the morrow he would launch an all-out attack to rid himself of that irritating digit for good.

Just as Boyer reached his command post a handful of exhausted men started to struggle through his lines. Some were unarmed and others were without their helmets and they were barely recognizable as American soldiers. Fortunately for them, the freezing cold slowed down the trigger fingers of the defenders. They were allowed through and identified themselves. They were last survivors of Colonel Cavender's 423rd Infantry Regiment.

Boyer had no exact figures of the size of the two regiments of infantry which had surrendered in the German Eifel, nor did he know their casualties. But he could make an educated guess at how large a regiment would be with its attached arms of engineers, artillery, tank destroyer men, etc. There must then have been between eight and ten thousand men on that hilltop, he guessed.

The knowledge shattered him. A larger number of soldiers had surrendered to the Japs in the Philippines back in 1942, but a lot of that number had not been Americans, but locals. So this had to be the biggest number of American soldiers to surrender to the enemy since the Civil War nearly a hundred years before.

About the same time that Major Boyer was doing his rounds, Hasbrouck was still in his office in Vielsalm wondering what had happened to his high-ranking courier to the 1st Army HQ, Colonel Schroeder. Finally, at eight o'clock Schroeder made his appearance after a hectic trip back. Hasbrouck was so glad to see him that he rose and shook him heartily by the hand. Coffee and sandwiches were brought and Schroeder told his C.O. that not only had he seen the Army Commander, Hodges, but he'd also spoken to Field-Marshal Montgomery. He, Hasbrouck, could expect a visit from Montgomery in the near future. Hasbrouck, who had served under Montgomery before in Holland when the Germans broke through the 7th Armored and nearly threatened the Field-Marshal's HQ, wondered if he would enjoy that visit. But for the time being he concentrated on the message Schroeder had brought from Hodges.

It read: 'Ridgway with armor and infantry is moving from west to gain contact with you. When communication is established, you come under command of Ridgway. You retain under your command following units: 106 Division (R.C.T. 112) and CCB 9th Armored Division.'

It was good news and Hasbrouck felt a sense of relief. At last aid for his hard-pressed command was on the way. At the same time, however, the message made his life more complicated. Now, according to Hodges' order, he was in command of Hoge of the 9th Armored who outranked him as well as Jones, who was a major-general.

At about the same time Hasbrouck received the message from 1st Army telling him that his command was to pass over to Ridgway's XVIII Airborne Corps, Jones received one from Middleton. It read: 'There is a large attack on Bastogne from the direction of Houffalize. It has reached a point six kilometres east of Bastogne. Can you send something small to attack the enemy in the rear? The 112th Infantry has a battalion near Gouvy. If it is not engaged ask the commanding general to have it advance in direction of Bastogne and hit the enemy from the rear.'

One hour later Middleton sent Jones another message relayed from 1st Army HQ. Dated the day before, it said that a defence line should be established from St Vith to Echternach, and 'enemy in rear of line will be isolated and destroyed where found. There will be no withdrawal'.

These messages indicate just how badly Eisenhower's plan had gone. A brigadier-general was giving orders to two other generals senior to him. The brigadier general was supposed to take orders from one corps commander, Ridgway, while one of his subordinate generals was accepting orders from another corps commander, Middleton. To cap it all, an army commander was ordering one of those subordinate generals, whose division was virtually decimated, to hold on to two towns, Echternach and St Vith, which were already lost, with a force that was surrounded and fighting for its very life. It was a scene of total confusion. Montgomery could hardly have imagined just how untidy 'the show' was.

Wearily, for he had not seen a bed since he had left Holland three days before, Hasbrouck tried to clear up the command mess. He wrote a note to General Bill Kean, Hodges' chief-of-staff: 'General Jones is a major-general and I am a brigadier. His being attached to me makes it look as though he had failed in some respect and I want to put myself on record as saying he is in the saddle in control of his outfit and that we are cooperating in the best possible way. If my note [he meant the one that Schroeder had taken to 1st Army HQ] gave any other impression, I want to correct it at once before an injustice is done.'

Then on the carbon copy Hasbrouck wrote a footnote to Jones stating that 'this is being dispatched at once with a copy to General Ridgway. I hope it will correct any misimpression my note to General Kean may have caused'.

We do not know General Jones's reaction on receipt of that carbon but he must have been greatly surprised to discover that he was no longer under Middleton's command, but under that of an airborne corps commander.

Hasbrouck no longer cared. His job on the morrow would be fighting the Germans, not making peace between the generals. He let his head sink to the desk. Next moment he was fast asleep.

The Supreme Commander slept too, though his sleep could hardly have been sound. All day he had been incarcerated in his locked and shuttered room at Versailles, guarded by a battalion of MPs. If he left his office, he must take a tank to go to another building. That was the order of his chief-of-security, worried by the fact that Skorzeny's killers were already congregating in Paris, waiting for a chance to assassinate Eisenhower.

But Eisenhower had other problems than that of the assassination threat. It had been his intention to keep secret the fact that Montgomery had taken over the northern shoulder of the Bulge, together with two US armies. But the secret had only lasted until the afternoon.

Worried by the confused events taking place in the Ardennes, Prime Minister Churchill had returned from a liquid lunch to worry Field-Marshal Sir Alan Brooke about the command set-up there. First he wanted to telephone Montgomery, but Brooke advised him not to go behind Eisenhower's back. For the Premier wanted to suggest to Montgomery that he should take over in the north. Instead Brooke, who knew he had to keep strict control of his political master when he was in one of his moods, suggested he make the proposal direct to the Supreme Commander.

Thus at five o'clock that afternoon Eisenhower was forced to reveal to Churchill that Montgomery had been in command in the north since ten o'clock that morning. Churchill was appeased. He and Brooke now waited expectantly for Montgomery's nightly telegram. (It had to be censored before Brooke dared show it to the Prime Minister, for it ended tongue-in-cheek with, 'We can not come out by DUNKIRK this time as the Germans hold that place'.)

But it wasn't the revealing of that secret alone that worried Eisenhower that night; it was that Montgomery was not going to stick to the strategy which he had hammered out at Verdun. As Commander Butcher, Eisenhower's PR man, recorded it: 'The general plan is to plug the holes in the north and launch co-ordinated attack from the south'. Already Eisenhower had indications that Montgomery had no intention of 'plugging the holes'. Nor did Monty seem ready to launch an immediate counter-attack as Eisenhower had planned the previous day.

Montgomery and his handling of the northern 'shoulder' were Eisenhower's main problems, but Patton was also causing headaches. At Verdun he had boasted he would attack with six divisions on the 22nd, but three of the divisions which they had earmarked for that attack (the 106th, 28th and the 7th Armored) seemed to have disappeared. Did this now mean that Patton would not be strong enough to break through the German flank guard in the south provided by the enemy's Seventh Army? If the enemy did stop Patton there or even delayed him, von Manteuffel's Fifth Panzer could well capture a bridge across the Meuse.

It was something that Bradley, who was providing Eisenhower with most of his limited information from the front, did not appear to be taking seriously. He had cabled Bradley in the early hours of the 20th that it was vital to secure the Meuse bridges against enemy attack. So far Bradley had not reported back that this had been done.

Eisenhower didn't know that his cable was considered so unimportant by Bradley's staff that they didn't give him it till hours later. Nor did he know that all Bradley was ever to do about securing the Meuse bridges was to send a staff officer to inspect them – and that was done on 25 December when the danger was over.

Nor did Eisenhower realize that, like himself, Bradley was virtually a prisoner of his own security men. He had given up his Cadillac with its three general's stars. Instead he rode around in an unmarked open jeep in the freezing December weather. He was also persuaded by his security chief to give up his helmet with its three general's stars. At his headquarters at the Hotel Alfa he entered through the back door and kitchen. He changed his bedroom at the hotel every night. Just as Eisenhower's security men felt that the Supreme Commander was a target for Skorzeny's killers, Bradley's thought that German assassins dressed in American uniforms might attack the Army Group Commander at any moment.

Besides, Bradley was depressed. The fact that Eisenhower had taken two armies from him and given them to Montgomery meant that the Supreme Commander had lost confidence in him. He had failed to execute the deception correctly. His aide, Major Hansen, noted in his diary that 'he [Bradley] has let paper work go hang itself ... Don't feel like looking at it.' A week before, Bradley had commanded sixty divisions. Now he was down to a mere handful, with Patton, his former boss, soon to emerge as the general who really made the decisions.

He, too, did not sleep very soundly that Wednesday. One man who *did* was Field-Marshal Montgomery. Fortune had favoured him once again. A week before he had been so bored with the war on the Western Front and his lack of ability to control the Allies' grandstrategy that he had asked Eisenhower for permission to go home at Christmas and visit his young son. Now, in a surprise change, he was in charge of two US armies in addition to his own British 21st Army Group. He exulted when Eisenhower gave him command of the northern 'shoulder'. Later he would signal Brooke that 'He [Eisenhower] was excited [when he called Montgomery to tell him he had been given the new task] and it was difficult to understand what he was talking about; he roared into the telephone speaking very fast. The only point I really grasped was ... that I was to assume command of the northern front. This is all I wanted to know. He then went on talking wildly about other things. I could not hear and said so; at last the line cut out before he finished.' The signal could not disguise Montgomery's contempt of Eisenhower as a ground commander. He had made a mistake. Now, as Montgomery saw it, he was panicking.

Every war, it is said, produces its own heroes. In the Second World War, the British had to wait a very long time for theirs. Three years of defeat after defeat until Monty made his appearance in the Western Desert and saw off Rommel. He was of a different type from the great national military heroes of the First World War. He possessed no inherited wealth, nor did he have important connections at Court as his predecessor, Field-Marshal Haig, had had. He didn't belong to one of the fashionable cavalry regiments as had Haig, Gough and Plumer in the First War. He had started his career in the Royal Warwickshire Regiment.

In a way Montgomery was a mixture of old and new. There was something plebeian about him. He was pushy and concerned with PR. His dress was deliberately sloppy. He cultivated a funny taste in baggy pants and would appear on the battlefield carrying an umbrella, just like the Duke of Wellington. He collected silly military hats and adorned them with several badges as his fancy took him. For him there were no official military dinners where the 'port was passed'. He usually served water to his guests.

He knew his ordinary British 'squaddie', or thought he did. He appeared to abhor 'bull' − 'if it moves, salute it; if it doesn't, whitewash it' sort of thing. His soldiers felt he wouldn't waste their lives unnecessarily. With him there would be no great blood-lettings like the Somme or Ypres. When, early in the war, his men of the 3rd Infantry Division started to catch V.D. in France, he said they should get free condoms and sent to supervised French brothels. That nearly cost him his job.

But there was plenty of the Imperial British past in Monty's make-up as well. In some respects he was the worst kind of Victorian prig. He was a non-smoker and non-drinker. In a profession given to drink, whores and profanity, Montgomery stood out as the exception. He might be liked by the men, but his fellow officers found him suspect.

Those same Victorian qualities did not endear him to the Americans either. He did not keep a mistress like most of his fellow American commanders. He wasn't 'one of the boys', who you could slap on the back and play cards with. Montgomery was clearly born to command and gave off that English air of superiority which so irritated his US counterparts.

Now for the last time in the Second World War he was in charge. It was the chance that he had been waiting for since the late summer, when he had been removed from control of the Allied land armies. He now had the opportunity to prove himself once more. Eisenhower had given him command. Bradley was out of the running. As for Patton's drive in the south, he shared Alan Brooke's opinion of it as 'a half-baked affair and I doubt it's doing much good'.

His strategy would be simple. As he explained it in his memoirs: 'I found the northern flank of the bulge was very disorganized. Ninth Army had two corps and three divisions. First Army had three corps and fifteen divisions. Neither Army Commander had seen Bradley or any senior member of his staff since the battle began [fourteen years after the battle, Montgomery still could not refrain from making the dig at Bradley] and they had no direction on which to work.

'The first thing to do was to see the battle on the northern flank *as one whole* to ensure the vital areas were held securely and to create reserves for a counter-attack.'

Montgomery would now run the battle his way. Eisenhower's plan to lure the Germans out of their fortifications and then strike them a decisive blow would not come to fruition now. Already the Eisenhower scheme had cost America 20,000 of its sons killed, wounded or captured. Before it was all over another 60,000 would go down that same path.

DAY SIX:

Thursday, 21 December, 1944

Weather: Heavy snowfall. Fog. Roads muddy and slippery.

'It looks like Custer's last stand to me.'

General Clarke.

Inside the perimeter at St Vith the defenders waited. They were tired and running out of ammunition. For the moment there was silence. Their own guns weren't allowed to fire. They had to save shells. But they could hear the rumble of German armour and the creak and jingle of horse-drawn transport as they brought up their limbers and cannon.

Now, in the morning stillness, they could hear the German NCOs shouting their orders. Signal flares sailed into the sky and exploded with a sharp crack, bathing the snow below in unreal light.

For the most part the Americans were spread out along the ridge lines and hills, but there were gaps between their formations, and in most cases the Germans would have the cover of the woods, save where here and there it was broken by a field. Some of the more enterprising of the defenders had placed marking sticks to give the range in the snowfields to their front, but the veterans of the Seventh Armored knew the attackers would come behind the protection of their armour; marker sticks wouldn't be much use for men armed only with rifles and automatics.

Although they had been expecting it since dawn, the beginning of the German bombardment startled the defenders. With a great howl, a battery of German *Nebelwerfers* opened up. Their huge shells sailed into the sky, trailing black smoke behind them. Next instant they were hurtling down to smash into the trees and fields all along the perimeter. The whole horizon erupted into flame. Shells and mortar bombs began to rain down on the Americans as they cowered at the bottoms of their foxholes, with the tree bursts snapping off the tops of the pines like match sticks.

The attack came in small groups – grenadiers in white smocks, grouped tightly behind tanks grinding forward in low gear, their machine guns chattering to keep the defenders' heads down. Everywhere they probed the defence looking for a weak spot. Here and

169

there were lone Germans sneaking forward to throw a stick grenade. As Major Boyer wrote later: 'The Krauts kept boring in no matter how fast we decimated their assault squads. Again and again there was a flare of flame and smoke as some Kraut got close enough to heave a grenade into a machine gun crew or launch a Panzerfaust. One calibre 50 squad which had been dishing out a deadly hail of fire was hit by a Panzerfaust, which struck the barrel between the breech and muzzle. The gunner fell forward on the gun with half his face torn off; the loader had his left arm torn off at the shoulder and was practically decapitated while the gun commander was tossed about 15 feet away from the gun to lie there quite still.'

But as Major Boyer remembered: 'Whenever a machine-gun crew was killed off, other men leaped from their holes to take over the guns. Always there were more Germans and more Germans, and then more Germans – attacking and reattacking for better than one and a half hours.'

The Germans had by-passed Captain Carl Mattocks' CP after knocking out the 57mm anti-tank they had set up outside. Now he wondered what he should do. The CO was still unable to act, a victim of combat fatigue, and he was lumbered with two civilians.

But now the Germans made up his minds for him. Suddenly two Germans blundered into the CP. Perhaps they were looking for loot. Sergeant Vaught, a communications NCO, reacted first. He whipped up his carbine and fired. The German slammed against the wall, dead before he could slither to the floor.

The other turned. '*Amerikaner*!' he yelled and made an attempt to bolt, but Mattocks was quicker. He fired a burst from his grease gun. The bullets ripped the length of the fleeing man's left side. He stumbled out. Then his knees gave way and he slipped to the snow.

Together with Sergeant Davies, Mattocks hurried to the German lying in the snow. His face was black with frostbite. Davies placed his fingers under the German's nose. 'He's not breathing, Captain.' Mattocks nodded. He grabbed the dead man's burp gun, smashed it up and threw ammunition into the deep snow. Just then the 'dead' man came to and mumbled weakly, '*Doktor*'.

But Mattocks had no time to find aid for the wounded German. He knew that he and what was left of his little command were fighting for their lives. The men hurriedly started to bury a few mines they had found in the snow. Perhaps, with luck, they might stop some unsuspecting German tank. Then they were off again, heading into the unknown.

Everywhere the American defenders were being forced back. Marching down a narrow road between banks of snow two foot high Harry Martin and his buddies of the 424th Regiment couldn't understand why. 'We withdrew in bewilderment. We wondered why we were retreating. We had stopped the Germans on the sixteenth and we had not been under German pressure since that first day of the battle. We hated like hell to retreat, knowing that whatever ground we gave up we would have to take back before this darn war would be over. We didn't even stop to eat but kept on the go while passing 10-in-1 rations from one man to the next.'

What Martin and his buddies didn't know was that by noon the Germans were successfully infiltrating everywhere and that two German assault groups were making a determined attempt to cut off the defenders' rear. In the case of Lieutenant Pennino's 48th Armored Infantry Battalion, a group of daring SS troopers sneaked into the positions of the Battalion's B Company. Before anyone was aware of it, the Germans had started up and driven off twenty fully equipped White halftracks, filled with the men's personal effects.

Some soldiers objected violently to being ordered to retreat.

Three days before, the 106th's 589th Artillery, which had escaped the débâcle in the Eifel, had been ordered to take up its positions at a roadblock in the tiny Belgian hamlet of Baraque-de-Fraiture.

Major Parker, acting commander of the 589th, set up his three remaining howitzers to defend the crossroads and waited; but nothing happened. The artillerymen could hear hundreds of guns firing elsewhere and see the scarlet flashes of cannonfire lighting up the night sky. But their positions seemed to be a little oasis of peace, forgotten by friend and foe alike.

But the Germans had not forgotten what was to become known as 'Parker's Crossroads'. They knew its importance; for the crossroads was situated on the inner flank of two US divisions coming up to support Clarke's hard-pressed men – Ridgway's 82nd Airborne and 3rd Armored Divisions of the XVIII Airborne Corps. If the Germans cut through the crossroads they'd stop any attempt to withdraw from the salient.

Not only that, Baraque-de-Fraiture was situated on what was probably the most important road in Belgium that December –

Highway N.15. *Route Nationale* 15 was one of the few wide, well-paved roads running through the Ardennes and the Germans vitally needed that road for their tracked vehicles for the drive on the Meuse. Unwittingly, when the divisional artillery commander had placed Parker and his men on that lonely crossroads he had put them right on the path of 2nd SS Panzer Division. *Das Reich* Division, one of the elite formations in the German Army, was heading on a collision course with Parker and his unsuspecting gunners!

All the previous day Parker and some volunteers from service units, one hundred and ten men in all, had been preparing their positions. He had sited each of his three howitzers to cover one road, thus forming a triangle. Each howitzer was supported by a handful of riflemen. There were also a couple of light machine guns to cover each position. Hacking and hewing at the iron-hard earth beneath the snow, the men had laid chains of anti-personnel mines. Then they had dug foxholes and laid telephone wires to connect each hole. It had been hard work, but at least it had kept them warm.

As the hours passed and nothing happened, Major Parker started to persuade other units to join him. They were either lost or stragglers, but they were glad to come under the command of someone who seemed to know what he was doing. In the end Major Parker had under command a reconnaissance company from the Seventh Armored, a self-propelled 37mm gun and an anti-aircraft battery, equipped with multiple-calibre machine guns. He was beginning to feel quite proud of his setup now. They were well sited and dug-in. They had food and ammunition and, although a little nervous, they had guts.

That morning the first contact came in. Twelve German cyclists were probing the perimeter from the west.

Ten minutes later the second contact report came in. Then another and another. After that the field telephone hissed repeatedly and men whistled softly into the instrument to attract attention and then gave their reports. German reconnaissance parties were prowling everywhere.

They were the men of Lucht's 58th Panzer Corps. The 2nd SS Panzer was experiencing fuel trouble, so Lucht had pushed ahead and sent in his men. Roads were scarce in the Ardennes. The arrogant bastards of the SS would have bumped him if they could, but they couldn't. So now he stole 'their' road.

The grenadiers came ploughing through the deep snow, greatcoat tails swinging, shouting and firing their burp guns from the hip. But if they thought they could roll over the green *Amis*, they were in for a disappointment. The GIs held their positions. What followed was short, sharp, and for the Americans, sweet. The Germans fled, leaving behind a dozen dead and fourteen prisoners.

The Golden Lions could fight too. They didn't need the constant messages coming in from the experienced 3rd Armored and 82nd Airborne, exhorting them 'to hold as long as you can'. They were paying back a score. They had suffered a defeat, unprecedented in the history of American arms in the Second World War, to avenge. They wouldn't budge.

That day Brooke sent a message to Montgomery which read: 'I want to give you a warning. Events and enemy action have forced on Eisenhower a more satisfactory system of command. I feel it is more important that you should not even in the slightest degree appear to rub this undoubted fact in to anyone at SHAEF or elsewhere. Any remarks you may make are bound to come to Eisenhower's ears sooner or later.'

But on that Thursday Montgomery had little time to concern himself with Eisenhower's feelings. His scouts, who he called his 'gallopers', were now returning from the various battlefronts. They brought with them a picture of the battle being fought in the old VIII Corps sector different from the one drawn by Hodges the previous day.

As Montgomery signalled to Brooke that day, it was all well and good for Patton to boast he would attack with six divisions, but three of those divisions were in chaos. 'I sent a Liaison Officer down that way yesterday and he returned tonight with a picture of a very disorganised front with divisions in bits and pieces all over the place.'

As a result, Montgomery viewed the chances of Patton's attack on the morrow with frank pessimism. 'My information about the situation in the south,' he wired Brooke that Thursday, 'about Bastogne is somewhat alarming and it looks to me as if the enemy columns are moving westwards, having passed that place.' What would be the value of Patton's attack then, even if he did succeed in breaking through the defensive screen provided by the German Seventh Army?

Montgomery had problems, too, with his new subordinate American commander, the hook-nosed leader of the US XVIII Airborne Corps. All that day, as Montgomery recorded, Ridgway had telephoned 'frequently, to say that he is being attacked in strength by an estimated two or three armored divisions'. Still Ridgway wanted to push on, link up with the battered units fighting desperately inside the perimeter and continue the battle on the same ground. That was not what Montgomery had in mind if he were 'to tidy up' the battlefield and defeat the enemy.

But Montgomery knew Ridgway and knew he didn't take kindly to orders from chairborne warriors, especially if they were British. Monty had first met the paratroop commander in Africa when the latter had been commanding the US 82nd Airborne Division. It, with the British 1st Airborne, was scheduled to jump over Sicily and lead the invasion of the island in July, 1943.

There, virtually from the start, Ridgway had clashed with Eisenhower's airborne adviser, the elegant General 'Boy' Browning. The open quarrel between the two men came to the notice of the Supreme Commander. Eisenhower tolerated no animosity between his American and British officers. As he was fond of saying, 'You can call the other guy a son-of-a-bitch. But if you call him a *limey* s.o.b., then pack your bags and go!'

At a meeting in Algiers Eisenhower had put Ridgway through the mill on account of his attitude to Browning. Ridgway had lost his temper and began defending his stand on the grounds that he was trying to defend the 'prestige of the US Army'. Now Eisenhower lost *his* temper. He had already got rid of one of his planning staff, General Huebner, on account of his anti-British stance. He hauled Ridgway over the coals, concluding by saying that Ridgway might as well 'start packing up, for he was going home'. Ridgway had appealed to Patton who had appeased Eisenhower and Ridgway had stayed in Africa at the head of the 82nd Airborne Division.

So Montgomery realized that Ridgway would be a prickly subordinate. He was an airborne soldier, trained in the airborne concept that paras were likely to be cut off in battle and would fight in this manner until help reached them. The perimeter *was* virtually cut off and he was battling to relieve the men in that perimeter. Once there, he would want to hold the ground that some of his soldiers had died to reach. Therefore, he would take unkindly to an order, especially from a British superior, to relinquish that ground. It involved, after all, the 'prestige of the US Army'.

Montgomery took Brooke's advice. He decided to keep his lips sealed and get on with the battle. He knew the Americans' almost pathological concern with not giving up ground, however worthless, which 'American blood has bought'. All the same he must not let Ridgway have his head. Once the link-up had been achieved, the battered defenders of the perimeter would *have* to be withdrawn.

It was Ridgway's old division, the 82nd Airborne which was in the van of the attack towards the perimeter – and they were finding it tough going. For they were faced with the premier division of the whole of the German *Wehrmacht*, the 1st SS – the Adolf Hitler Bodyguard – heavily armoured and led by commanders who had been fighting constantly since 1939.

All that the men of the 82nd (which was equally tough, for it had fought in Italy, France and Holland) had to fend off the German armour was a truckload of captured German panzerfausts. But the men of General 'Gentlemen Jim'* Gavin's 82nd were undismayed. They had fought the SS before and beaten them. They'd do it again.

They did so, but the cost was high. At Cheneux they bumped into a well-prepared enemy position, held by the 2nd SS Panzer Grenadier Regiment. The fanatical young German grenadiers were supported by flak cannon in a ground role. The paras decided to wait for darkness before they attacked.

Now, supported by two tank destroyers, Colonel Harrison's 1st Parachute Infantry Battalion started to cross four hundred yards of open ground to the Germans' front. The first wave of Americans stumbled forward. It was shot to pieces. The second wave suffered the same fate. But nothing could stop the 'All Americans', as the 82nd was called. The third wave got as far as the wire. They stumbled into the coils of wet barbed wire. But they had no wire-cutters!

But, as the survivors went to ground, still firing at the SS dug in and around the white houses above, the two tank destroyers worked their way to the side of the village. Their huge 90mm cannon started to thump. German machine-gun posts disappeared in balls of flame.

* 'Gentlemen Jim' on account of his handsome features and natty appearance. Marlene Dietrich always swore he had parachuted into the Ardennes to rescue her that December and they may have had a love affair afterwards when Gavin was in command in post-war Berlin.

Then the third wave was up and taking advantage of the opportunity offered them. They sprinted into the village street, littered with dead. Here and there they sprang onto the flak wagons which had shot up their comrades. No quarter was given or expected. Then they were through. The SS were pulling back and they had a few minutes to count the cost. It was high. One company was down to eighteen men and no officers. The other had thirty-eight men and three officers. The total in dead and wounded was 225 men. Only a handful of Germans were captured. They, too, had fought to the end.

But the survivors were proud, not only of their achievement, but of the fourteen German flak wagons which they had captured. Now, as 'Gentleman Jim' went up to visit them this Thursday, the survivors told him proudly, they were the 504th Parachute *Armored* Regiment. Later that day the Germans counter-attacked. Some of the very young German attackers were captured. They were asked by the battalion intelligence officer 'why they had come straight across open ground – shouting and yelling?' The prisoners replied that they had been doing it ever since the start of the offensive and up to now 'everybody has run away or surrendered!'

Gavin had to smile at that, but he made no comment. He knew his paras held the ordinary infantry of the line in contempt. So he left and crossed the Salm River to visit Jones's CP at Vielsalm. He was impressed by the CPs parking area which was packed with brand new administrative vehicles, including two huge trailers for making doughnuts!

Jones turned out to be 'the picture of dejection'. He told Gavin about his two lost regiments and said he was 'uncertain of what he had remaining'. Gavin decided he didn't particularly like the 'feel' of the 106th's CP. He left as soon as he could and went over to Hasbrouck's, who told Gavin that he was holding back several German divisions, but they were already moving around the flanks of the perimeter, heading west. He had been able to get a staff officer through to 1st Army to let HQ know how bad his situation was. He was cheered by the arrival of Gavin's 82nd, but still the problem was – either he was reinforced or he was withdrawn.

Gavin took the information to Ridgway who told him that the perimeter force would be probably withdrawn through the 82nd. Gavin could see that Ridgway was not impressed by Hasbrouck's remark that either he was reinforced or withdrawn, but he didn't comment on it. Instead he listened to Ridgway's order to make a reconnaissance of a good divisional defensive position for the 82d when the time came.

Gavin said he would and departed, leaving Ridgway to his thoughts, which weren't particularly pleasant. Hasbrouck's remark to Gavin made the 7th Armored's commander sound like a quitter – and Ridgway didn't like quitters. Neither did he like Montgomery's intention to withdraw. His airborne troops had been caught in situations like that of Hasbrouck more than once since they had first gone into action in Sicily. Why give up valuable ground? Why not stick it out and fight? Ridgway's distaste for Montgomery's plan began to harden. The fate of the 20,000 American troops trapped in the perimeter now hung in the balance.

Inside the perimeter things were going badly wrong. Hasbrouck had just received a signal from Ridgway in reply to his letter on the problem of command. Ridgway ordered the 'discontinuing' of the attachment of the 106th to Hasbrouck, but directed Jones to 'co-operate with 7th Armored Division to carry out court orders'. Hasbrouck must have thought he was going mad. He and Jones had been co-operating all the time. But there was no time to ponder the absurdity of the signal. His perimeter had been pierced in at least three places.

Up front, Major Boyer watched in fascinated horror as a line of German tanks rumbled across a ridge. Out of nowhere five Shermans came squelching through the snow to take up the challenge. At pointblank range the Germans fired blinding white flares. It was an old trick they had learned in Russia. Blinded by the sudden flash, the American tankers groped helplessly. One by one the Shermans were knocked out while Boyer watched impotently. The Panthers started to move forward. Boyer ducked into a snow-filled ditch. He waited with bated breath. But the German tanks moved past him in the glowing darkness with an uncanny sense of direction. Later Boyer guessed the Panthers were equipped with some kind of new night sight. He was right. The Germans did indeed have a top-secret infra-red night sight.

Desperately Clarke and Hasbrouck, both groggy now from lack of sleep, sought to hold their positions. Time and time again the Germans attacked them after a regular fifteen-minute artillery bombardment, against which the Americans could offer no counterfire;

they had virtually run out of shells. Relentlessly the enemy pushed into the perimeter.

Now there were no replacements for those killed or wounded. Up in the St Vith area Clarke had perhaps a hundred infantrymen left. Most of his tank destroyers were burning hulks or had vanished to God knows where. In that immediate area he had exactly four tanks left, one commanded by Lieutenant Will Rogers Junior. But on that day the son of the famed American humourist could find nothing to laugh about.

Now Clarke started to shorten his line. He ordered his men to the east and south-east to begin pulling back as soon as darkness fell. They set out in the blinding snowstorm, led by officers carrying a compass. But the enemy seemed to be everywhere and not many reached their destination.

Boyer held his positions to the very last. He had ordered that no more men would risk their lives to rush forward and take over the machine gun when a crew was knocked out. But at eight o'clock that night Boyer was told he could pull out his survivors; a new defensive line was being formed a thousand yards to the rear.

Wearily Boyer crept from foxhole to foxhole to relay General Clarke's order to his men: 'Save what vehicles you can. Attack to the west. We're forming a new line west of the town [St Vith]'.

He set off with them behind him in a single file. An intense snowstorm raged. They plodded on, their boots heavy with snow. All around them there were triumphant Germans, shouting, shooting off flares, looting what they could find in the newly abandoned American positions. After a while Boyer realized that so many men would be discovered sooner or later; the Germans were too close. Like Riggs before him, he ordered his men to split up into groups of four and five and make their way back to the new defensive line independently.

They said their goodbyes and set off once again. But, like Riggs, Boyer, 'the unsung hero', as Mattocks called him, was not fated to reach his own lines. On the following morning he and his little group reached a road leading out of St Vith. It was filled with German traffic. Boyer decided to hide out until it was safe to cross. He led his men up a snowy hillside to a stone wall. But as one of his soldiers crawled up the hillside he loosened a rock. It clattered noisily to the road below. Someone shouted in German. Then another voice cried in English that they'd better come out. They were surrounded. They would be mortared if they didn't surrender – *at once!*

Boyer knew he was finished. Exposed as they were on the hillside, it would be suicide to continue the fight. Slowly he stood up and raised his hands. Wearily he started to plod down the hillside in the deep snow.

Below on the road a smiling German officer waited for him. 'Just the fortunes of war,' the German told the bespectacled American officer sympathetically. 'Maybe I'll be a prisoner tomorrow.'

Desperately Clarke and Hasbrouck laboured to form the new defence line before the Germans attacked again. The enemy must know by now that the Americans had withdrawn. But they, too, were hampered by the heavy snowfall and the lack of good roads leading west for their armour. But once the snow stopped they'd attack once again and both generals knew that their troops, after five days of battle, were becoming very weary. As we have seen, Clarke had been forced to send several officers, up to the rank of Colonel, back to the rear on account of 'battle fatigue'.

But as Clarke, who had been without sleep for two nights, sweated it out in the new position, Hasbrouck brought up with him the last message from Ridgway. Earlier General Kean (Hodges' Chief-of-Staff) and an old friend of Hasbrouck, had told Ridgway that Hasbrouck could not be 'expected to sacrifice his command out there'. It was for Hasbrouck alone to decide whether to hold or withdraw. Ridgway had taken no notice.

Now Hasbrouck explained Ridgway's latest order to Clarke. He expected the defenders to withdraw to an oval position, later to be called 'the fortified goose-egg'. Here they would fight on until they were relieved by the 3rd Armored. Further, the 7th Armored and the 106th would now come under the command of General Jones. It was obvious that Ridgway had lost confidence in Hasbrouck's will to fight.

Hasbrouck, Clarke and Hoge, who was also present, didn't like the plan one bit. The Ridgway plan admittedly shortened the length of front they would have to defend. But the terrain was rough. Most of it was hilly forest. What might look like roads through the forest on the map were in reality only tracks, now snowbound: not suitable terrain for mobile defence. In addition there was only one good road through the area leading to the rear at Vielsalm. What if it was cut?

That would mean the end of the supplies. Then there was the question of the 82nd Airborne to their rear. If the paras were pushed back for just two short miles, again they would be cut off from all supplies.

Clarke expressed the feelings of the other two generals when he growled, 'It looks like Custer's last stand to me'.

Nonetheless, orders were orders. Hasbrouck told Clarke to prepare to execute the Ridgway plan, but not yet. He drove back to Vielsalm and sent a long message to the Corps Commander. He explained the dearth of roads in the 'goose-egg' and how all supplies had to come over a single bridge at Vielsalm. He explained that Clarke's CCB had been reduced to half its strength. If 'another all-out attack comes against CCB tonight [the night of 22 December], we can't prevent all-out breakthrough. P.S. A strong attack has just developed against Clarke again. He is outflanked and is retiring west another 2000 yards, refusing both flanks. I am throwing in my last chips to help him. Hoge had just reported an attack. In my opinion if we don't get out of here and up north of the 82nd before night we will not have a 7th Armored Division left. Hasbrouck.'

That evening, as Hasbrouck and Clarke pondered over what seemed the imminent destruction of their 7th Armored and brave men fought for their lives in the 'fortified goose-egg', while others tried to stay alive deep behind enemy lines, the Supreme Commander put the finishing touches to several important messages he would send off on the morrow.

One was to General Marshall in Washington in which he recommended that Generals Bradley and Spaatz should be promoted to four-star generals, pointing out that the time would be particularly opportune in the case of the former. He said that Bradley had 'kept his head magnificently and [had] proceeded methodically and energetically to meet the situation. In no quarter is there any tendency to place any blame upon Bradley.' Eisenhower was correct. It was *he* who should take the blame for what had happened in the Ardennes, *not* Bradley.

He had been the cause of the deaths of thousands of young Americans, and the many thousands still to come. But it did not appear to bother Eisenhower greatly. He worked at his special Order of the Day, which he hoped would encourage his hard-pressed men in the Ardennes. It was an order which, unwittingly, revealed his strategy and plan all along. It read: 'By rushing out from his fixed defences the enemy may give us the chance to turn his great gamble into his worst defeat. So I call upon every man, all the Allies, to rise now to new heights of courage, of resolution and of effort. Let everyone hold before him a single thought: to destroy the enemy on the ground, in the air, everywhere – destroy him! United in this determination and with unshakable faith in the cause for which we fight, we will, with God's help, go forward to our greatest victory.'

That 'greatest victory' was being reviewed by the Belgian renegade and SS General Leon Degrelle that afternoon. He had been sent back to Belgium by Hitler to take over the administration of the newly recaptured eastern provinces of his native country. It had been a long journey and when he had a chance, on the road from Andler to Schönberg, to look around him, he seized the opportunity.

Degrelle, who had worked his way up from private to general in the harsh fighting on the Russian front, winning the Knight's Cross in the process, knew real soldiers when he saw them. Now he stepped out of his car and walked into a field. He came across a trench. 'In it were dead Americans, lined up just as when they were alive and with their cheeks still pink from good food and exposure to fresh air. Tank fire had mown them down and two of them had their faces flattened, but with a noble expression. The trench was full because everyone had stuck to his post, in spite of the wave of fifty or a hundred tanks which had swept upon them, leaving the tracks which I could see in the snow.'

Thoughtfully the renegade SS general walked back to his car. He had seen some real soldiers.

DAY SEVEN:

Friday, 22 December, 1944.

Weather: Conflicting reports. In the north, 6th Panzer Army experiences rain and mud. In the south, the 5th Panzer Army encounters fog and snow. Limited air activity.

'A mission well done. It is time to withdraw.'

Montgomery to Hasbrouck
22 December, 1944.

That Friday morning Hemingway rose from his sick bed at last. He had exhausted the stolen wine and the little cellar of that remote house on the stream was filled with 'Schloss Hemingstein 1944'. The author, who had made war and violence his special subject, decided he'd go and have a look at the battle; after all that is why he had hurried to Luxembourg in the first place.

In the event he was actually 'invited' to go and view a battle. In Hemingway's circles that is how they fought the war. Colonel Luckett of the Fourth Infantry's 12th Regiment and Hemingway's good friend, the commander of the Division's 22nd Regiment, Colonel 'Buck' Lanham, invited the author to drive to a hilltop some two miles away. There the three men would view part of Patton's attack into the southern 'shoulder' of the Bulge.

General 'Red' Irwin's 5th Infantry Division of the 3rd Army would follow up an artillery bombardment with an attack from the hamlet of Michelshof in the direction of Echternach on the River Sauer. The attack would go in with a strength of two battalions. Still, it was a tough assignment. Not only didn't the men of the Fifth Division know much about the enemy's strength, but also the terrain was rugged and difficult. To make matters worse, fog started to roll in before the assault began.

As the guns began to thunder and the infantry prepared to advance, everything which could go wrong did. The Fifth's advance party got lost in the fog and then came under heavy enemy artillery. Control in the heavily wooded area was difficult and the lead battalion got a little out of hand. Then the main body, which was following, experienced the same difficulty. Casualties mounted, but the fifth pressed on.

Colonel Luckett, who had been in the line since D-Day, found 'this magnificent display of force', as he described the attack tongue-in-cheek, 'all very amusing. They [the Fifth's infantrymen] were dressed in snow camouflage made from sheets and went across the plateau two or three miles conducting marching fire. What they were shooting at, I don't know. Ernie and I had a pleasant time joking about it!'

The Fifth's attack ended in total confusion, with disorganized infantry unable even to reach the start line for the real attack. Hemingway and his military pals had seen enough and Hemingway returned to the headquarters of General 'Tubby' Barton at the Luxembourg town of Junglinster. There the war was soon forgotten. 'Tubby' was being sent home, officially on account of ill health, but most of his senior officers believed it was because he had handled the Fourth Division badly during its time in the Hurtgen Forest. So a farewell Christmas Eve party was being planned for him and the talk was all of the food and drink needed for it: meanwhile, four miles up the road young Americans died in the mud and the fog.

At his headquarters in Luxembourg City, Patton knew little of what was happening to his Fifth Division, but he was delighted with his III Corps which was leading the attack up to Bastogne. 'Drive like hell!' he ordered the Corps and now, despite the fog and the rain, they seemed to be doing that.

The III Corps' attack had kicked off at six o'clock that Friday morning. Three divisions strong, it had as its objectives Wiltz, Bastogne and St Vith. Now Patton boasted, 'We'll be in St Vith by 26 December.' In fact, American troops wouldn't recapture St Vith until one month later. But Patton's main attention was directed to his 4th Armored Division which had kicked off its attack from Martelange. Under normal circumstances a Sherman tank could reach Bastogne from Martelange in thirty minutes. Now Patton, who had personally designated the composition of the leading strike force, waited expectantly for news of his favourite division's progress towards Bastogne.

That morning an event took place in Bastogne which would enter the American history books and become, for most Americans, *the* abiding memory of the whole Battle of the Bulge. A Sergeant Butler of 101st Airborne's 327th Glider Infantry Dvision was at his post in the basement of a lonely farmhouse on the Arlon–Bastogne road when he saw four figures coming up the road from the German positions to the south. They were carrying what looked like a bedspread on a pole. He picked up the phone and called his CO,

Captain Adams, 'There's four Krauts coming up the road. They're carrying a white flag. It looks like they want to surrender.'

Then Butler and two other airborne troopers went out to meet the Germans. One of them, a stocky man wearing medical insignia, said in careful English, 'We are parlementaires. We want to talk to your officer.'

Then another of the group, who wore the insignia of a major said something in German which the smaller officer translated into English: 'We want to talk to your commanding general.'

Puzzled but interested, Butler tore two strips of cloth from the white flag, blindfolded them, and led them to the rear.

Half an hour later Colonel Ned Moore, acting Chief-of-Staff of the 101st Airborne, woke up his chief, General McAuliffe, and said, 'Some Germans have brought in a document which they'd like to read out to you.'

It ran as follows: 'To the USA Commander of the encircled town of Bastogne.

The fortunes of war are changing. This time the USA forces in and near Bastogne have been encircled by strong German armored units. There is only one possibility to save the USA troops from total annihilation: that is the honorable surrender of the encircled town. If this proposal should be rejected, one German Artillery Corps and six heavy AA Battalions are ready to annihilate the USA troops in and near Bastogne. All the serious civilian losses caused by this artillery fire would not correspond with the well-known American humanity.
The German Commander.'

'They want us to surrender,' Moore said.

'Nuts,' said McAuliffe, and, dropping the paper on the floor, he went off to inspect his front. When he returned one of his officers, Colonel Harper, said, 'Say Tony, those two Kraut envoys are still in my command post. They say they brought a formal military communication and they're entitled to an answer.'

'What the hell shall I tell them?' McAuliffe asked.

'That first remark of yours would be hard to beat, General,' another officer suggested.

'What did I say?'

'You said "nuts".'

Everyone in the room liked that answer.

McAuliffe scribbled something on a piece of paper and handed it to Harper. 'Here's the answer,' he said.

Harper read the message: 'To the German Commander. *Nuts!* The American Commander.'

'Will you see that it's delivered?' McAuliffe said.

'I'll deliver it myself. It will be a lot of fun,' answered Harper.

The legend of the 'battered bastards of Bastogne' had begun. It would soon deflect from the 'defeat' at St Vith and all that had gone before it. It was a legend that Patton, with his eyes always set on gaining personal publicity, would soon home in on. That afternoon he ordered the Fourth Armored Division to continue advancing throughout the night 'to relieve Bastogne' and his III Corps Commander contacted Middleton to tell him that his Third Army troops were expected to link up with the 101st Airborne 'by tonight'. But it would be another four days before the Fourth managed to slog its way to a link up with the 101st. Montgomery's prediction would prove to be correct. Patton's attack from the south into the 'Bulge' was a 'bit of a dead duck'.

Friday was a day of bitter battle and almost total confusion inside the 'fortified goose-egg'. Hasbrouck's message to Ridgway reached the airborne commander just after Jones, the new overall commander in the goose-egg, had phoned Ridgway to say that he agreed that the salient should be evacuated. It angered Ridgway immensely. As he sat there fuming, an aide came in bearing yet another message. It was a memo from Jones which made it clear he had changed his mind about pulling out. It stated: 'My intentions are to retain the ground now defended.'

It was too much for Ridgway. He had had enough of all this pussy-footing around. Bastogne was surrounded, but was holding out. Why couldn't Jones and Hasbrouck? Those two subordinate commanders obviously lacked guts or didn't know what they were doing. Ordering his jeep, strapping on the somewhat showy hand grenade he always wore on his webbing and carrying his First World War Springfield rifle, he set off for the front.

'By hearing their voices and looking into their faces,' he wrote later, 'there on the battlefield, it was my purpose to get from them on the ground their own sensing of what they were up against.'

At about one-thirty Ridgway arrived in Vielsalm and began his 'hearing of voices and looking into faces'. Right from the start he liked neither. He stood in front of the big wall map of the area and drew a large goose-egg shape on it. 'What do you think of making a stand inside this area?' he asked. 'You'd hold out until a counter-attack caught up with you. You'll soon be surrounded, of course, but we'll supply you by air.'

Hasbrouck replied first. 'I don't like it. The area is heavily wooded, with only a few poor roads. Besides, the troops have had over five days of continuous fighting in very trying weather. My people are only fifty per cent effective. And I'm sure that goes for the infantry too.'

Ridgway didn't like Hasbrouck's answer. He was used to being cut off. All the parachute operations he had been involved in since 1943 had meant his men had been cut off for some time. There was no problem about being cut off. As long as the Allies controlled the skies and the weather was suitable for flying, they could be supplied by air. He looked at Hasbrouck with scarcely concealed contempt. The man obviously lacked backbone.

Suddenly Jones, whose moods varied by the hour, cut in: 'I think it can be done.'

That angered Hasbrouck. Jones the infantryman didn't understand the tactical use of armour one bit. The fortified goose-egg simply wasn't tank ground. Too few roads and too many trees – that was the problem. In that kind of ground, with no infantry support, a tank was a sitting duck for any German infantryman armed with a panzerfaust.

'Tanks can't manoeuvre in there,' Hasbrouck protested. 'We could only use them as pillboxes.'

Ridgway ended the discussion there. He slapped his helmet on and reached for the Springfield. 'Come on Bob,' he said to Hasbrouck. 'The two of us will go up front and see just what the hell the situation is.'

Followed by an equally angry Hasbrouck, he left, leaving Jones staring at his broad back in open bewilderment. Why hadn't he also been invited to go up front?

Montgomery's Liaison Officer, Major Harden, had been at Has-brouck's HQ in Vielsalm when Ridgway's order telling him to form the 'fortified goose-egg' had arrived. Now he reported to his master what he had seen in the little Belgian town. 'The 7th US Armoured

Division was very shaken but only really because their commander was so shaken.'

Now, despite the fact that he was commanding forty divisions, Montgomery decided to go and have a look at the situation himself. Throughout this first week of battle neither the Supreme Commander nor his Army Group Commander (Bradley), nor his 1st Army Commander (Hodges) had visited the fighting troops. Montgomery was different. As Major Harden wrote afterwards: 'Lesson for Hodges was that when you move in a hurry and lose all your communications then get a set of able and young liaison officers who should be able to keep you in the picture and issue your orders and get about your troops *without a tin hat* so that they can see you and believe they have an able commander.' Harden concluded, 'In my opinion [it was] Monty's greatest battle'.

So, accompanied only by an aide and two outriders on motor cycles, Montgomery set off in his heated Rolls, flying 'the largest Union Jack possible' to 'visit with', as General Clarke put it, 'the Seventh Armored.'

'General Montgomery,' Clarke remembered, forgetting that Montgomery had been made a Field-Marshal the previous September, 'was impressive to me . . . very cool in battle.'

As the guns thundered, for the Germans were attacking into the goose-egg yet once again, Montgomery chatted with Clarke. He reviewed the Ridgway plan. He learned from Clarke that his neighbour Hoge's Combat Command A had run out of fuel and was low on ammunition. He saw, too, that the men were virtually exhausted. He did his best to encourage them and, as Major Harden noted, 'I must say the effect of his talk to all ranks had an electric effect. At least they knew what it was all about and that they were on the winning side and not on the other.'

Without making any criticism of Ridgway's plan, but with his mind made up, Montgomery left.

It was now half past three in the afternoon. Clarke was walking the fields just outside his new CP at Commanster. Clarke had spent most of his pre-war military career as an engineer. Now he was testing the ground to check whether it would bear the weight of a 30-ton Sherman tank or even a 5-ton halftrack. After some time he decided that it wouldn't. So much for armoured warfare that night. He returned to his CP to be told that General Ridgway was on his way for a commanders' conference.

Impatiently Clarke waited for the arrival of Ridgway and Hasbrouck. He knew that time was running out. If some decision were not made about a withdrawal soon, the Seventh Armored might well be overrun. The only chance of escape now was under cover of darkness. A withdrawal in daylight might well spell suicide. He needed an order, and he needed it *very soon*!

At four-thirty Ridgway faced his subordinate commanders. He snapped at Colonel Reid of the 424th Regiment, 'What's the combat efficiency of your unit, Colonel?'

'About fifty percent, sir.'

Ridgway turned to Clarke. Like Reid and all the other officers present, Clarke was an unknown quantity to Ridgway. For the last two years Ridgway had associated mainly with airborne officers who regarded themselves as a special kind of elite. Ridgway knew little of armoured tactics and logistics. 'And yours, Clarke?'

The big armoured general pulled no punches. Clarke was never one to be impressed by rank. 'Forty percent, sir,' he answered promptly.

Ridgway frowned. After what he had seen during these last three days in the Ardennes (twice he had seen men break down and refuse to fight), he was beginning to suspect everybody's motives and courage. One of the men who had broken down, an officer, he had had arrested, and shortly thereafter he had threatened *personally* to shoot the other one, a sergeant. Were these officers just as weak, or were they giving him the unvarnished truth? Ridgway realized that he needed someone he knew and trusted to give him an honest assessment of the situation.

Then he remembered General William Hoge. He had known Bill Hoge since their cadet days at West Point. He knew what 'a calm, courageous, imperturbable fellow' he was. 'I knew nothing would ever flurry him and so above all I wanted to talk to him, to get his feel of the situation'.

He asked why Hoge wasn't at the conference. One of Clarke's staff said that he was still on the road to Commanster. Ridgway nodded and asked to be put in touch with him by radio. This was arranged and Ridgway talked with his old friend in plain speech, but using double talk, 'making allusions to West Point football days', until it was clear Hoge knew who he was. Then Ridgway gave him the grid coordinate of a farmhouse where he wished them to meet.

Hoge arrived at the farmhouse just as the light was beginning to fade. Ridgway took him to one side out of earshot of the other officers and said, 'Bill we've made contact now.' He meant the defenders with his own XVIII Airborne Corps. 'This position is too exposed to try to hold it any longer. We're not going to leave you in here to be chopped to pieces, little by little. I'm going to extricate you with all the forces of the 7th Armored and the attached troops, including your own. I plan to start that withdrawal tonight. We're going to get you out of here.'

It must have cost Ridgway dearly to say those words. It went against the grain to withdraw, but he must have known by now that Montgomery would not tolerate any further loss of life in defence of the salient.

Hoge didn't reply for a moment. His inexperienced CCB had done well, but the price had been high. In one battalion there had been three commanders in five days. The men were about at the end of their tether. Finally he just said, 'How can you?'

As Ridgway recorded after the war: 'That one sentence revealed more to me than anything any commander out there had said, or any amount of reports I could have gotten, because here was a man in whom I had absolute, implicit confidence – in his personal courage, in his professional competence and in his stability of character.'

Firmly but emotionally, Ridgway said to his old friend, 'Bill, we *can* and *will*!'

Undoubtedly angry at being overruled by Montgomery and knowing that he had been wrong to sack Hasbrouck, which he had done early that morning, Ridgway drove straight to Jones's CP. Now he found the General he had appointed to command the fortified goose-egg 'strange'. He appeared too casual, almost indifferent, little interested in the fact that that night we were going to bring his people out of the trap.'

After talking to Jones for a few minutes, Ridgway sent everyone out of the room save general officers and his Deputy Chief of Staff, Colonel Quill. At Ridgway's direction, Quill wrote on a scrap of paper the order relieving Jones of his command. Then he re-instated Hasbrouck and gave him overall command of the salient. So within a space of twelve hours Hasbrouck had lost his division and been given it back. It was symbolic of the confusion at the top in the US Command.

Even 'Gentleman Jim' Gavin was struck by the way the US treated its senior officers, how 'unfair and thoughtless' it was. 'Montgomery congratulated all those who fought at St Vith. *We relieved* the two senior commanders.'

Years later Gavin went on to reason: 'In the case of General Jones and his 106th Division . . . higher command knew of his dispositions and approved of them. His leading green regiment were overwhelmed before they could afford much resistance and there is little that he – or anyone else for that matter – could have done about it.' Gavin concluded: 'Summarily relieving those who do not appear to measure up in the first shock of battle is not only a luxury we cannot afford – it is very damaging to the Army as a whole. We have much to learn from the British about senior command relationships.'

With Jones dealt with, Ridgway turned to a shaken Hasbrouck, who still could not get over the fact that he had been relieved at dawn and re-instated at dusk, and snapped, 'Bob, start pulling your people back as soon as possible. I want them all withdrawn under cover of darkness tonight.'

But it wasn't going to be as easy as that. As Hasbrouck passed on the message he had just received from Montgomery – 'You have accomplished your mission, a mission well done. It is time to withdraw' – Clarke found that he probably wouldn't be able to withdraw. He was heavily engaged. If his command attempted to withdraw with the enemy at its heels, his men would be slaughtered. Besides his vehicles were up to their axles in mud and snow.

Hoge reported the same to Hasbrouck, but Hasbrouck was adamant. Time was running out fast. He radioed back to Clarke and Hoge: 'The situation is such on the west of the river [Salm] south of the 82nd Airborne that if we don't join them soon, the opportunity will be gone. It will be necessary to disengage, whether circumstances are favorable or not. Inform me of your situation at once with regard to the possibility of disengagement and withdrawal.'

Clarke replied that his armoured vehicles could not possibly get out that soon. Hasbrouck signalled back that the escape bridge at Vielsalm would probably be blown by noon on the 23rd. Then all hope would vanish.

Clarke answered, 'I don't know how we can do it, General. But I'll go over and see Bill Hoge again.'

Hoge was realistic but glum. 'We'll never make it out, Bruce,' he said. 'Let's just stay and fight. Our vehicles are up to the hubs. Haven't got a chance of getting out.'

Clarke got on the radio again. He told Hasbrouck with a note of weary finality in his voice, 'We have to stay'.

To the rear there were other problems. It was clear that 'Parker's Crossroads' would soon come under all-out attack. All day long the SS had been shelling and mortaring the American positions. Major Parker himself had been badly wounded and had first refused to be evacuated, but in the end he had been forced to and had been succeeded by his second-in-command.

Gavin, who realized the danger quicker than some of his fellow commanders in the XVIII Airborne Corps, hurriedly sent a battalion of airborne infantry to support the artillerymen. Unfortunately, at roughly the same time the 3rd Armored Division of the same corps, which was coming under severe pressure itself, had to withdraw the tanks its commander, General Maurice Rose, had dispatched to help the defenders of that snow-swept crossroads which was now becoming vital. For if the Germans broke through there, not only would the XVIII Airborne Corps be endangered, but also the men who were soon to retreat from the goose-egg.

Gavin made a personal reconnaissance of the place, then he conferred with General Rose and asked him to send whatever armour he could find. Rose, who would be killed in action himself in 1945, promised he would. While a company of airborne men under the command of a Captain Woodruff drew a tight defensive circle around the crossroads, a platoon of tank destroyers rolled towards the junction. Unfortunately the tank destroyers lost their way in the fog. Pausing to find their bearing, they were attacked and overwhelmed by a bunch of marauding SS troopers.

It was one more sign that the Germans were testing the defences. But a little later it was the Germans' turn to be unlucky. An officers' patrol of the 2nd SS was surprised by some airborne men. There was a small firefight, but then the Germans surrendered. As was usual with German prisoners, especially the arrogant SS who were given to boasting, they talked. They told their captors that their attack was being held up by a lack of fuel, but that would soon be rectified. Then the SS would attack – *in divisional strength*.

It was not an idle boast either. If necessary the commander of the 2nd SS Panzer was prepared to use his whole division to gain the vital crossroads. His Army Commander, Sepp Dietrich, was breathing down his neck. Indeed the burly Bavarian had given him a 'Zigarre' (Cigar), as the Germans called 'a rocket' that very morning. So now he was busy assembling the whole of his 4th Panzer grenadier Regiment for the coming assault.

Everywhere in the surrounding fields the SS lurked, jockeying for position, waiting for the order to attack. They were hard young men, some no more than seventeen, from a dozen different countries, nearly a third of them from France. These were Alsatians, who had been declared German in 1940 when France had surrendered. But all of them, whatever their age or nationality, were imbued with overweening arrogance of the SS. 'Our honour is loyalty' was their motto, and they meant it. They would be loyal to the death. Gavin's airborne troopers had seen that all right the previous day when they had attacked the fortified SS village. And now the lone company of the airborne men, Captain Junior R. Woodruff's F Company, stood in the path of the whole 4th SS Panzer Grenadier Regiment.

Inside the fortified goose-egg both Hoge and Clarke were under heavy attack. The German tankers were employing the same trick they had used east of St Vith when the now captured Major Boyan had seen them shoot up five Shermans in rapid succession. They fired blinding white flares to dazzle Clarke's tank gunners and then, while the latter dithered, unable to see, blasted great holes in the Shermans.

Desperately Clarke laboured to get his survivors out, retreating all the time, trying to save as many men as possible. But again the Shermans were at a disadvantage. To combat the mud and snow of Russia, German tank designers had given their armoured vehicles very broad tracks. The Panthers and the few Tigers used in the battle could plough through even the deepest mud. The Shermans, on the other hand, with their narrow tracks, designed to British specifications for the fast-moving war of the western Desert, were often hopelessly bogged down in the muddy trails of the forest.

Frantically Clarke appealed for more infantrymen to protect his retreating tanks. Hasbrouck, working flat out in Vielsalm to prepare the withdrawal plan, now agreed upon by Ridgway, could only spare him one single company of riflemen, plus a few armoured cars. With that Clarke had to be content.

Although Clarke and Hoge didn't know it, the Germans were in trouble too. Not only did von Manteuffel want to use the road network out of newly captured St Vith, but the SS of Dietrich's 6th SS Panzer Army did too. The result was a monumental traffic jam on all roads leading in and out of the town. Field-Marshal Model, Army Group Commander, went to St Vith himself to see what was going on. The chaos staggered him. He was forced to get out of his staff car and walk into the town packed with vehicles from a score of different units, edging along at a snail's pace. Just as Clarke had done before him, the Field-Marshal, who at the beginning of the offensive had commanded 1,800 tanks and assault guns, was reduced to playing traffic cop in a vain attempt to keep the vehicles moving.

As he did so, he thought bitterly, as he told Albert Speer* the following day, that 'the whole scene showed that the Army had lost its erstwhile famous talent for organization, surely one of the effects of Hitler's three years of command'. Model was bitter too, because he saw that all this effort was being wasted. For he knew something that none of the Allied commanders and few of the German ones did.

Secreted on the island of Nordostland off Spitzbergen in the Artic, a German weather team had been radioing back weather information ever since mid-November. Their weather data had helped Hitler to pick the date for the start of the last offensive in the West. Their predictions had been correct and had allowed Model's armies to enjoy what was called 'Führerwetter' (Führer's weather): cold, damp, overcast weather which prevented the Allies from using their air superiority. On the morrow, however, the weather would change. A 'Russian high' was predicted. With it it would bring bright, but very cold weather, ideal for planes. Model knew, even as he stood there ankle-deep in mud, monocle firmly clenched in his left eye, face red with cold and fury, that on the morrow the *Ami jabos* (dive bombers) would be out in their thousands. That would be it, and as British and American bombers came winging in over his headquarters in an old hunting lodge in the Eifel, he would confess to Speer, 'The offensive has failed'.

Unaware that Nature itself was coming to their rescue, Hasbrouck and his staff officers laboured that night on the details of the

* German Minister for Armaments, the man mainly responsible for producing the weapons needed for the great counter-attack.

withdrawal. Ridgway had estimated that the men in the fortified goose-egg had fourteen hours of darkness to complete their withdrawal. But Hasbrouck knew it would take at least four hours just to work out the plan and issue orders to the main forces involved – Hoge's and Clarke's commands and the two infantry regiments, the 112th and 424th.

In all some 22,000 men would be coming out with their trucks, tanks and other heavy equipment. They had just three roads at their disposal, all narrow and winding and all ending at two small bridges over the River Salm. The Germans on both sides of the goose-egg could rush those roads at any time, for during the withdrawal only small holding parties would be left behind to stop any such attempt. Once a road was cut, tragedy would result. As General Perrin, the new commander of the 106th Division, or what was left of it, commented: 'Leavenworth [US Army Staff College] never contemplated such a problem.'

While Hasbrouck worked on the withdrawal plan, Colonel Craig, the divisional artillery executive at Vielsalm, had contacted his boss General McMahon at Commanster to organize artillery cover for the retreat. But at Commanster no one had the usual encoding device, the Slidex. Craig was desperate. Time was running out. He dare not, however, use plain English in case the Germans were listening to the US radio traffic.

He tried double talk. 'We're going to do what the Blues did in the third operation in Tennessee,' he cried, referring to a retirement operation the 106th had practised during manoeuvres. But no one at Commanster remembered that operation.

Desperately Craig said, 'Well, remember what the Reds did in the fourth operation. We're going to do that.'

The General grew angry and snapped that this was no time for double talk. Craig also grew angry. Remembering a simple code which the 106th had once used, he barked, 'I'm going to write this in Tennessee code and you'd better find somebody who remembers it!'

In the end General McMahon found somebody who remembered the code, a snoring aide who had been woken up to decode the message. The planning went on. It was a race against time as the hours of darkness ticked away.

*

While his former staff sweated and laboured, their one-time commander, General Alan Jones, was being carried away in an ambulance, bound for Liège. According to some chroniclers of the battle he had fallen to the floor after the interview with Ridgway and had suffered a heart attack. Others say that, for a while and to save his reputation, Ridgway had made him deputy commander of the XVIII Airborne Corps.

Was the 'heart attack' a polite fiction to save face, not only Jones's but that of Ridgway and those other senior officers who had lost their heads in the first week of the Battle of the Bulge? Soon the Inspector General's Branch would start inquiries into the conduct of officers and units involved in the initial stages of the Battle, but for the time being senior officers must present a united front.*

Whatever the explanation, General Jones was yet another 'victim', and a particularly tragic one. He had spent the whole of his adult life in the US Army, a quarter of a century of preparing for war. Year in, year out, when the US Army had been thought of as a refuge for fools, reactionaries and the workshy, he and his kind had plodded through the hundred and one picayune tasks that made up the life of the peacetime soldier in some godforsaken garrison town. He had sweated through morning parades in the harsh sun of Texas; he had hiked through the choking dust of those manoeuvres in Tennessee; he had faced the resentful eyes of two generations of young soldiers 'gigged' for some military crime or other; he had listened to the same boring small talk in half a hundred officers' clubs on a Saturday night.

Year in, year out, to find out in one short week that he was a military failure. Within seven brief days he had seen a lifetime's work vanish as inexorably as he had seen his young division vanish too.†

Thus General Jones, 'the man they'd never take alive' passes out

---

* As late as 4 June 1993, the US Department of the Army denied there were any records of an IG investigation into the conduct of the 106th Division, 14th Cavalry, etc. But there were, which the author managed to get declassified on 23 February, 1993. The inquiry, dated 22 January, 1945, and stamped 'secret' censures Colonel Devine *indirectly* for having withdrawn without telling the 106th Division. Why then all the secrecy, maintained for nearly fifty years?

† The 106th Division was reconstituted in France. But apart from some local patrol action, its main task was to guard the massive concentration of German POWs on the Rhine. It must have given those veterans who had been German POWs themselves a great deal of satisfaction.

of our picture, driven slowly over the snowbound road that led to the Meuse and Liège, a casualty of the battle as surely as if he had been struck by a bullet.

At dawn Colonel Strickler and his survivors of the 28th Division's 110th Regiment had broken out of the forest and stumbled on to a narrow road. Now they were too exhausted and hungry to care whether they were spotted or not. They had been on the run behind enemy lines since the night of 19 December when they had fled from Wiltz. They had to have food and warmth.

Ahead of them there was a little hamlet. Throwing caution to the wind, they advanced on it groggily. The first house they came to was empty. Desperate now, they moved on to the next house. This time their knock was answered and they asked the Belgian at the door for food. He saw their piteous conditions and invited them in. Over bread, butter and jam, which they wolfed down, and warmed by hot coffee (ersatz), they listened carefully as he explained the local situation. Two days before, the Americans had blown the bridge just beyond the hamlet and gone. Nervously their host told them to hurry up; he was expecting the Germans at any moment.

With renewed strength now they set off again. They had managed to dodge the enemy for so long; they were determined not to be captured now. Three miles down the little road they were suddenly challenged – *in English*! They had reached their own lines.

They found themselves at Vaux-les-Rosières astride the highway leading out of Bastogne towards Neufchâteau to the south-west. Surprisingly enough the town was the temporary HQ of no less a person than General Cota, their old commander, who was now without a division to command.

But at Cota's HQ Strickler was welcomed like someone who had risen from the dead. His hand was shaken repeatedly and he had drinks and hot coffee thrust at him as he sat wearily on a hard chair spluttering out his tale.

Strickler was one of the few lucky ones. Later both Bradley and Middleton would heap praise on the 28th and, in particular, on the 110th Regiment: 'it did a splendid job. Had not this regiment put up the fight it did the Germans would have been in Bastogne long before the 101st Airborne.' But the bill had been very high.

The 110th Regiment had lost the tanks and men of five tank companies; two field artillery battalions had been decimated; one engineer battalion had nearly vanished, plus two battalions of infantry virtually wiped out. On 15 December the infantry had had 150 officers and 2,923 men on strength. The day after Colonel Strickler finally staggered into divisional headquarters that Saturday the 110th had exactly 55 officers and 730 men left for duty. In effect the infantry had lost two-thirds of its strength in a week!

From divisional commanders like General Alan Jones, with thirty years' service behind him, to obscure teenage privates who had come up as reinforcements after the Hurtgen Forest blood-letting with not more than three months' training, these men had been sacrificed to an evil, ill-conceived strategy.

Now the question was – were those thousands of brave, weary, half-starved men still fighting in the fortified goose-egg going to be sacrificed to that same strategy as well?

As a half-moon started to creep up the sky, the forward artillery observers stole into their positions along the sides of the 3,000-yard corridor still left in American hands. It would be their job to direct the covering fire that would protect the troops as they started to withdraw.

The ground was still soft and muddy. They could feel it as they crouched in their holes waiting for it all to start, listening to the brisk snap-and-crackle of yet another fire fight. For the German infantry were still boring in on the flanks of Hoge's and Clarke's battered commands. But it seemed to be getting colder. An icy wind was beginning to blow and the clouds were disappearing.

Now the sky was clear. The forward artillery observers tucked their heads deeper into the smelly warmth of their collars. Every now and again, they rubbed the tips of their noses which were beginning to tingle. Their breath started to fog on the air. It was definitely getting colder.

It was midnight, 22/23 December 1944.

DAY EIGHT:

Saturday, 23 December, 1944

Weather: Clear and cold. Snowdrifts block the Eifel roads. No snow ploughs. Engineers and troops burn fences for fuel. Cleared road surfaces icy.

'A miracle has happened!'

General Bruce Clarke, 23 December.

At 0030 hours that Saturday morning, the plan for the withdrawal was finally completed and handed out to the commanders within the fortified goose-egg.

It envisaged a gradual withdrawal along three roads, being funnelled into the two bridges over the River Salm. There, to the rear, the 82nd Airborne held the line. But any breach in the airborne's thin defensive crust as, for instance, at Baraque de Fraiture – 'Parker's Crossroads' – could spell disaster. The three German divisions, one of them armoured, plus Remer's Führer Escort Brigade, grouped around the goose-egg, would push in and massacre the men trapped on the wrong side of the River Salm. The last time Montgomery had attempted a withdrawal action on this scale had been at Arnhem and that had been suicidal.

Up front Clarke's men were still fighting hard. The Germans had launched yet another night attack. Advancing along the railway line, they had knocked out tank after tank. But Clarke's supporting artillery was rallying quickly. The Seventh's 434th Armored Field Artillery opened up with a monstrous roar. Shells started plunging down just three hundred yards in front of the foxholes held by what was left of the American infantry.

That barrage stopped the German armoured thrust. But, on both left and right flanks, determined teams of Germans armed with panzerfausts infiltrated the Seventh's positions. Now the Germans were 'tank-cracking', as they called it, hunting out the bogged down Shermans.

In that moonlit night, slashed by the glow of tracer fire, the American tankers without infantry protection were powerless to stop them. The rockets slammed into the Shermans at close range. The hollow boom of metal striking metal was followed almost instantly by the screams of burning men as the American tanks with their flammable petrol engines burst into flames.

Clarke called Hoge, who was also under attack. He said he couldn't disengage under these circumstances. The Germans were too close. Hoge agreed. That was his position too. He told Clarke, 'I'm supposed to start moving at zero three hundred hours, but I'm getting hit hard in at least two places. I can't possibly disengage.' Both men radioed Hasbrouck at Vielsalm that a withdrawal at the scheduled time was out of the question.

A few miles away, Colonel Robert Erlenbusch was trying to shore up the north-eastern corner of the goose-egg. Driving through the hamlet of Braunlauf he spotted a yellow light flickering in one of the local cottages and ordered his driver to halt. He went into the cottage and found a dozen men slumped on the floor in apathetic gloom. 'What the hell are you doing here?' the Colonel demanded.

Nobody knew. They turned out to be men of the 106th's surviving regiment, the 424th, which had been retreating since 17 December. Now Erlenbusch gave them some purpose.

'Come with me,' he barked.

Grateful for any kind of leadership, the infantrymen followed him into the village street. Then within minutes he had rounded up several hundred Golden Lions. Just then a convoy of empty trucks came ploughing through the mud. Erlenbusch stopped them and asked a sergeant from Hoge's command where they were going. The NCO said that the Germans had broken through and they were trying to get back to the railhead at Beho. Erlenbusch was not having that. He commandeered the trucks and filled them with his new 'battalion'. 'Now move back to Commanster', he ordered the men.

That done, he returned to his own command post, called Clarke and told him of the breakthrough on Hoge's front.

'Yes, yes I know,' Clarke said soothingly. 'The Jerries have broken through at several places. Just hold *your* lines.'

Things were beginning to fall apart in the fortified goose-egg.

Tough Mike Klimick of the Seventh's 87th Recon could see that all right. As he and what was left of his outfit pulled out, he met an infantryman who was crying as he marched. He said he was 'a cook and hadn't fired a gun in three years'. All the same he had a big Luger hanging from his belt. Klimick, thinking the Germans might capture the man soon, advised him to get rid of the 'Kraut weapon'.

Some time after that he came across a 'bunch of infantry lying in the mud and snow', shot down as they tried to hold onto their positions. 'Blood was splattered all over the place.'

That one-eyed machine gunner with the highly developed nervous system, Harry Martin of the 424th Regiment, also thought things were going badly wrong. After days of trudging around in the mud and snow, he and his company finally contacted Hoge's Combat Command in the early hours of that Saturday morning. Still not aware of what was going on, they were suddenly alerted to the fact that they were being withdrawn by their Captain Bartel crying 'frantically', 'Jump on anything that's moving out! Every minute counts. *Every man for himself!*'

Martin sprang on a tank destroyer carrying a 90mm gun. He was lucky and he knew it. That great overhanging cannon was the only one used by the Western Allies which could stop a Tiger, and already there were Tigers milling around to their rear. If any vehicle was going to get through, it would be this one.

Calvin Boykin was in that column of the 814th Tank Destroyer Battalion. Up front, Lieutenant Bill Rogers Jr, who had given up his seat in Congress to join the army and had rejected a staff appointment for an active command, was leading the tank destroyers in their attempt to break out. Boykin was in the middle of the column in an armoured car. Now, as the vehicles ground their way up a muddy slope, he spotted 'a burning tank that had just been hit. A wave of panic seemed to envelop those around me. Vehicles started backing. Others tried to turn round. It seemed as though our worst fears were being realized. We were trapped. A voice – I recognized it as being Colonel Jones – came through on our 608 radio, urging us to burn our vehicles if necessary and get out on foot.'

Panic was about to break out, it seemed.

Now General Hoge called Colonel Erlenbusch and told him, 'I can't get through to General Clarke. Part of my front has been broken through. If any of my units come through your area, take charge of them.'

Erlenbusch told him that he had already taken over fifteen of his trucks and filled them with infantrymen from the 424th, adding, 'I'll keep an eye out for anything else.'

Minutes later Erlenbusch had bad news from his own subordinates. Lt-Colonel Wemple, commanding his right flank, reported that he was engaged in heavy action with the enemy. To his left flank, Major Lohse reported that he was being shelled by tanks and artillery.

Erlenbusch called Clarke: 'My whole area is being surrounded. The Jerries are softening up Lohse and will hit him at any moment. Wemple is already under heavy attack. Don't you think they should pull out now, sir?'

Clarke told him, 'I can't authorize a withdrawal yet. General Hoge is under heavy attack. If you pull out first, he'll be outflanked.'

'But sir,' Erlenbusch protested, 'if my people are going to get out at all, it'll *have* to be at first light!'

But Clarke was firm. 'You've got to hold on. The area in the south has to be cleared first. Besides, the roads to the rear are awfully muddy.'

Erlenbusch was about exhausted. He had been in constant combat for seven days. His nerves were ragged. 'But sir,' he protested, 'my men will be sitting ducks.'

Clarke kept calm. He soothed the distraught Colonel. 'Don't worry. I'll do everything to get out just as soon as possible.'

Erlenbusch sighed and called Lohse. He told him, 'We're not moving out right away. Get ready for a Jerry attack.'

Lohse took the phone from his ear. 'Do you know what it's *really* like out here?' he yelled.

Erlenbusch listened. He could hear the snap and crack of a firefight, dominated by the louder explosions of shellfire.

Erlenbusch borrowed Clarke's calm manner. 'Don't worry,' he said, 'We'll get you out.'

At five that morning, with the temperature sinking steadily, Clarke received a radio message from a very worried Hasbrouck in Vielsalm. It read: 'The situation is such on the west of the river (Salm) south of the 82nd that if we don't join them soon the opportunity will be over. It will be necessary to disengage whether circumstances are favorable or not if we are to carry out any kind of withdrawal with equipment. Inform me of your situation at once particularly with regard to possibility of disengagement and execution of withdrawal.'

Clarke knew he had to make the crucial decision. Probably the fate of 22,000 men depended upon making it correctly. He called Erlenbusch to find out his situation.

'There's a firefight just south of me,' the Colonel replied. 'We've got to get out *now*!'

Still Clarke hesitated. If his men got bogged down on the muddy roads and tracks, the Germans would just eat them up. 'You'll probably be able to take off at daylight,' he said without too much conviction. 'If you'll hang on another ten minutes, I can give you the good word.'

Erlenbusch promised he'd try.

Clarke went outside his CP. The sky was tinged with scarlet from the guns, but it was greying too. Dawn wasn't far off. Suddenly he felt a thrill of recognition. The ground beneath his feet crackled and snapped. *The many ruts made by his vehicles had frozen!*

Just then Hasbrouck called him, impatient to know when Clarke could move out. 'Bruce,' he demanded, 'do you think you can get out?'

For once Clarke let his pent-up emotions loose. 'A miracle's happened!' he exploded. '*The road's frozen*! We're chopping the vehicles out of the ice. At zero six hundred, we're going to start rolling.'

At 'Parker's Crossroads' the SS were attacking in force, something which worried General Hasbrouck immensely. If the 82nd crumpled under German pressure or even withdrew, he didn't give much of a chance for the success of the retreat out of the goose-egg. But Ridgway and his subordinate divisional commanders still didn't seem to take the threat to 'Parker's Crossroads' seriously. So Major Goldstein, who had now succeeded Parker in command of the embattled force, decided he'd make them understand. Taking a captured SS officer and NCO with him, he drove to Manhay where the leading elements of the XVIII Airborne Corps' Third Armored Division were located. There he showed his prisoners to Lt-Colonel Walter Richardson of a task force from the 3rd Armored.

Richardson realized immediately the inherent danger of the situation and sent a company of tanks to the aid of the defenders of the crossroads. He also sent a company of the 509th Parachute Infantry, the oldest parachute battalion in the US Army, which had been in action constantly since 1942 and whose men sometimes wore the red beret of the British Parachute Regiment with whom they had fought in North Africa.

General Gavin, worried about the crossroads, went up to see the situation for himself. As always 'Gentleman Jim' commanded from the front. But this time Gavin was unlucky. 'I went to the town of

Fraiture,' he wrote after the war, 'and proceeded from there toward the crossroads. I encountered such a tremendous volume of fire that it was suicide to go any further. Small arms fire was ricocheting in all directions. Interspersed with this was artillery, mortar and tank fire.' Gavin was forced to retreat, concerned now as to whether the position could be held. If it weren't, then the men now beginning the withdrawal from the fortified goose-egg would retreat to find themselves involved in another battle to their rear.

Gavin worried unnecessarily. Parker's Crossroads would hold all that day. But when the mixture of gunners, paras and tankers did pull back, only one third of their number would return. Again the butcher's bill would be too high.

Erlenbusch was on the phone again. 'Sir', he began, but Clarke didn't give him a chance to speak. He cut in with, 'All right, Bob, *crank up!*'

Erlenbusch needed no further urging. He ran out of his CP shouting his message. At once the tank drivers were starting their motors. Truck drivers started up and cold engines spluttered and coughed.

Shells began to fall around the CP. Erlenbusch ordered two tanks that were bogged down to be set on fire. A shell exploded nearby and he feared that this was artillery softening up. The Germans would attack soon.

He looked for his jeep, but to no avail. His driver had taken off without him! He spotted another jeep parked in a farmyard, pelted across the road and sprang into the driver's seat. Two figures huddled in sleeping bags were fast asleep, despite the bombardment, in the back.

Erlenbusch pressed the starter and slammed the gear home. The jeep shuddered. Its wheels were frozen in a rut. He jammed the accelerator to the floor and with a lurch the jeep came free. Close by a German emerged from the trees and raised his Schmeisser. Slugs pattered the length of the jeep like tropical rain bouncing off a tin roof. Erlenbusch looked at his sleeve. It was riddled by bullets, but he was unhurt. He rolled the jeep onto the street. Behind him his two passengers continued to snore. He would not learn till he reached Vielsalm that he had been the chauffeur to a chaplain and his assistant!

*

General Hoge's withdrawal started smoothly enough at ten minutes past six. His rearguard broke off contact with the enemy, who reacted slowly to the Americans' retreat. When they did so, they were stopped dead in their tracks by another tank company which Hoge had posted at the village of Maldingen. The Germans faltered and the Shermans pulled out with ease, not losing a tank. Then they too were rolling after the main column speeding along the paved highway to Vielsalm.

Behind him General Hoge left one small unit – Task Force Lindsey, commanded by a captain of that name. This little cavalry unit would screen the withdrawal all that morning. It was a suicidal mission, but Hoge knew that Captain Franklin Lindsey would be prepared to take the risk. But Clarke's withdrawal was not going smoothly at all. Acting as traffic cop once more, he stood on the side of the road urging his drivers on. Not that they needed much urging. The Germans were too close and even over the roar of their engines they could hear the boom of enemy artillery fire close by. It wouldn't be long before the Germans overran their positions.

Harry Martin of the 424th knew that all right. Luckily for him, the commander of the tank destroyer on which he rode had told him to get inside the vehicle. 'We've just received word on the radio that there's a small arms fight ahead. Come on inside. You'll be safer.' Now as Martin enjoyed the warmth, pressed up near the breech of the 90mm cannon, bullets started to bounce off the tank destroyer's side.

The commander looked grim. Martin, who had just told himself that the difference between armour and infantry was that the former carried 'warm clothing, blankets and food with them', knew why. He was fearful that some German infantryman might sneak out of the trees and pot the vehicle with those devilish bazookas of theirs. Suddenly he didn't envy these tankers one bit.

Further up the column, they weren't so fortunate. The tank destroyers of the 814th Battalion were in constant action warding off attacks by German Panthers and infantry. Lieutenant Hugh Bertruck engaged the Germans in a furious firefight. Time and again, they fired their huge cannon, the solid-shot armour-piercing shells slamming into the enemy tanks, rocking them back on their bogies. One of Bertruck's men, a Sergeant Glen Hoop, succeeded in knocking out three Panthers in rapid succession. Then his vehicle was hit. Hoop was wounded, but insisted he was going to fight on, which he did.

But the Germans were pressing home their attacks with ever more determination. At a fork in the trail the 814th moved to left and right. Just then firing broke out on both sides. They had run into an ambush. 20-year-old Calvin Boykin took the wrong fork with his armoured car. He swerved past three shattered jeeps, all blazing furiously, and tried to escape from the confused mêlée. Skidding and slithering, the armoured car, plus two jeeps, left the icy road and landed right in an area of marshy ground. The drivers gunned their engines. Mud flew everywhere. Men cursed and pushed. But they were well and truly bogged down.

They sabotaged the armoured car's 37mm gun and shoved a lighted rag soaked in gasoline into the tank. With a muffled crump, the armoured car burst into flame. Next moment the men were pelting furiously after the other vehicles. This was their last chance to escape.

In Vielsalm Hasbrouck waited anxiously at the bridge. Mud-splattered tanks and trucks trundled past him, laden with exhausted soldiers. Then he was told of a new threat. Remer's elite Führer Escort Brigade had bumped the 28th Division's 112th Infantry. They needed help urgently, but what could he do? He had no reserves.

In what he later described as 'one of the funniest orders I ever issued', he sent the 'Seventh Armored's divisional reserve' into action to restore the situation. It consisted of exactly two tank destroyers!

Fortunately the 'divisional reserve' arrived just as the lead German tanks approached the village of Cierreux where the hard-pressed men of the 112th were fighting a desperate holding action. This time the American gunners fired the first shots. Within minutes their great 90mm cannon had put two German tanks out of action and the remaining five turned tail and fled.

In the lull that followed, a platoon of light US Honey tanks and a section of towed tank destroyers turned up out of the blue and helped to restore the situation. The panic which had threatened to engulf the men still inside the fortified goose-egg eased. Order was re-established – but not for long.

That afternoon the Germans began crossing the River Salm and infiltrating into Vielsalm itself. Hasbrouck himself escaped death by inches. A German tank suddenly appeared a hundred yards from his schoolhouse HQ and started to shell the vehicles parked outside. A halftrack went up in flames and the commanding general of the 7th Armored had to make a run for it.

As the sun appeared for the first time for a week and the sky turned blue, it occurred to General Hasbrouck that he had once been faced with this problem, a withdrawal under enemy pressure, at the Staff College in Fort Leavenworth. Then he had suggested that the trapped force should withdraw at once, even in daylight. He had been given a bad mark by his examiners. They had maintained that a withdrawal should always be conducted under the cover of darkness. Had he been right then or was the examiners' decision the correct one?

Bruce Clarke knew only that he was getting his men out. Now, tied to the front seat of a jeep, driven by his faithful Sergeant Jenderewski, he catnapped, totally exhausted. He had done his best. The men were coming out.

This was the nadir of his career. Within days of receiving his first general's star, he had fought a battle which had ended in retreat and defeat. Immediately after the event, all talk was of the brilliant defence of Bastogne and how Patton had thrust forward to save 'the battered bastards of Bastogne'. America needed a victory. No one wanted to talk of the 'defeat' at St Vith. Besides, that withdrawal had been executed at the command of a 'limey' commander, Field-Marshal Montgomery.

In fact, using armour in a role for which it had never been intended, defence, he had stopped von Manteuffel's drive dead. On that day Field-Marshal Model had conceded defeat. The spirited defence of St Vith and later the fortified goose-egg had put the German attackers well behind their scheduled time table. Now the 'shoulders' were firm, the Meuse was defended along its length in Belgium and France and the Germans were running out of fuel for the armour. The sleeping general of two weeks' standing, who one day would go to the top of the US Army, had done his job well. He deserved his rest. Thanks to Bruce Clarke there would be no further victims in his section of the Battle of the Bulge.

About seven o'clock that night Colonel Boylan, in charge of the 7th Armored's rearguard, arrived at Vielsalm. Just as he crossed the River Salm he was stopped by an MP and ordered to report to

General Hasbrouck *immediately*. The Colonel thought he had failed, but when he entred Hasbrouck's CP, the General threw his arms around the surprised Boylan and exclaimed, 'Thank God, Boylan, you're here! You've got everyone out!'

But he hadn't. Out in the fortified goose-egg there was still a mixed force of riflemen from the 112th Infantry Regiment and light Honey tanks from the Seventh, which had beaten off a German armoured attack early that afternoon. Now this force was trapped with German tanks to their front and others from Remer's Führer Escort Brigade to their rear.

Weary and demoralized, knowing that time was running out fast for them, the Americans flung themselves into a desperate attack. Their aim was to open a path to the River Salm before the second bridge over the stream passed into Germans hands. For an hour they tried. Each time they were beaten back. Then Remer's panzers to the rear hit them hard. This time Remer brought up his Ferdinands, great lumbering assault guns.

Using their old high velocity flare trick, the Germans got off the first shells. They couldn't miss. The American vehicles were trapped in a narrow defile. In that tight valley the crump of the great German assault guns and the explosion as the ammunition racks of the Honeys went up was magnified a hundredfold. The night was made hideous by the sound as tank after tank was shattered by the German fire. Here and there the light cannon of the Honeys cracked into action. But their shells made little impression on the thick steel hides of the Ferdinands.

Now most of the survivors concentrated on saving their skins. They started to back down the road. Unfortunately for them American engineers had just blown a culvert in their path. Now it was blocked by huge chunks of concrete. They were trapped! Ill-armed and badly disorganized, they were no match for Remer's elite. One by one they were knocked out. The official history of the campaign records no survivors.

Part of the badly beaten column discovered an escape route. Led by Colonel Nelson of the 112th, the survivors thrust westward out of the trap. Luck favoured them now. The snow stopped falling. A bright half moon tinged the sky a hard silver. Guided by this icy light, Nelson led his men over snowy fields and frozen marshes.

Later some of the survivors remembered it as a beautiful winter night, but at the time they had no eyes for the beauty of the scene. All their attention was concentrated on spotting the forward positions of the 82nd Airborne which they knew were to their rear. Now they began to file into the hamlet of Provedroux.

It appeared peaceful. Then the commander of the lead tank spotted some tanks parked further up the street. He ordered his Honey to halt and surveyed them in the silver light. They weren't American tanks. They were German!

'*Fire!*' he barked to his gunner.

The Honey's little gun cracked into action. Immediately all hell broke loose in the hamlet. Germans came pouring out of the houses on all sides and started firing wildly at the *Amis* who had appeared so surprisingly in their midst. Equally startled, the Americans began returning their fire. In an instant chaos and confusion reigned in the narrow street.

But again the column's luck held. They fought their way through the hamlet and by midnight the first of the survivors began to drift into the lines of the 82nd Airborne. They were exhausted bunches of men from half a dozen different units – engineers, tankers, infantry. All were in frank disorder, tired beyond belief. They had seized any kind of vehicle in their frantic attempt to escape from the trap. By midnight two hundred of them had passed into the 82nd's lines. How many didn't make it was never assessed. Now they were fed and allowed to sleep. But not for long. That night they'd be in the line again, fighting off the threat to Ridgway's XVIII Airborne Corps.

Clarke staggered exhausted out of his jeep. But, cornered as he was, he had a few words for the wounded as they were checked by a surgeon. The doctor noticed Clarke's blood-shot eyes and sunken cheeks and said, 'General you'd better get some sleep or you could be in serious trouble.' He obviously thought that Clarke might have a heart attack.

Clarke shook his head wearily and said he didn't think he could sleep; there was too much going on his mind.

'I can fix that,' the surgeon said confidently. Immediately he gave Clarke a drug which knocked him out, as his biographer has written, 'like a sack of sand'.

But Clarke's sleep was not going to be undisturbed. Just about the same time that the men of the 112th Infantry Regiment began to pass through the 82nd Airborne's lines, a staff officer tried to shake Clarke awake. 'General,' he said urgently. 'General Ridgway wants you immediately.'

'The hell with it,' Clarke mumbled dreamily and, turning over, fell asleep again at once.

Later when Clarke was completely awake he was told once again to report to Ridgway. He did so in the same uniform, dirty and stained, that he had worn back on 16 December when he had rushed from Holland to St Vith. To his surprise the airborne corps commander was dressed in garrison uniform complete with ribbons.

He saluted and snapped, 'General Clarke reporting to the Corps Commander.'

Ridgway stared up at the big tanker coldly. He didn't offer him a chair. Instead he said icily, 'I'm not used to having brigadiers tell me they won't report to me.'

Clarke looked down on him, 'Well General, the fact is I hadn't been to sleep for a week. I've been fighting a battle that I'm sure you know about. Last night the surgeon told me I had better get sleep or I'd be in trouble. He gave me dope. Then they tell me this morning that I refused to get up last night, but I can't remember it. Maybe I said, "The hell with it", but I don't know.'

Ridgway, still smarting at the fact he had been forced to withdraw the defenders from his fortified goose-egg, wasn't appeased and started to lecture Clarke on army discipline.

Clarke listened for a while, face grim and set, and then he'd had enough. He snapped, 'General, I came to this command against my wishes. I got nine decorations for bravery in twelve days in my old outfit. I've got a good record in the Third Army and I can go back there tomorrow morning and General Patton will be glad to see me. I'd like your permission to leave.'

Ridgway didn't react. So Clarke tried again, 'I've done my job up here. History will give our unit credit for the job we did at St Vith. I'd like to leave.'

Finally Ridgway spoke. 'Well,' he said, 'just don't let it happen again.'

Clarke saluted, did an about-turn and stalked out. As he did so, there was a low rumble from about a mile away. It was the bridge at Vielsalm. US engineers had just blown it up. The Battle for the fortified goose-egg was over.

*

In Versailles Eisenhower finished writing a telegram to Hodges of the US 1st Army. It read: 'Please transmit the following personal message from me to Hasbrouck of the Seventh Armored. QUOTE. The magnificent job you are doing is having a great beneficial effect on our whole situation. I am personally grateful to you and wish you to let your people know that if they continue to carry out their mission with the splendid spirit they have so far shown, they will have deserved well of their country. UNQUOTE. EISENHOWER.'

It appeared that the Allied Supreme Commander did not even know that the Seventh's 'mission' was already over.

Nearly four thousand men failed to return from the fortified goose-egg. Together with the eight to nine thousand of the ill-fated 106th Division who were killed or captured, plus the 2,000-odd lost by the 28th Division's 110th Regiment, the Supreme Commander sacrificed nearly 15,000 men that first week of December, 1944.

On Sunday, Christmas Eve, Eisenhower was allowed home briefly to get a change of clothes. He called another general to ask for the release of a sergeant from the 5th Infantry Division who was under sentence of death at Cherbourg for murder and rape.

Curfew in Paris that night was nine o'clock. Not that there was much to do in the French capital. Everyone was scared of the German assassination teams reputedly lurking in wait for the Top Brass. So the Supreme Commander stayed in the security of his HQ. It was recorded that he enjoyed a modest little party that night. After all, it *was* Christmas Eve.

ENVOI

'Now they rest tranquil and secure in the friendly soil of the Netherlands. May our great debt to them and to all the others who gave their lives in that great crusade serve as an inspiration.'

President Dwight D. Eisenhower, 7 July, 1960 on the occasion of the dedication of the US Military Cemetery at Margraten.

The survivors of the 422nd and 423d Regiments were being taken even deeper into Germany now. In the last couple of days they had seen some terrible things: American dead stacked like cordwood, prisoners huddled in snowy fields all night long, forced marches with precious little food or water, dive-bombing attacks by their own planes.

Donald Britt, aged 19, had seen half his platoon killed before the rest had surrendered. Now he was huddled in a packed boxcar somewhere outside Limburg. Fifty years later he recalled, 'We hadn't had anything to eat or drink for days. We were so thirsty that our tongues were thick.' Suddenly they heard what sounded like running water. One of the prisoners who spoke German called to the nearest guard 'Wasser'. The guard ignored him.

Then somebody said, 'Hey, it's Christmas Eve. Why don't we sing some Christmas carols? Maybe we can attract some attention and get some water.'

So the weary young prisoners launched into 'Silent Night' Other prisoners in other boxcars took the carol up. Soon the whole long train was singing.

'We heard a murmuring from the crowd further up the platform. They were telling the guards to let the Amis have water. Their guard agreed to do so if they didn't attempt to escape. Men were allowed out with canteens and helmet liners to fetch the precious water. When every man had had a drink, the doors were locked once more.'

In Britt's car someone said, 'Let's pray.'

Quietly, as the crowd dispersed, the young men said The Lord's Prayer together, 'and 70 men leaning on each other for support inside a cold boxcar far from home, somehow drifted off to sleep.' On this last Christmas Eve of the war, it seemed that all decency and compassion had not been lost.

Eighty miles away Frau Vincken and her 12-year old son Fritz were startled as a knock came on the door of their lonely cottage. They opened it to find two steel-helmeted men there, with another lying wounded in the snow. Frau Vincken told the two to come inside and bring their wounded comrade. They told her that they had lost their battalion; they had been on the run for three days without food or shelter.

The woman tut-tutted and, after the wounded *Ami*, whose name was Harry, had been placed in Fritz's bed, she commanded: 'Get Hermann and six potatoes.'

Fritz looked surprised.' This was a serious departure from our pre-Christmas plans,' he remembered many years later. Hermann was a plump rooster named after the immensely fat *Reichmarschall* Hermann Goering. The Vinckens had been fattening him up for weeks just in case Father got leave for Christmas. Now it was obvious that Frau Vincken was going to feed the Americans with the rooster.

Hermann was duly dispatched and plucked and the house started to fill with the smell of roast chicken and potatoes. Suddenly there came another knock on the cottage door. Fritz answered and went white. Four German soldiers stood there. Even at 12, Fritz Vincken knew the penalty for harbouring enemy soldiers. They could all be shot. But his mother reacted correctly. She said '*fröhliche Weihnachten*' and when the leader of the little band explained that they had lost their outfit and asked whether they could spend the night, she agreed. She said, 'You can have a fine warm meal and eat till the pot is empty.'

The soldiers smiled in anticipation.

'But,' the little woman added, 'we have three other guests who you might not think of as friends.' Her voice hardened and her son thought he had never seen her look so stern. 'This is Christmas Eve and there will be no shooting here.'

The Corporal in charge knew at once who the other 'guests' must be. '*Amis?*' he snapped.

Frau Vincken looked at their frost-chilled faces. 'Listen,' she said slowly, 'You could be my sons and so could those in there. A boy with a gunshot wound, fighting for his life. His two friends – just like you and just as hungry and as exhausted as you are. This night, this Christmas Eve night, let us forget about killing.'

The corporal could not decide what he should do, but Frau Vincken made up his mind for him. She clapped her hands and said,

'Enough talking. Please put your weapons there on the woodpile and hurry up before the others eat the dinner.'

Now the Americans and the Germans sat side by side on the hard wooden chairs in the kitchen. While Frau Vincken finished the chicken and boiled some more potatoes, the Corporal, who had been a medical student until the previous autumn, had a look at Harry. He said he had lost a lot of blood. He needed rest and warmth.

Then they sat down to eat. The Corporal brought a bottle of wine from his haversack and another soldier produced a loaf of dark army bread. Frau Vincken cut the loaf into small pieces, but said half the bottle of wine had to go to the wounded soldier. '*Komm Herr Jesus.*' She said the old familiar grace with tears in her eyes, 'Come and be our guest.' They ate till there was nothing left, conversing somehow in a mixture of German, French and broken English.

Just before midnight on this most holy of German religious festivals, the woman asked the men to come outside and look up at the Star of Bethlehem. Wordlessly, their breath fogging on the icy air, they stared up at the starry heavens, German and American. 'For all of us during that moment of silence,' Fritz Vincken remembered long afterwards, 'looking at the brightest star in the sky, the war was a distant, almost forgotten thing.'

1944 gave way to 1945 and still the killing went on. With the Allies now on the offensive and recovering the ground they had lost in the first week of December thousands of American dead were now being found in the woods and fields, some still frozen solid and glowing with what appeared ruddy good health; others buried under two foot of snow. Captain Shomon at Margraten opened more and more burial fields. He went to visit his colleague, Captain Pearson of the 607th Graves Registration Company, to see if he had any extra space at his cemetery in Henri Chapelle in Belgium.

Pearson said he hadn't. He had already expanded to 15,000 graves and his men were working 'day and night. Some days they had as many as five hundred bodies to bury'.

So Shomon returned to Margraten. The cemetery was growing ever faster. Another company was rushed up to help. The ground was frozen iron hard. Freezing winds lashed the burying fields. More clerks were brought in to fill in the ever growing pile of 'Report of

Burial and Inventory of Personal Effects' forms. In the Army, even in death, a form had to be completed. Now, as Shomon recalled after the war, 'No longer were ten acres adequate for our ever-increasing number of burial plots; we needed twenty acres, thirty, possibly more.'

The population of a medium-sized American town lay beneath that alien soil under simple white wooden crosses – and still the killing continued.

By the morning of 23 January, 1945, General Bruce Clarke was once again back with his CCB on the outskirts of the little Belgian town where he had spent that fateful week in December. That morning Combat Command A of the Seventh Armored was waiting at Hunningen, two miles to the north, ready to attack St Vith.

But some time that icy January morning General Hasbrouck changed his mind. Picking up his phone he called Clarke and said, 'Bruce, you got kicked out of St Vith. Would you like to take it back?'

Clarke said he would. He put down the phone and ordered his staff to start planning the attack.

Half an hour before Combat Command B was to assault St Vith, Clarke walked up a hill which overlooked the town. It had been completely flattened by two terrible RAF raids since he had fled the place. Only three buildings were left standing. Indeed it was clear the Germans had been forced to build a road around it, so bad was the destruction. And everywhere there were craters, almost lip to lip.

At fourteen hundred precisely the artillery bombardment began. In a few minutes his three-pronged attack on St Vith would begin. Clarke knew he'd be needed back in his CP to control the operation. Turning, he started to walk back to his jeep. Suddenly he stopped. A few yards away, almost covered in snow, was his old looted German Mercedes with the defective gear-box. It was the same car he had driven from Holland to St Vith on 17 December, 1944, to take over command. For a minute he stared at it. That Sunday back in December must have seemed like another world now. A whole American dream had been shattered. The war had not been won in 1944. Victory was still some way off. Once more they'd have to attack that dreaded Siegfried Line just as they had done back in October.

Bruce Clarke clambered back into his jeep and got on with the battle. Three hours later St Vith was taken. The front was restored.

The Americans were almost back where they had been on 16 December, 1944. It had cost America 80,000 men, dead, wounded or captured.

They met on 10 May, 1945, two days after the surrender of the Third Reich. All around, the German city of Frankfurt was in ruins. But not the building in which they assembled, the *IG Farben Building*, Eisenhower's new HQ. To some of the Americans who worked there that seemed surprising. Then the *IG Farben Haus*, built in 1928 on the site of a former lunatic asylum, had a sinister reputation. Until the previous month it had been the headquarters of the German chemicals conglomerate which had manufactured the gas for the extermination of Jews and others in Nazi Germany's concentration camps.

There now were the US Army's top brass – Eisenhower, Hodges, Patton, Simpson and Patch (of the US Seventh Army). They were the victors; they had beaten the Germans. The war in Europe was over at last. But already some of the generals had new worries. Hodges knew he was being sent to fight in the Pacific against the Japanese. Patton would like to rearm the newly surrendered German division and use them to fight the 'Mongols', as he called the Russian 'allies'. Patch was having trouble with his French allies in Austria and Germany, where the latter wouldn't surrender Stuttgart which was supposed to be part of the new US zone of occupation.; and Simpson too had his problems. Seemingly no employment had been found for him in this new world, now that he had helped to defeat Germany.

But it seemed that Eisenhower had the most worries of all. After the gala dinner which he had given for his victorious generals was over and the flunkies had departed, he cleared his throat and began to speak. He told the other four that what he had to say was 'very confidential'. In due course some of them might well be called to testify before a Congressional committe of inquiry. Congress might want to know details of the kind of war they had conducted in Europe between 1944 and 1945. Eisenhower went on to explain that there was an urgent need for them to continue to maintain the same solid and united front to the outside world as they had done throughout the compaign. 'Let's agree on the right form of organization,' he said.

They knew what that meant. Eisenhower wanted them all to tell the same story if they were ever questioned about what had happened in Europe. Patton, in particular, realized that Eisenhower was talking solidarity like this to his top commanders because the Supreme Commander had begun the 'big cover-up.' As the former wrote afterwards in his confidential papers, 'Eisenhower's talk sounded like covering up probable criticism of strategical blunders which he unquestionably committed during the campaign.'

And Patton certainly knew something. But, as he again stated in his private papers, 'I feel that as an American it will ill become me to discredit Ike yet. That is, until I shall prove more conclusively that he lacks moral fortitude. This lack has been evident to me since the first landing in Africa, but now that he has been bitten by the Presidential Bug it is becoming ever more pronounced.'

By the autumn of 1945, having been sacked from his beloved Third Army, Patton's resolve was weakening. Now he disliked Ike intensely for what he thought the ex-Supreme Commander had done to him and his life. He confided to his diary, 'I will resign when I have finished this job, which will be not later than December 26th. I hate to do it, but I have been gagged all of my life and whether they appreciate it or not, Americans need some honest men who dare to say what they think, not what they think people want them to say.'

That November of '45 he allegedly told his chief-of-staff General Hobart Gay over dinner, 'I have given this a great deal of thought. I am going to resign from the Army. Quit outright. That is the only way I can be free to live my life.' Later he said, 'I'm going to do it with a statement that will be remembered for a long time. If it doesn't make the headlines, I'll be surprised!'

But what would that statement be? Could it have been about Eisenhower's mistress, Kay Summersby? Hardly likely. Patton wasn't a petty man. After all he currently had a mistress himself – indeed he had three of them during his time in Europe. No, that statement, which would make 'the big headlines', had to be about Eisenhower's conduct of the war. But for most of the campaign in Europe the Supreme Commander had been an office man. His generals had won – and sometimes lost – his battles for him. There had been only one period throughout 1944–45 when Eisenhower had actively taken over as ground forces commander. That had been in the period leading up to the Battle of the Bulge.

Would Patton, then, have recited that whole damning indictment of what Eisenhower had known prior to the great German 'surprise attack'? The Oshima decodes telling of an attack in the West; the

Reichsbahn decodes detailing the trains laden with troops and armour heading for the Eifel; the Ultra decodes of the *Luftwaffe* signals sending large numbers of fighters to the Western Front when they were urgently needed in the north to protect Germany's cities against relentless Allied bombing; the 100th Group's spotting of the German armour grouping between Bitburg and Losheim opposite Middleton's VIII Corps. Would Patton have revealed the great secret: *that Eisenhower had been prepared to sacrifice a whole US corps to get the Germans to come out of their prepared defences and fight in the open?*

The world was never fated to know. Now that Patton had made his decision to speak out as soon as he had resigned from the US Army, he began to grow increasingly nervous. His old friend 'Hap' Gay suggested that in order to take his mind off the 'statement', they should go pheasant shooting together.

Patton accepted with alacrity. On Sunday 9 December, 1945, he set off to go pheasant shooting in the woods around Speyer, the old German city in the Rhenish Palatinate. He never reached those woods. As the world knows, he was involved in an accident with an American Army truck just outside Mannheim. Hurried by ambulance down the autobahn to nearby Heidelberg, he was discovered to have a fractured spine, with complete paralysis of his lower body as a result.

For twelve days he lingered, fighting hard against death. But at ten to six on the evening of 21 December, exactly one year to the day when he had launched his attack on Bastogne, he died in his sleep of a massive heart attack. As the US Army paper *Stars & Stripes* headlined the front-page story: 'General Patton Dies Quietly in Sleep'.

For the warrior who eight months before had declared, 'The best end for an old campaigner is a bullet at the last minute of the last battle' it was an incongruous end. So the secret of what Patton might have said on that day after Christmas, 1945, died with him.

In that November when Patton had first pondered leaving the Army and then telling what he knew, Eisenhower had returned to Washington. There he had taken up Marshall's old job as Chief-of-Staff. There his boss as Secretary of State for War was Robert Porter Patterson, a civilian and also new to the job.

On 16 December, 1945, a year after the Battle of the Bulge had started, Patterson told Major-General Bissell, Eisenhower's Chief-of Intelligence, that Senator Tom Connally, a Texan Democrat and chairman of the Foreign Relations Committee, felt the 'American public had never been satisfied with the explanation the War Department made concerning the German break-through in the Ardennes about this time last year and that he thought it would be most appropriate just now to release a comprehensive explanation to the Press'.

Patterson ordered Bissell to prepare 'a narrative account of the conditions leading up to and the operations of the Battle of the Ardennes. 'Bissell was to give a report on the German activities during this period, as well as an intelligence summary'. The Secretary of State wanted the document ready for release on 23 December.

When Bissell informed Eisenhower what Patterson wanted, he must have been very alarmed indeed. It was the kind of request for information that he had been fearing all along. On the afternoon of the following day Eisenhower discussed the matter with Patterson. Although Eisenhower, for obvious reasons, was strictly against going ahead with the 'Bulge release', Patterson insisted the former should prepare a memo for him.

On the following day Eisenhower wrote Patterson a confidential letter. In it he stated: 'I am unalterably opposed to making any effort to publicize at this time any story concerning the Ardennes Battle, or even allowing any written explantion to go outside the War Department. To do so would inevitably create the impression that there was some reason for seizing upon a flimsy excuse, such as the anniversary of the outbreak of the Battle, to defend something where no defense is necessary.'

On that same day, Eisenhower followed his confidential letter with a confidential memo to Patterson. In it he again protested in the very first paragraph, 'I have been informed that many of the Army's sincere friends,' he wrote, 'are considerably disturbed by certain implications and insinuations that occasionally appear in the press concerning the so-called "Battle of the Bulge".'

Eisenhower went on to state that he had taken a calculated risk in the Ardennes. 'I consulted with my principal subordinates* concerning the probable effects of a German offensive in that region

* These were obviously those mysterious meetings in early November 1944, when Eisenhower was completely out of touch with the outer world for three days.

(the Ardennes) since I had received warnings from my intelligence system that there were indications that such an attack might take place. The Army Group Commander (Bradley) believed, *and I agreed*, that such an attack if it came about could be confined to the area east of the Meuse in which damage to us would be relatively light.'

Then Eisenhower went on to make an astonishing statement. 'General Bradley actually traced on the map, many days in advance of the attack, the line to which he estimated the Germans could penetrate if they succeeded in concentrating considerable forces under conditions of very bad weather. The line he traced coincided in remarkable detail with the one they actually reached.'

He stated further: 'In spite of the knowledge that this kind of an attack could eventuate, I refused to pass on to the defensive, preferring to take the chance of meeting the enemy forces in the open if they should venture on a heavy attack west of the Siegfried. The alternative was to permit the advantages that would accrue to him through our settling down to the so-called winter defensive.'

Eisenhower concluded, 'I should like to repeat that I consider myself solely and exclusively responsible for this portion of the campaign . . . It happens that in Washington today are several of my principal combat commanders that participated in that struggle. If you should like to have an informal personal conference with them or with me I should be glad to assemble them and discuss the matter at length with you.'

Patterson thanked Eisenhower for the memo on the 19th and wrote that he was sure 'the whole performance [in the Bulge] was highly creditable to the Army and to you'. All the same, he still thought that the main features of the Battle should be made known to the public. 'Otherwise they will hear nothing but fault-finding and many of them will think that the Army is covering up.'

Eisenhower was getting his first experience in Washington of how politicians were scared of public opinion and how they scuttled for cover when they thought some failing or other was about to be exposed. It was to be useful 'on-the-job' training for him for the years to come when he would be President of the United States.

In the end the two of them compromised. There would be no press release on the Battle of the Bulge that Christmas. Instead Patterson accepted that there should be 'a series of short narratives on the European campaign, with one of them being devoted to the Ardennes.'

Eisenhower had won. The Battle of the Bulge was no longer of special interest. It was, as Eisenhower had insisted to Patterson in his memo of 18 December, 'a mere incident in a large campaign' about which one should '*say nothing whatsoever except in response to casual inquiry from our friends.*' (author's italics)

Since that time, nearly fifty years ago now, there have been more than enough Inquiries into the Battle of the Bulge and they haven't been 'casual' in the least. But Eisenhower's luck has held over that half century. They have all been 'friendly'. Dwight D. Eisenhower had got away with it.

Bibliography

BEFORE THE STORM

J. J. Shomon: *Crosses in the Wind*, Privately printed Holland, 1991.
Correspondence with John Marshall, 1992.
Correspondence with Richard Petersen, 1992.
J. Petersen: *Heal the Child Warrior*, Privately printed Cardiff by the Sea, Calif, 1992.
Harry Martin: *I Was No Hero*, unpublished manuscript.
Correspondence with H. Martin, 1992.
S. Frank: *The Glorious Collapse of the 106th*, Saturday Evening Post, 8 Nov, 1946.
F. J. Price: *Troy H. Middleton*, Louisiana State University, 1974.
J. Nobusch: *Bis zum bitteren Ende*, Privately printed, 1978.
Edited: *Ardennen 1944/45*, Luxembourg, 1983.
M. Shulman: *Defeat in the West*, Ballantine, 1968.
R. Merrian: *Dark December*, Ziff Davis, 1947.
C. J. Malinowski – correspondence, 1993.
R. Gaul: *Schicksale zwischen Sauer und Our Diekirch*, Privately printed, 1986.
Correspondence with James Thorpe, University of Maryland.
The Cub, 1943–93. Published by the 106th Divisional Association 1993.
Correspondence with B. Rutledge, Adjutant 106th Assoc, 1992.

DAY ONE

Bis zum bitteren Ende, op. cit.
I was no Hero, op. cit.
Crosses in the Wind, op. cit.
Correspondence with M. McIntyre, 1992.
J. Toland; *Battle*, Random House 1958.
C. Whiting: *Death of a Division*, Leo Cooper, 1983.
J. Kreisle: *Forty Years After*, Privately printed.
Correspondence with Dr Kreisle, 1992.
Correspondence with H. Miller, 1992.

E. Dupuy: *The Incredible Valor of Eric Wood, Saturday Evening Post*, 12
    February 1947.
Correspondence with J. Marshall, 1992.
R. Phillips: *To Save Bastogne*, Stein & Day, 1983.
Correspondence with J. Cope, 1992/93.
C. MacDonald: *The Battle of the Bulge*, Weidenfeld & Nicolson, 1983.
Correspondence with M. Dillard, 1993.
Ardennenschicksale, op. cit.
Correspondence with Bruce Clarke Jnr, 1990–93.
Conversation with Will Cavanagh, 1992.

DAY TWO

Ellis: *Clarke of St Vith*, Dillon, 1974.
Letter from Gen. Bruce Clarke.
Conversation with Mike Tolhurst.
Marshall MS op. cit.
Correspondence with Carl Mattocks.
R. Lewin: *The Other Ultra*, Heinemann, 1982.
C Boyd: *Hitler's Japanese Confidant*, University Press of Kansas, 1993.

DAY THREE

C. Whiting: *Papa Goes to War*, Crowood, 1990.
H. Mayer: *Kriegsgeschichte der 12 SS Panzerdivision*, Muniverlag, 1982.
Marshall MS op. cit.
R. Allen: *Lucky Forward*, Manor Books, 1977.
B. Horrocks: *A Full Life*, Leo Cooper Ltd, 1974.
Martin MS. op cit.
Peterson MS op cit.
T. Bird: *Americans POWs of World War II*. Praeger 1992.
Death of a Division, op. cit.
Clarke of St Vith op. cit.
R. Gaul: *Schicksale zwischen Sauer und Our*, Privately printed, 1985.
Decision at St Vith, op. cit.

DAY FOUR

Death of a Division, op. cit.
Petersen MS op. cit.
C. Whiting: *Decision at St Vith*, Ballantine, 1969.
C. Whiting: *Operation Northwind*, Leo Cooper, 1990.
D. Belchem: *All in a Day's March*, Collins, 1978.

The Cub, 45–91. Selection of articles etc from the 106th Div. 1991.
American POWs of WWII, op. cit.
Battle, op. cit.
N. Hamilton: *Monty*, Vol III, Hamish Hamilton, 1986.

DAY FIVE

Decision at St Vith, op. cit.
All in a Day's March op. cit.
Letter from Bruce Clarke Jnr.
Martin MS, op. cit.
Letter from Walter Pennino.
Mattocks MS, op. cit.
The Cub, op. cit.
Monty, Vol III, op. cit.
Schicksale Zwischen Sauer und Our, op. cit.
Marshall MS, op. cit.
American POWs in WWII, op. cit.

DAY SIX

Clarke of St Vith, op. cit.
Time-Life: *The Battle of the Bulge*, no date.
Mattocks MS, op. cit.
Martin MS, op. cit.
Letter from Mr Pennino to author.
Decision at St Vith, op. cit.
Monty, Vol III, op. cit.
C. Whiting: *Slaughter over Sicily*, Leo Cooper Ltd, 1992.
J. Gavin: *On To Berlin*, Ballantine, 1979.
R. Phillips: *To Save Bastogne*, Stein & Day, 1983.
Interviews with various villagers at Meyrode, 1993.

DAY SEVEN

Clarke of St Vith, op. cit.
To Save Bastogne, op. cit.
Papa Goes to War, op. cit.
Decision at St Vith, op. cit.
Hugh M. Cole: *Ardennes: Battle of the Bulge*, Washington, 1964
Battle, op. cit.
M. Ridgway: *The Memoirs of Matthew B. Ridgway*, Harper, 1956.
Monty, Vol III, op. cit.

C. Whiting: *The Ardennes: the Secret War*, Century, 1984.
A. Speer: *Inside the Third Reich*, Weidenfeld & Nicolson, 1970.

DAY EIGHT

On To Berlin, op. cit.
Martin MS.
Correspondence with Calvin Boykin.
Soldier: Memoirs of Matthew Ridgway, op. cit.
Battle of the Bulge, op. cit.
Battle, op. cit.
Clarke of St Vith, op. cit.

ENVOI

Crosses in the Wind, op. cit.
Letter to author from Peter Russo.
St Petersburg Times, Dec 25, 1992.
Reader's Digest, Jan, 1973.
Edited: *The Papers of Dwight D. Eisenhower*, Johns Hopkins, 1978.
M. Blumenso: *Patton*, William Morrow, 1987.
The Unknown Patton, op. cit.

Index